Second Edition

What Is It About Me You Can't Teach?

An Instructional Guide for the Urban Educator

ELEANOR RENÉE
RODRIGUEZ

JAMES
BELLANCA

Foreword by
ERIC COOPER

CORWIN PRESS
A SAGE Publications Company
Thousand Oaks, California

For information:

Corwin Press
A Sage Publications Company
2455 Teller Road
Thousand Oaks, California 91320
www.corwinpress.com

Sage Publications Ltd.
1 Oliver's Yard
55 City Road
London EC1Y 1SP
United Kingdom

Sage Publications India Pvt. Ltd.
B-42, Panchsheel Enclave
Post Box 4109
New Delhi 110 017 India

Printed in the United States of America.

Library of Congress Cataloging-in-Publication Data

Rodriguez, Eleanor Renée.
What is it about me you can't teach? : an instructional guide for the urban educator /
Eleanor Renée Rodriguez, James Bellanca. — 2nd ed.
    p. cm.
Includes bibliographical references and index.
ISBN 978-1-4129-3763-4 (cloth) — ISBN 978-1-4129-3764-1 (pbk.)
    1. Education, Urban—United States. 2. Children with social
disabilities—Education—United States. 3. Teaching—United States. I. Title.
LC5131.R63 2007
370.9173′2—dc22

                                      2006002892

This book is printed on acid-free paper.

10 11 12 13   10 9 8 7 6

Acquisitions Editor:	Cathy Hernandez
Editorial Assistant:	Charline Wu
Production Editor:	Jenn Reese
Copy Editor:	Barbara Coster
Typesetter:	C&M Digitals (P) Ltd.
Proofreader:	Kris Bergstad
Indexer:	Elllen Slavitz
Cover Designer:	Michael Dubowe
Graphic Designer:	Scott Van Atta

Contents

Foreword

On too few occasions does one have an opportunity to read a book that approaches the most important questions regarding student achievement and school reform. *What Is It About Me You Can't Teach?* by Eleanor Renée Rodriguez and Jim Bellanca is a book that faces the domain given short shrift in the nation's analysis of what is going wrong with many schools, that is, the importance of preparing and keeping good teachers. Though a national publication by Linda Darling-Hammond, *What Matters Most: Teaching for America's Future* (1996), addresses the centrality of teaching and learning and its impact on achievement, very few school reform publications give attention to the issue of classroom instruction.

Rodriguez and Bellanca have made an important contribution to the school reform literature. In this book they acknowledge (through the "voices of children") the impact that teacher attitudes and performance have on the learning of the urban child. Poignant examples abound here, which force the reader to consider how teachers behave differently to many urban students. As has been reported by the authors in their examples, teachers often tend to slow down the pace of learning, persist less strenuously in helping students, and view urban children as disadvantaged, unruly, unsocialized, slow, and backward—thus perpetuating a self-fulfilling prophecy. Teachers who expect students to be successful will work toward that end, and usually they will produce results that justify their optimism, for example, providing strategies that deliver subject matter in interesting ways and helping the students to cognitively adapt and process information.

The legacy of research shows that urban teachers must change their teaching practices in the direction of concentrating more time and effort on concept and cognitive development, reasoning, thinking, and higher-order comprehension skills when engaged in subject matter instruction. A strong base of research linking cognitive development to prior knowledge in learning emerged in the late 1970s. Those studies concluded that, particularly when reading is the learning mode, those students with much prior knowledge and experience relevant to a subject have less difficulty learning new material and retain more than those with inadequate or incomplete prior knowledge and experiences. Urban students need the benefit of teachers who know how to access prior knowledge that students might not be aware of and that might help them with the material to be learned.

Through illustrative examples, Rodriguez and Bellanca guide the reader through integrated and interdisciplinary lessons that use much of the cognitive research referred to above. The reader is guided on a virtual tour of relevant topics and ideas that will work well with all students, but particularly with urban children. The use of predictions, graphic organizers, elements of Feuerstein's Instrumental Enrichment program, concept themes, problem-solving strategies, and concept attainment models are all embedded in content-area instruction. This synthesis provides the conceptual foundation necessary for appropriate classroom mediation.

The lasting contribution of this book is that it also gives the reader a clear portrait of the educator best able to serve urban students. This educator is sensitive, empathetic, confident, knowledgeable about appropriate teaching methodologies and subject matter, and is acclimated to the nuances of learning used by many urban children. This educator also provides a strong role model for the students, maintains high expectations for all students served, and is able to integrate academic learning into structured applied learning opportunities. Thus the context of schooling becomes one of nurturance, guidance, leadership, and support, in spite of the harsh realities of everyday life continually faced by many urban students in our schools.

I am pleased to introduce the revised edition of this book to our many partners in urban school systems across the country and to thank the authors for their outstanding contribution.

—Eric Cooper
National Urban Alliance for Effective Education @ Lake Success,
New York, Council of Great City Schools, Washington, D.C., and the
University of Alabama, Birmingham

Preface

How would you feel if your teacher greeted you with first-day frowns that suggested, "I sure hope you can learn something in this class, but I doubt it." "Why did she assign him to my room in the first place?" What would you think if your teacher told you in so many words, "You're not someone who will ever learn in my classroom"?

Such are the feelings and thoughts of thousands of young children and older students who are greeted with subtle body language and words that say, "I don't believe you can learn." It is these children who have to be asking themselves, "What is it about me you can't teach? My shabby shirts/baggy pants? My accent? My skin color? My braids/locks? Because I'm a girl? My parent(s)' low income? . . . Just what is it?"

How a teacher answers these questions for any child who feels or thinks them is a critical determinant of how well that child will succeed in that classroom. Ideally, teachers' first responses will communicate, "There is nothing that prevents me from having the highest of expectations for you." In a like manner, the second response will be, "And to demonstrate the sincerity of my belief that you can learn anything I have to teach as well as anyone else in this class, I am going to use the best instructional practices that will make your success a reality."

The first purpose of this book is to show future and present classroom teachers that there are practical instructional methods to ensure that all children have the benefit of the best teaching. The second purpose is to provide teachers who need to expand their instructional repertoires with the tools to best help children who come to their classrooms not quite ready to meet the challenge of high expectations for all. In this way, all teachers can better respond to the question by saying, "There is nothing I can't teach you or any other child assigned to my classroom."

We have built this book on a foundation of research especially applicable for teachers working in an urban setting with students whose academic lives are marked by low performance, whatever its reasons. The first research is our own multiyear experience with students, teachers, paraprofessionals, and administrators in these settings. The second is the alignment of our experience with the meta-analytic studies of researchers. These researchers have looked at effect sizes and given a statistical rank order designating which instructional approaches are most likely to make a positive, large impact on students struggling to learn in the school setting. The third, and most important, is the research and effectiveness studies completed on the theory and practices of cognitive psychologist Reuven Feuerstein.

Because we ourselves have learned the importance of understanding well the learning challenges many urban students face, we have organized the text around Feuerstein's theory of Mediated Learning Experience. This theory, based on the concepts of Structural Cognitive Modifiability, which Feuerstein developed as a student of Piaget, holds that intelligence is flexible and changeable, not fixed and static. In the theory of Mediated Learning Experience, Feuerstein details the characteristics of those interactions between teachers and students that will best help all students become more efficient and effective learners. Originally developed with children of the Holocaust who were proving too difficult for their teachers to help via conventional instruction, Mediated Learning Experience has successfully been applied to students with special needs, including learning disabilities, behavioral disabilities, Down syndrome, and autism; African American children of poverty in urban centers such as Cleveland and Hartford; in rural areas such as Bahia (Brazil) and the Aleutian Islands; with Native American (Arizona), First Nation (British Columbia), Inuit (Alaska), Ethiopian (Israel), and Hispanic (Los Angeles, Mexico City) students; incarcerated youth (Bronx); as well as with gifted underachievers and students struggling with reading and mathematics in American schools from Portland (Oregon) on the West Coast to Wilmington (Delaware) on the East Coast.

In this book, we have used the characteristics of Mediated Learning Experience as the organizational guide for the chapters. Each chapter focuses on one of the characteristics and shows how it provides teachers with the tools that best promote "high expectations" instruction. We have selected those instructional strategies that align best with each characteristic. For each we provide the what, the why, and the how so that teachers can understand the characteristic, know why it is important, and understand how to use it in the classroom. Finally, at the end of each chapter, we provide three sample lessons to show how teachers can integrate the strategies into their daily lessons. These models are differentiated to show use with primary, middle, or secondary students.

Chapter 1 outlines the characteristics of the urban learner and details the unique steps necessary to overcome the students' instructional needs.

Chapter 2 reexamines the data on teaching tactics that enable teachers to put high-expectation words into instructional practice. Special attention is paid to the importance of Teacher Expectation Student Achievement (TESA) practices that are viewed as basic tools necessary for every urban teachers classroom.

Chapter 3 takes note of how the teacher's intention to develop each student's thinking skills and to apply those skills to subject matter balances with the teacher's ability to gain strong student engagement or "reciprocity." It identifies important strategies that engage students and maintain reciprocity throughout a lesson.

Chapter 4 targets the mediation of "meaning," an essential characteristic required in every lesson. It discusses the importance of prior knowledge and the design of lessons that help students construct meaning.

Chapter 5 explains the importance of mediation for "transcendence," in which the teacher enables students to form generalizations and draw conclusions about the facts they are learning. It shows how reciprocal teaching is an effective tool for providing students with the "learning to learn" skills needed to bridge concepts one to another.

Chapter 6 provides insights into the mediation for "self-regulation" that helps students learn how to take control and responsibility for their own learning behaviors. It outlines the tools in Feuerstein's Instrumental Enrichment programs for older students (STANDARD) and young students (BASIC), which help teachers mediate self-regulation more successfully with low-performing students.

Chapter 7 discusses the importance of using Mediated Learning Experience and Instrumental Enrichment to build the underlying feeling of competency that students need to learn well. It identifies behaviors of students who feel incompetent with and the importance of academic success as the basis for mediation of the feeling of competence.

Chapter 8 shows the connection of the mediation of sharing behavior with the use of informal and formal cooperation as a preeminent strategy for developing sharing behavior in the classroom and the home.

Chapter 9 connects Mediated Learning Experience with Gardner's theory of multiple intelligences to illuminate the need for teachers to individuate student learning. It outlines how teachers can structure lessons so that the locus of control for learning grows strong in all students and shows teachers how to differentiate instruction so that students are the ones who personalize learning experiences to align with their own needs.

Chapter 10 highlights the need for students to frame and pursue their own learning goals and provides a variety of instructional strategies that enable teachers to mediate goal planning and assessment.

Chapter 11 details what the mediator does and avoids doing to create challenges for all students as they build their skills and their competence. It focuses on the three-story intellect as a model for setting increasingly challenging lessons in various content areas.

Chapter 12 discusses self-change, which calls for teachers to eliminate labels that categorize students and lock all put-downs out of the classroom. This is the first step in enabling students to self-talk about their own capabilities and to move to positive reflection and self-assessment that guides them to change their own behavior without the need of teacher mediation. Strategies are provided to facilitate positive self-assessments that will lead to improvements in learning.

Chapter 13 notes that the task of transforming classroom instruction from teacher talk and low-expectations methods to student-centered mediation requires a change in teacher belief. For this transformation, teachers will benefit most from a comprehensive professional development program that includes intensive coaching and follow-up.

For those who have used the first edition of this book, there are several noteworthy changes. These include the following:

- Updated description of the challenges of urban teaching and learning in Chapter 1
- The addition of Chapter 13 on professional development
- Three sample lessons for each chapter
- The updated description of the new BASIC tools for Instrumental Enrichment
- Clarification of the Mediated Learning Experience and its role as the organizational structure of this book
- Inclusion of updated research with a focus on the meta-analyses on effective teaching strategies that were completed since the first edition
- Key points to remember at the end of each chapter

In this revised edition, we have taken the opportunity to update the material we introduced in 1996. Since that time, additional research on how to best transform urban students from passive learners and low performers into active, engaged learners who are more willing and able to increase their academic achievement has helped us refine our thinking. In turn, we have passed on what we have learned from this research and from listening to feedback from multitudes of teachers throughout the United States and abroad who have told us what worked best to promote higher achievement for these students and what needed refinement in the original text.

More than ever, we are convinced of the need for the contents of this book. It is our fervent hope that what we advocate will make each of our readers stronger educators as mediators. We know that our points, as strongly as they are supported by effectiveness studies and research, run counter to some trends to turn teachers into script-reading automatons unable to meet the most important needs of their students. Quality instruction, especially in those schools where low-performing students struggle to learn, requires strong instructors who are skilled in making important decisions about how they teach each different child. They are the teachers who never have to face the question "What is it about me you can't teach?" because they have mastered the use of those skills that most announce, "In my classroom, I know there is nothing about you that I can't teach. I am going to help you transform your learning potential from words to actions. I will refuse to accept any gap in your achievement that separates you from the advantages that any others may have."

—James Bellanca
—Eleanor Renée Rodriguez

Acknowledgments

The framework for this book is based on Reuven Feuerstein's seminal work with the Mediated Learning Experience. Especially helpful are Reuven's 10 criteria for high-quality mediation. These criteria served as the major guide for linking the many strategies and structures to each other and to their meaningful use in the classroom.

Additional acknowledgments must be made to those who encouraged this work. Special thanks in this new Corwin Press edition to Kate Bellanca. Kate took time out from her winter school vacation and used her search engine skills to find, double-check, and update citations wherever she could. We thank her for this work and for helping us upgrade our technology skills.

We would like to thank those who have assisted us at Corwin Press in preparing the second edition of *What Is It About Me You Can't Teach?*

This book is dedicated to our ancestors, parents, extended family, and friends. It is hard to describe the special effect they have on our mission. Countless friends and colleagues have been supportive throughout the years. They have helped us stay focused on the children.

Finally, we dedicate this book to all the young learners and their families throughout the nation who are doing the best they know how to do and to the educators who appreciate the positive influence they can have on their lives.

—James Bellanca
—Eleanor Renée Rodriguez

I acknowledge the many blessings I have received, starting with my personal board of directors. First and foremost, Ms. Mayme B. Anderson, my mother, for her continued support and love, and I thank my sister, Leola Natalie Jackson, for her nagging and harassment. I give thanks to friends who have been particularly supportive, both personally and professionally, including, and certainly not limited to, Dr. Denise L. King-Miller, B. Anne Lovelady, Dr. Noah V. Rogers, Dr. John Brown, Deborah M. Brown, Patricia A. Cowen, and Debbie "Superfantastic" Baker. I could not have received more support and love than they provided.

—Eleanor Renée Rodriguez

Publisher's Acknowledgments

Corwin Press gratefully acknowledges the contributions of the following reviewers:

Ellen Brantlinger, Professor, Special Education Program Area
Indiana University, Bloomington, IN

Eric Cooper, National Urban Alliance for Effective Education @ Lake Success, New York, Council of Great City Schools, Washington, D.C., and the University of Alabama, Birmingham

Judy Deiro, Faculty
Western Washington University, Bellingham, WA

Edward Fergus, Director of Research, Metropolitan Center for Urban Education
New York University, New York, NY

Rosalind Pijeaux Hale, Professor of Education
Xavier University of Louisiana, New Orleans, LA

Rosanne G. Henderson, Principal
North Star Elementary School, Salt Lake City, UT

Ellen Herbert, Art Studio and Art History Teacher
Longview High School, Longview, TX

Tracy Huziak, Assistant Professor, Teaching and Learning
Bowling Green State University, Bowling Green, OH

Montie Koehn, Principal
Sequoyah Elementary School, Oklahoma City, OK

Marie Kraska, Mildred Cheshire Fraley Distinguished Professor of Educational Foundations, Leadership, and Technology
Auburn University, Auburn, AL

Barbara Rudiak, Principal
Phillips Elementary School, Pittsburgh, PA

Anne Smith, Education Research Analyst, Office of Special Education Programs
U.S. Department of Education, Washington, D.C.

About the Authors

 **Eleanor Renée Rodriguez**, PhD, a professional developer with Rodriguez and Associates, has provided consulting services and training to school districts, national associations, and state departments in 48 of 50 states and abroad. Her concentration is on research-based teaching and leadership strategies. She has served in positions from substitute teacher to superintendent, with assignments that included preK through adult education and with an emphasis on meeting the needs of students with special needs. In addition, she has directed, reviewed, and evaluated seminars and institutes for the American Association of School Administrators. Her mission is to eliminate the achievement gap and to help educators believe, behave, and achieve so *all* truly means *all*.

 **James Bellanca** founded SkyLight Professional Development in 1982. As its President, he mentored more than a dozen author/consultants as he led SkyLight in pioneering the use of strategic teaching and comprehensive professional development. Prior to meta-analyses that marked the effectiveness of cooperative learning, graphic organizers, and other cognitive strategies on student achievement, he coauthored more than a dozen texts that advocated the application of these tools across the curriculum with the theme "Not just for the test but for a lifetime of learning." Currently, he is building on the theories of cognitive psychologist Reuven Feuerstein to develop more effective responses to the learning needs of those low-performing students whose academic achievement continues to lag behind those who have greater learning advantages.

A Special Note

A wise man knows a proverb reconciles difficulties.

—Yoruba

Storytelling in Africa is an important oral tradition, and each story contains a lesson that highlights history, customs, and/or traditions. I love African proverbs. To me, they are the short and concise means to an end. The Nigerian proverb "It takes a village to raise a child" is remembered and used as a way to say that it takes everyone to educate everyone. Proverbs or sayings are used throughout this book in places where emphasis or additional attention is needed to reinforce a point. Enjoy!

—Eleanor Renée Rodriguez

To the children placed in our care.
We change lives.
Thank you for doing your best.

Children don't care how much you know until they know how much you care.

—Author unknown

My New Friend

I found someone who inspired me to fulfill my dreams. She challenged me to go out and reach my goals. And that it's okay to be different. I always thought that if I showed my true self, no one would be my friend. I thought that being smart was something to be ashamed of or hide. Until she helped me look inside myself. I found a person that was trapped in a prison. A prison where there was no sound, light, or one true person. When this person was released, it was like letting out a beast. Like a whole world of risk and chances opened up for me. I found a world I was never introduced to; before it always felt like the end for me. I never thought one person could change your life, but thanks to me allowing such a loving and caring person in my life, things have just begun. Thanks to my new friend.

—Rachell King, 16 years old
Hurricane Katrina Evacuee
Norfolk, Virginia
August 28, 2005

1

I Never Promised You a Rose Garden

Andrea remembers the day it happened. "I was sitting in geography class. I was a sophomore. The day had started out really bad. My mother was on my case for my bad grades. My teacher was handing back our tests. When he got to me, he threw the test on the desk. All I saw were the red marks. 'Your kind,' he said, 'don't deserve a desk.' I didn't even hear what else he had to say. I snapped. Just snapped when I heard that 'your kind.' It was the last straw. I didn't say anything when he ignored my raised hand or all the times he pretended I wasn't there. When I snapped, I just glared and said in my meanest voice, 'Mr. Rossi, just what is it about me you can't teach?'"

THE CHALLENGE OF URBAN EDUCATION

Andrea's angry question brings into the open the issue central to teaching and learning in urban classrooms: the nature of what teachers bring with them in dealing with their diverse student populations. Teachers in the affluent suburban schools may have well-equipped classrooms and laboratories, extensive counseling, and tutorial services in place, up-to-date textbooks, community support programs, extensive extracurricular programs, and cutting-edge technology at their disposal. These are what contribute to giving suburban students the "achievement advantage" and contribute to their superior performance.

On the other hand, many urban teachers struggle to keep aging walls graffiti free, work with textbooks bound together with tape, and labor to keep students safe from wayward bullets and drug-dealing miscreants. More often than not, the urban teacher who cares about making a difference buys her own supplies, counsels troubled children, resolves intense physical and verbal conflicts, and invents ways to include special challenge students for whom no other resources are provided. The urban students' lack of opportunity to have these resources contributes to their "achievement disadvantage" and the widening of the achievement gap. Working in an ER trauma center or air traffic control tower may seem like a dreamland compared to teaching and learning inside an urban classroom.

REFORM EFFORTS

Aided by the national reform movement begun with *A Nation at Risk*, there has been a plethora of organized reform efforts in urban school districts. Legislators, parents, teachers' organizations, professional educators' organizations, community agencies, and universities have joined the movement. From these efforts have come national standards, alternative and charter schools, site-based management, community service agency-school collaboration, public and parental engagement, teacher empowerment, choice plans, professional development schools, financial rewards for school-based improvement, lengthened school days, state takeovers, and privatization. In some cases, there even have been attempts to improve the resources available for teaching and learning that urban schools regularly lack.

This book is not about any of those efforts. It makes no judgment about which of these efforts help or don't help urban students. It also is not about the sociology of the urban students' community and its impact on student learning. These are givens that others address better than the material in this book. Rather, this book addresses the great, unforgotten, and often ignored issue of high-quality instruction in the urban classroom that can best attack the achievement gap and provide urban students with at least some of the means to share in the achievement advantages of their more affluent peers

Most effective teachers and most effective students are made, not born. Some students may be born with more natural ability than others to calculate, to read, to interact with others, or to excel at sports, but most learn how to succeed through the sweat of their brows and the sweat of their teachers' brows. In like manner, some teachers are born with more ability to motivate learning than others, but most improve how they teach through hard work and advanced study. Thus just as all children can learn to function in school more successfully through their own intense work and the skills of their teachers, so too all teachers can learn to teach more skillfully. Every basketball player is not Michael Jordan, but Michael Jordan didn't become a great player without developing his talents; every person who writes a poem is not a Maya Angelou, but Maya Angelou didn't become a great poet by neglecting her natural talent. Basic ability in children is not a limit, but a starting place. The same is true of teachers.

FOCUS ON RESEARCH

This book focuses on research conducted in the last 20 years that shows what teachers can do to add new knowledge and skills to their repertoire of teaching talent so that they can help students increase their own talents and achievements.

What happens with instruction in the urban classroom does not negate the importance of those reform efforts, which in fact help make productive teaching more likely; good instruction alone will not save our schools. However, all of the reform efforts are tangential to the central issue: the need for 100 percent attention to, and improvement of, instruction. Instruction that is connected to a meaningful curriculum and sound assessment is the most essential ingredient. Without improvement in instruction, there will be no improvement in student achievement and no development of student talents.

STUDENT ACHIEVEMENT AND TEACHER EXPECTATIONS: MORE THAN WORDS

Most of the research on student achievement asserts that improvement begins with the expectations of the classroom teacher. This book is not addressed to teachers in urban classrooms who believe that there is nothing they can do to improve their students' learning performance. Please don't scoff at the seriousness of the issue. The fact that such beliefs permeate urban schools is not to be minimized. For instance, at a recent meeting of high school mathematics teachers from a large urban system, in a room dominated by a bulletin board imprinted with the motto "We Believe All Can Learn—So Go for It," the responses to the question "How do we get more than 60 percent of our students to pass the state finals?" illustrate how subtle and deep are the low expectations held by the teachers:

"Get their parents involved."

"Get them to do more homework."

"Weed them out sooner."

"You can't teach lazy folks."

"Most belong in special education."

"They can't think."

"It's a dead-end street."

"They don't care. They don't have important goals."

"They're not like the students we used to have."

These comments, delivered by a mixture of African American, Hispanic, and Caucasian teachers, experienced and skilled in the teaching of mathematics, show frustration and the belief that nothing could be done for the 40 percent who were failing the test. These teachers' low expectations and ironclad vision—that students of the poor, students of color, students with special challenges, or students who speak other languages cannot learn—will continue to hold true. These students will not learn because they are not expected to learn, they are "excused" from learning, and they are instructed in ways that guarantee that they will not learn.

However, this book is addressed to teachers who do believe that all children can learn. Some of these teachers have great natural ability to teach all children, including urban children with diverse backgrounds, children with special challenges, and children with little wealth. These teachers are the Michael Jordans, the Maya Angelous, and the Martin Luther King Jrs. of the teaching profession. Most teachers, however, know they must continue to develop their talents to find ways to put the words "All children can learn" into practice. Many perform well without being superstars; but they do want all children to learn. They work in districts with the poorest classroom resources spread thinly among many challenged youngsters; they often have the least opportunity for the professional development that will help them learn about "best practice," the most recently discovered methods, and alternative instructional strategies. Their motto is, "Yeah, we do believe all children can learn"—their question is, "How?" Teaching in the modern urban classroom may be the most difficult challenge in the most difficult profession, but it also provides the greatest opportunity for a teacher to make a difference. Our focus here is on the knowledge that will help those committed to teaching all children who enter their classrooms.

In this book are many examples of practical strategies for immediate implementation. Some of the approaches to learning that are described here will require more practice and support over a longer period. These are balanced by sample lesson designs that delineate how to couple effective practices with course content and assessment in a lesson or unit design that will have the most impact on students. All of these are described in the context of research that shows how each approach is effective in urban classrooms. However, there is a "caveat," a "beware." All the instructional approaches are described with the forewarning that no single approach will help in every classroom every time. Each practice needs judicious decision making on the teacher's part. The teacher will make the chosen strategy appropriate for the content, the students' needs, and the situation. As the urban teachers select the appropriate strategy, they will make it an important part of their repertoire, their tool kit of approaches, that they will apply more and more skillfully as they grow in experience. With successful application of the tools will come the proof that indeed all children, including the much-maligned urban children, can learn because they, their teachers, have the tools, the talent, and the commitment to make it happen.

URBAN CHILDREN AND THE CHALLENGES THEY FACE

The development of a classroom teacher is a lifelong journey. An integral part of that journey is understanding the children in the classroom. As urban teachers progress on their journey, it is important they review the five main characteristics of the urban child. Who is the urban child? What are the truths, and what are the myths?

The first thing to know is that the urban child is a human being between the ages of birth and 18. Often, when referring to young adults receiving special education services, the age is extended to 21. These ages generally encompass the early childhood primary, intermediate, junior or middle, and high school grades. Although it is becoming more difficult to recognize preteens and teenagers as children nowadays, they are still children. In fact, one of the main problems encountered in educating urban children is the speed with which they are expected to grow up. Urban children are having more intense and different life experiences as children than most adults have had. These types of experiences can, and more than likely will, physically and psychologically age anyone. However, chronologically, the urban child, or any child for that matter, is still a child, regardless of the number or types of experiences.

Victims of Labels

Second, the urban child (the adjective used to be *inner city*) is likely to be, more than most children, a victim of labels that communicate and allow low expectations. The list on the following page covers excuses that teachers, principals, social workers, parents, and even the children themselves use to escape the challenge of rigorous learning and the assistance of strong instruction. More often than not, the labels are preceded in very subtle ways by some other phrase that is the heart and soul of low expectations.

The Scourge of Low Expectations

Third, the urban child is the individual (especially when male) most likely to end up in prison. How does this occur? Consider two examples that trace part of the responsibility to low-expectation practices in a school.

Abdul played his way through middle school. With 22 days of truancy his previous year, a failure in PE and Industrial Arts, and barely passing grades in his academics, Abdul ended up with a basic high school schedule for ninth grade: Practical Math, Basic English, Data Entry, Wood Shop, and General Science. After the first week of classes, Abdul told his sister that he was done with school (Abdul's mother was dead, his father lived out of state). Upset, the sister dragged Abdul into the counselor's office. After hearing the sister's complaints about Abdul's schedule and noting recorded remarks from teachers such as, "You are in Data Entry so you can get a job where you can succeed," "This is your fifth time through this basic math. I hope you get it this time," and "Stupid is as stupid does—this class is for the most stupid," the counselor commented, "Look, he's obviously not able to do this minimum work—if he could, he'd be in class now. We're doing the best we can. But he has to be able to do the work."

At this point, Abdul's sister pulled a copy of Abdul's test record from her pocket. Under "IQ," she pointed to the number 147. The counselor, stunned only for a moment, said, "This can't be Abdul's. No kid in this school ever got that score."

Abdul left school the next month. Three years later, he was in prison. The ability he was thought not to have appeared in his street activities. Within a month of going full-time to the streets, he became an accountant—organizing the books for his 450-member gang that specialized in crack sales totaling millions of dollars per year.

Jose's experience was no better. A gifted athlete who played on the all-city, all-star team in the sixth grade, he was turned down for admission to the junior high Spanish class. When he asked why, the principal responded, "You people are good athletes, but you'll never cut it in a language class." Five years later, Jose received a 20-year sentence. His crime? Jose had become a skilled forger, earning several hundred thousand dollars for his gang each year.

"I Can't Teach You Because You Are . . ."

black

brown

yellow

red

white

of interracial background

a Chapter 1/Title I student

not a native English speaker

bilingual

monolingual

Limited English Proficient

a free lunch student

a reduced lunch student

a neighborhood walker

a latchkey kid

an oldest child

a youngest child

an illegal resident

an immigrant

fatherless

motherless

homeless

federally connected

a left-brain learner

a right-brain learner

a refugee

an evacuee

of low SES (socioeconomic status)

of high SES

from a rural area

from an urban area

from a suburban area

learning disabled

visually impaired

orthopedically handicapped

speech impaired

emotionally disordered

attention-deficit/ hyperactivity disordered

autistic

hearing impaired

lesbian

gay

dyslexic

medically fragile

asthmatic

hyperactive

overactive

inactive

slow

backward

basic

a nonreader

illiterate

an underachiever

a gifted underachiever

a migrant

a transient

"at risk"

a jail bird

a ward of the state

an orphan

an adoptee

a truant

the child of middle-aged parents

HIV positive

not immunized

a dropout

born after September 18

not ready for kindergarten

a Head Start recipient

a food stamp recipient

a welfare recipient (Aid to Families With Dependent Children, AFDC)

a WIC (Women, Infants, and Children) program participant

a public housing resident

a Section 8 resident

physically abused

sexually abused

a head trauma victim

wheelchair bound

paralyzed

afflicted with Down syndrome

behaviorally disturbed

emotionally disturbed

educationally deficient

educationally handicapped

Children of Single Parents

Fourth, the urban child is likely to be the child with a single parent, who is most likely female, and most likely trapped in a low-pay, dead-end job or else fighting to survive on welfare. Many teachers who work in the urban schools look at this parent and make superficial judgments, and these judgments translate to low expectations:

"How can you expect Mario to do better? His father is in the state pen."

"Her mother didn't even finish Grade 8. Where does she think she's going?"

"Antonio's mother never comes to school. She doesn't care."

Fifth, the urban student is likely to be the child of immigrant parents who live in a community from the same country or region. Often, these children return home from school to share a small apartment with cousins, aunts, and uncles. They live near friends from the same villages in Russia, Poland, Mexico, Guatemala, Vietnam, Africa, or China. They hold on to the traditions and values of the "old country."

THE TASK AHEAD

When these children of different cultures, backgrounds, and languages come into the same classroom, the teacher is faced with more than differences in knowledge and skill. Urban teachers face a heterogeneous mix in their classrooms that runs deeper than language. They face a plethora of obstacles to instruction that can overwhelm even the strongest. What to do? Where to start?

While it is important for districts to continue their efforts to remake the size of schools, align the curriculum, and strengthen assessment, they cannot forget the quality of instruction. In this, it is important that urban districts pay attention to that research that makes the most difference in the improvement of test scores for urban students.

This research starts with the high expectations of studies begun several decades ago with the Los Angeles Teacher Expectation Student Achievement (TESA) project. When teachers learn to use the TESA behaviors well, they lay the foundation for the understanding that how students learn is more important than how they teach. The selection of the strategies and tactics they use to promote better learning follows from what works with the different students they face.

When teachers make this substantive change in perspective, they ready themselves to become mediators of learning. A mediator, as defined by cognitive psychologist Reuven Feuerstein, is a teacher who helps students better understand the world by developing the students' ways of knowing, or "cognitive functions." Very often, as a result of the urban students' lack of preschool mediation, these children come to school with poor cognitive readiness to learn. The mediators see this and use the principles and practices of mediated learning to help these children develop the prerequisite cognitive functions they lack.

The chapters that follow provide teachers with information on the principles and practices of mediation. There teachers will find road maps to understanding each of the mediation criteria, why it is important as a way to increase the quality of student learning, and how to build the mediating experience into meaningful lessons.

This book will not provide all the answers to moving urban students along the pathway to higher achievement. Part of those answers must come from the ways teachers and their school leaders apply the information in a systematic way. Part will come from new research on what works to help urban children become better learners so that they are in charge of their own educational destiny. And part will come from the other reforms that urban districts are putting in place. What must not be forgotten, however, is the essential idea that the most gain will come from the quality of mediated instruction that targets high achievement for all students.

2

High Expectations for All

They expected nothing, gave little, and got the same in return.

—Charlayne Hunter-Gault (Carson, 1991)
Resurrection City, Washington, D.C., 1968

Most educators will say it: "All children can learn." But what do they mean? Some qualify their statements by saying, "All children can learn, providing . . ." Others say, "All children, except for . . ." Still others add various phrasings of "if," "but," and "when" in order to qualify the statement. Does the statement work for classes filled with just blossoming roses, or does it apply also to classes in which weeds and thistles abound?

ALL CHILDREN CAN LEARN

The statement "All children can learn" is a popular declaration. The best instructional practices and stimulating programs that make this statement a reality are not so readily demonstrated in urban classrooms. The well-documented scarcity of these practices says more about the lack of conviction behind the espoused belief than it does about the sentiment itself. When the discrepancy between the "talk" and the "walk" is noted, the conversation often turns quickly to excuses, rationales, and other evasions as defenses for explaining why it is that "these children" can't be taught. "This is not what I thought teaching would be," says one surprised novice.

"It's certainly not why I spent my tuition money for a lifelong job," adds another. "My school was never like his, " chimes in a third. "Compared to this, my school was a rose garden."

Happily, there are many educators who do talk the talk and walk the walk. They have found many ways to put their unqualified beliefs into successful practice. Just as Henry Higgins followed his words with actions when he transformed Eliza Doolittle from a street-talking flower girl into a polished socialite who fooled the experts into thinking his protégé was a Hungarian princess, so too many educators work to transform all their students, including those who present the most significant learning challenges, into active, engaged, and successful learners. They don't look for a gifted rose garden; they make their little plot of land into a rose garden.

The belief that all children can learn springs from a positive point of view about learning potential. When the pessimists look at children and see a glass half empty, they go into a blue funk. "See," they say, "these children have limited intelligence. According to the statistics graphed on the bell curve, people with limited intelligence contribute the least to our gross national product and the most to crime and to welfare. Education, then, does no good." On the other hand, the optimist looks at the glass and sees that it is half full. "There is much we can do," they beam. "It may take more work, but let us use the best tools we have to educate each child to the fullest." Unlike pessimists such as Jensen, Murray, and Hartenstein, the optimists know that solid research supporting their view does exist, and they dedicate themselves to putting high expectations into practice.

In the last two decades, the optimists have demonstrated that there are strategies for dispelling the myths that only those measured to be bright or those who are given strong, early education at home can learn. Two of these optimists, Samuel Kermin (1972), director of the Teacher Expectations and Student Achievement (TESA) project for the Los Angeles County School System, and Reuven Feuerstein, the Israeli cognitive psychologist who created Instrumental Enrichment, have made especially valuable contributions. More recent contributions include Gardner's theory of multiple intelligences and the growing movement toward authentic learning and assessment.

> Colorism, like colonialism, sexism, and racism, impedes us.
>
> —Alice Walker (Riley, 1993)

TESA: THE TRIED AND TRUE

In the mid-seventies, Samuel Kermin and the Los Angeles County School Board introduced the results of a multiyear study, TESA. Having reviewed the early research on how teacher behavior influenced student performance, Kermin and his associates devised practical means for teachers of poor and minority students, long thought of as impossible to teach, to help all children learn. Kermin and his associates identified 15 teacher behaviors that seemed to have the greatest impact on how students improved their performance in reading and mathematics testing and created a training program to enable teachers to practice the belief. For the first time on a large public scale, the TESA program demonstrated what it takes to transform the belief into a reality. High expectations, as implemented through the 15 teacher behaviors, showed that poverty and race were not insuperable barriers to learning. The real barriers were created by the low-level expectations with which these children were taught. With new teacher behaviors, substantive learning was as possible for these children as for the children of affluence and influence.

Following the initial success of TESA with the children of Los Angeles County, Kermin and his associates designed and disseminated a teacher training program, now also universally known as TESA, to expand the impact of the initial research. In this training program, they outlined the research on each of the behaviors, modeled how a teacher might effectively implement each behavior, conducted guided practice, and set up coaching teams to provide classroom observation and on-the-spot feedback.

Following the lead provided by the "wait-time lady," Mary Budd Rowe, and by Robert Rosenthal's study *Pygmalion in the Classroom*, the TESA program's studies showed how selected teaching behaviors such as wait time, proximity, higher-order questions, and constructive feedback were missing in classrooms where the teachers lacked the belief that all children can learn. Most notably, the researchers found that teachers behaved differently toward students whom they believed had low learning ability. Most often, these judgments were based on stereotypes of class, race, and family. For these children, the teachers asked low-order, factual questions such as "Who is the main character?" or "What year did Columbus sail from Spain?" or else asked them to choose the correct answer to fill in a blank. When teachers perceived children to be slow, they used less wait time, reinforced correct responses less, and provided less individual attention.

> Researchers found that teachers behaved differently toward students whom they believed had low learning ability.

On the other hand, the TESA researchers noted changes in behavior when teachers believed that certain children had the capability for high performance. For these children, the teachers were more likely to make regular and consistent use of the high-expectations behaviors. For these students, a teacher was more likely to ask a question that required the student to think ("Why do you think Lincoln freed the slaves?"), wait more than five seconds for the student's response, and provide positive and expansive feedback ("That was an excellent answer. I especially liked your inclusion of the description of the political pressure").

Kermin and his associates demonstrated that once teachers were provided with new ways to interact with students for whom they held low expectations, the teachers themselves would interact differently with those students. The students, challenged to respond in new ways, would improve their own performance and behavior in the classroom. In a sense, the new teaching behaviors forced a different type of teacher-student interaction. The new interactions resulted in the students' responding in more positive ways. The students' responses changed the teachers' perceptions of what their students could do and learn. The more the teachers changed how they taught, the more they transformed students into engaged learners. For instance, when low-expectations teachers ignored misbehavior, noncompliance with task instructions, failure to complete tasks, or exhibition of "who cares?" behavior, or when they merely shouted and screamed at the students, they saw instant but short-lasting changes in the students. Compliance was swift, but disappeared once the sound and fury were over. When these teachers—who had once argued vociferously in defense of their scream-and-punish tactics—learned how to use cues, higher-order questioning, wait time, and the other TESA strategies, they saw new, lasting results with their students. Buoyed by the positive responses, the teachers increased praise, proximity, and other reinforcers, which resulted in additional positive responses. Indeed, Kermin's hypothesis about high expectation practices proved that changed teacher behavior could change student performance.

TESA's success had a major impact on how educators thought about students from poor families and children of color. First, the project demonstrated clearly that teachers' high and low expectations directly affect the learning of children. Second, the project developed a systematic method that enabled teachers to revise their low expectations in favor of high-expectation behaviors. Third, the project destroyed the myth of the "natural" teacher that had dominated American education. The project's results made a solid argument for improving the quality of teacher training and development, improvements that would provide teachers with successes in teaching, and transform their attitudes about student potential for learning. This in turn would fuel additional successes in their work with at-risk children. Fourth, the project provided easy-to-use, easy-to-learn teaching tools that produced strong, measurable, and significant results in the achievement level of students often claimed to be "unmotivated" or "not teachable." Finally, the project demonstrated how poverty, family history, and race are too easily used as excuses by educators who get low-performance results from students, largely because they teach with low-expectation strategies.

The magic of high expectations is neither novel nor limited to formal education. George Bernard Shaw first popularized them in a Greek mythological story for modern audiences in his pre-twentieth-century play *Pygmalion*. Decades later, Broadway adapted the story in the popular musical *My Fair Lady*. Around the world, audiences thrilled to the rise of the cockney flower girl, Eliza Dolittle, to the ranks of royalty. They watched as her mentor, convinced that he could teach anyone, anything, first changed Eliza's pronunciation and vocabulary and then her demeanor and dress so that all were convinced of her royal blood. At times, she doubted, but he persisted until her triumph.

THE FIFTEEN BEHAVIORS

What were the teacher behaviors (and the expectations they evidenced) that Kermin and his associates found to have the greatest impact on low-performing children in the classroom? There were 15 that they researched in the classrooms of Los Angeles and that became the heart of the TESA training program.

1. Equitable Distribution. Thomas Good's (1987) research had shown how teachers tended to call more often on students who sat in the front row and middle seats in the classroom (the T) and ignored students outside the T seating pattern; students in the back corners had the least likelihood of being asked to answer a question. Moreover, by the middle grades, many students learned the strategy of distribution and sat themselves, given the choice, according to their desire to participate or not participate. High performers went to the T, low performers to the corners.

To correct the unequal distribution of questioning, TESA taught teachers to make a conscious effort to direct their questions to the corners and the back of the room. When put into effect, the strategy put students on notice of the expectation that all students, regardless of seating, would have an equal chance to be called on. There would be no hiding in a TESA classroom.

2. Affirm/Correct. In his study of teacher behavior, Good (1970) had noted that teachers gave less accurate and less detailed feedback to students they perceived as low achievers, giving students perceived as high achievers more detailed and accurate feedback. He also noted that Anglo students were more likely to get accurate and detailed feedback than Mexican American students. Rubovits and Maehr (1973) had noted a similar pattern when black and white students were in the same classroom.

In the TESA project, teachers were trained to make accurate comments about each student's response. The feedback would note that an answer was correct or incorrect and, in the best circumstances, would explain "why."

3. Proximity. Using a variety of research studies, the TESA project showed how the teacher's physical closeness to the student affected time on task. In the project, teachers learned how to reseat students, how to rearrange seating for easier access, and how to move closer to students who were off task.

4. Individual Help. Sadker and Sadker (1985) noticed how the assertiveness of high-achieving students, especially males, resulted from more individual help. In the TESA project, teachers learned how to identify the two or three students who received the least amount of attention, even when they called for help in a proper manner.

5. Praise. Rosenshine (1971) and Good (1987) both documented how teachers were less likely to praise perceived low achievers for academic performance and more likely to praise perceived high achievers. Moreover, researchers noted that teachers tended to protect low achievers from criticism about wrong answers. The TESA project trained the teachers to give energetic, positive feedback and rewards to all students, with a special *concentration of attention for the perceived low performers.*

6. Wait Time. Mary Budd Rowe provided the research that showed the importance of teacher silence after asking a question. She noted how often teachers answered their own questions or jumped to a new question in less than eight-tenths of a second. She also noticed how student involvement increased when teachers extended the wait time or silence to two or three seconds. In the TESA project, teachers were trained to keep quiet for two or more seconds, to not answer their own questions, and to not add additional questions.

7. Courtesy. A number of researchers, including Brophy, Good, Hillar, Sadker and Sadker, and Rist, have observed that many teachers were discourteous and disrespectful toward "low-status students" yet demanded that those students show respect to them as teachers. More often than not, high-status students, those who received the most attention from the teacher, copied the teacher's behavior toward the low-status students. This included interrupting answers of the low-status students, high use of put-downs, and sarcasm. The high-status group members were mostly white males; minority females were the lowest status group.

In the TESA project, teachers were taught to identify how they created or contributed to high- and low-status groups by the way they gave attention, responded to students with courteous statements such as "thank you" and "please," and avoided the use of sarcastic tones and belittling phrases.

8. Reasons for Praise. After helping teachers in the project change their patterns of praise (see Item 5 above), the project deepened their understanding of how offering reasons for praise corresponded to the equal distribution of status. Brophy (1986) had already noted that many teachers gave fewer reasons for praise to low achievers; teachers tended to give low-status students "static" praise that was overdone and simplistic, such as "Good job," "Yes," and "OK." When teachers distributed praise and provided reasons, Brophy noted a change in students' achievement.

TESA trainers prepared teachers to follow Brophy's criteria for giving praise at selected appropriate times, such as when students would make genuine and significant gains or when students would fail to appreciate their own progress. The trainers also provided criteria for judging the quality of praise. These criteria included the notions that sincere praise is appreciative, applicable to a specific accomplishment, natural, private, and attributed to effort and ability.

9. Personal Regard. Brophy (1986) observed that teachers in his study paid less attention in academic and social situations to the socioeconomically disadvantaged students. The more advantaged students received more smiles, more eye contact, more questions that asked them to connect academic content to personal experiences, and more positive responses to personal examples. Outside of class (as in the lunchroom or on the playground), teachers gave less time and attention to the personal well-being and interest of disadvantaged students.

In the TESA project, teachers in training learned how to develop content-related questions that connected to what they knew might be of interest to a student. For instance, a science teacher might ask Raphaela to explain how water temperature affects her swimming; a social studies teacher might ask Juan to compare the means of transportation used in his native Mexico to the means used in Los Angeles. In neither case would the teacher limit these interest-connected questions to select students. The teacher's challenge with these questions and other displays of personal regard are equitable distribution.

10. Delving. Brophy (1986) had also noticed how low achievers were asked fewer and easier questions than high achievers. If the low achiever showed signs of bewilderment, the teacher more readily turned to another student or answered the question. When high achievers were questioned, the teacher more readily gave clues, probed for evidence or reasons, or encouraged a more extensive response. TESA teachers were trained to push students to expand on their answers, to ask all students a second or third follow-up question that forced them to delve more deeply into course content, and to provide clues that would help all students, especially the lowest performers, to give a full response.

11. Listening. In 1964, Flanders noted how teachers spent more time talking to low-status students and less to the high achievers. In contrast, perceived high achievers spent more time sharing ideas, conversing with the teacher, and engaging in activities that required student talk.

12. Touching. Relying on studies that showed how a teacher resting a hand on a student's shoulder or forearm was more effective in focusing a student's attention on a task than simply reprimanding or talking to the student, the TESA project researchers anticipated later learning style research that identified the needs of kinesthetic learners for physical contact. (Obviously, this research also antedated unfortunate classroom incidents that have made any touch by a teacher an act to avoid or to be very cautious about.)

13. **Higher-Level Questions.** TESA brought to the forefront the issue of lower- and higher-order thinking as expected of low- and high-performing students. The researchers noted how low performers were limited to factual questions: who, what, when, where, and how. High performers were given the questions that asked them to process, apply, and evaluate ideas. To counter this tendency, TESA prepared teachers to use tools such as Bloom's (1956) taxonomy of cognitive objectives to frame the complete range of questions for all students. In this way, teachers would communicate that all students were expected to perform complex thinking tasks.

14. **Accepting Feelings**. TESA research distinguished between a teacher's indifferent response to a student's task performance and the teacher's acknowledgment of the affective dimension of the student's performance or response. For instance, with less effective feedback, the teacher would acknowledge minimally that the student had given a correct answer; with more effective feedback, the teacher would acknowledge the joy or pride with which the student had communicated the answer or response. If the teacher had to give corrective feedback, he or she would also acknowledge the student's disappointment. When this occurred consistently in a classroom, students were more open and responsive to feedback from the teacher and consequently more likely to act on improving and/or correcting their work.

15. **Desisting**. In high-expectation classrooms, the TESA study described how teachers maintained on-task behavior by directly confronting off-task behavior. This direct confrontation identified the specific misbehavior, expressed the teacher's feeling about it, and instructed the student to stop the misbehavior and replace it with a specified acceptable behavior. In contrast, teachers with low expectations allowed students to continue misbehavior and often justified what the students were doing with statements of low expectation such as "What else can you expect?" or by increasing voice volume to a scream.

> Children respond to the expectations of their environment.
>
> —William Grier and Price Cobb (Riley, 1993)

Because the TESA behaviors were identified and the program introduced more than three decades ago, it is not uncommon for some educators who are more enamored with fluff and fads to dismiss TESA as out of date. However, somewhere in this country there is a large number of students who still fall victim to low expectations.

RESTORING CHILDREN OF WAR: THE MEDIATED LEARNING EXPERIENCE

At the same time that Kermin was working with TESA, Reuven Feuerstein (1980) was paralleling the TESA successes with a very different approach in Israel. Having studied with Piaget in France, Feuerstein developed a system of learning for the children of the Holocaust who arrived in Israel from all parts of the world following

World War II. Working in kibbutz schools, Feuerstein faced the challenge of teaching children devastated by concentration camp life and the destruction of their families and cultures.

The children had come from the deserts of Ethiopia, the fields of Lebanon, and the ravaged nations of Europe and Asia. Few brought formal learning with them; many brought the remnants of emotional devastation and cognitive deficits. Most lacked what Feuerstein called "the prerequisites of learning."

> Feuerstein found that his special students lacked "the prerequisites of learning."

When placed in the classrooms of the kibbutzim, these children caused their teachers to throw up their hands and declare, "You are impossible to teach, you cannot learn!" What the teachers experienced were children and young adults whose impulsive behavior, inability to connect information, and passivity blocked all attempts at formal schooling.

The Jar of Learning

Rather than deny the perceptions and low expectations of these experienced teachers, Feuerstein, a classic optimist, saw that the "jars were half-filled. I knew from my diagnoses that these were giant jars. We had much to do, but we were not sure how to do it." In his commitment to find ways to open "these minds locked and chained against learning," Feuerstein adapted traditional IQ assessment instruments to the task of discovering why these children functioned so poorly. After all, he noted, they had survived far more serious threats to life and limb before getting to Israel. Using his collection of test tools, which he later named Learning Propensity Assessment Devices, Feuerstein identified 14 cognitive functions that were prerequisites for significant achievement. Comparing the early childhood experiences of his special students with students who were having success in school, he found that the children who were struggling lacked the prerequisites. In addition, Feuerstein found that parents were the primary providers of the "mediation" that developed these prerequisites. Because the war and the camps had so destroyed their families, the children Feuerstein was attempting to assist had never experienced the necessary mediation.

Having identified the problem, Feuerstein next faced the challenge of finding the possibilities for introducing the weak cognitive functions that could give older children the cognitive foundations they had missed. These investigations led to the development of his theory of mediated learning and the instructional practices that made the theory work.

The theory of mediated learning begins with the presupposition that all children can learn. For Feuerstein, there are no qualifications to this belief. There are only the limits imposed by those who desire excuses to avoid the challenge of mediating success for all.

The Two Wellsprings of Learning

Feuerstein's systematic approach to teaching and learning begins with a rejection of Skinner's behavior modification theory, with its belief that learning is merely a response to external stimuli. Taking his cue from Piaget, Feuerstein teaches that learning springs from within the individual's heart and mind. Without internal motivation, there is no learning for humans.

B. F. Skinner's Theory

S — R

Stimulus   Response

Piaget introduced the concept that the teacher's major role is the creation of a rich learning environment appropriate to the student's cognitive development. In this scenario, later expanded by Vygotsky (1962) in his early explanation of idea construction, the learner makes "meaning" from stimuli provided by the teacher in the classroom. Feuerstein also adopted the belief that learning is centered in the active mental engagement of the learner with past knowledge and new experiences. In this engagement process, the learner melded new with old, and the result was "learning."

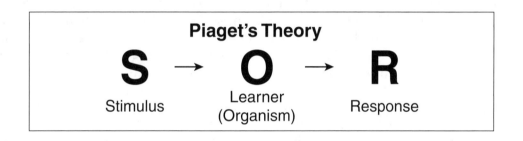

Piaget's Theory

S → O → R

Stimulus   Learner
(Organism)   Response

Feuerstein parted ways with Vygotsky, however. Feuerstein postulated that the best quality of learning does not occur in an environmental vacuum. He noted how parents, siblings, and other significant individuals can impact the learner from the earliest years. He also noted that many children, denied this interaction by poverty, racism, or other negative environmental conditions, failed to develop their learning capabilities. As a consequence of his observation, Feuerstein proposed an extension of Piaget's S-O-R model. Between the stimulus and the learner and the response and the learner, Feuerstein added the mediator. This mediator is a person who captures the many stimuli that bombard a learner every day, strains the stimuli, and helps children develop their own way of filtering those stimuli that promote learning from those that distract. For Feuerstein, parents are the first mediators. They are assisted by peers, siblings, teachers, counselors, and other helpers who assist learners in developing their learning propensity.

> Learning is centered in the active mental engagement of the learner.

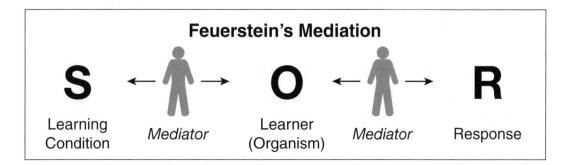

Feuerstein's Mediation

S ← *Mediator* → O ← *Mediator* → R

Learning   Learner   Response
Condition   (Organism)

The Content-Free Curriculum

To assist the mediation process, Feuerstein developed a curriculum of "content-free" print materials that he called "instruments." In actuality, the content of each instrument is "thinking" itself. Feuerstein wanted this content-free approach so that the student would not be blocked by language deficiencies or by a lack of prior knowledge in any specific discipline. Such a lack, he argued, would distract from the cognitive restructuring.

The mediator helps learners concentrate on the thinking processes they are using to solve the increasingly difficult problems on each instrument. In addition, the mediator, relying on selected open-ended questions and positive feedback, helps learners identify how they are planning to solve the problem, how they are assessing the process for solving the problem, and what tactics were most successful. Guided by additional open-ended questions from the mediator, the learner identifies the successful process and applies the critical elements to the next, more difficult problem.

Noting how "teacher talk" and mindless seatwork with their low expectations of what students could do had failed with these children, Feuerstein adapted the inquiry strategies that he had learned as a child psychologist and teacher. These strategies, which he labeled "mediation," became the essential tools for enabling classroom teachers and parents to uncover the cognitive functions necessary for all children, especially children challenged to learn how to learn.

As Feuerstein and his colleagues developed it, mediation is a mutual interaction between the mediator (a parent, teacher, coach, or counselor) and the student. The mediator purposefully directs the interaction toward a specific goal by focusing attention, selecting, framing, interpreting, and cuing the student on specific stimuli. Consider the example of a young student walking home from school. A parent or teacher at his side as he walked through the dilapidated neighborhood could focus his attention on the sights, sounds, and smells. By highlighting what they were experiencing together, the parent or teacher could interpret his experience, establish cause-and-effect relationships, and give meaning to the events. The student's attention could be directed toward different people, and he could make comparisons to other individuals at other places who are similar. Cutting short the student's impulsive and shallow judgments would help him sort through the plethora of experiences systematically. In short, Feuerstein would argue that this caring mediator ensures that the child learns how to learn in a purposeful and complete way. The mediator builds the foundations of cognition, the thinking processes that ensure that the student will learn no matter what means of instruction—direct, indirect, constructive, or collaborative—the child might receive in future schooling. With such mediation, the child develops the internal controls that enable him to learn how to learn.

> The mediator helps children develop their own way of filtering those stimuli that promote learning from those that distract.

The Criteria for Successful Mediation

Feuerstein developed 10 criteria of interaction that are fundamental for skilled mediation. The first three criteria—(1) intentionality and reciprocity, (2) meaning, and (3) transcendence—Feuerstein believes are necessary for successful mediation in any instructional situation. The remaining seven—(4) competence, (5) self-regulation and control of behavior, (6) sharing behavior, (7) individuation, (8) goal planning, (9) challenge, and (10) self-change—Feuerstein saw as helpful in specific situations. Because they teach children how to learn, all of these mediative efforts, he argues, are essential for making high expectations central to every classroom. They are especially important to counter the poor instruction that is provided in classrooms dominated by workbooks, laissez-faire busywork, teacher lectures, and recall tests. The teacher-as-mediator, therefore, is the person who initiates active learning, the mental processing that transforms incidental learners into students grounded in the prerequisites for learning, and leads students to success in each and every content area.

When considering the use of mediation, there is a variety of key points that distinguish a teacher from a mediator.

- *The mediator builds the foundations of cognition,* the thinking processes that ensure that the student will learn.
- *Mediation of intentionality starts from the mediator; the student being mediated must reciprocate or respond.* If there is not a balance of intentionality and reciprocity, there is no mediation. If the mediator fails to obtain the desired response, there will be little or no learning.
- *Mediation of meaning is the second required component.* Although memory may be a tool that facilitates meaning, recall by itself is insufficient for learning. For the student to grasp the meaning of a concept or idea, the student must understand that concept and its implications.
- *Mediation of transcendence is the third constant in the process of mediated learning experiences.* It is required in every lesson along with intentionality, reciprocity, and meaning. The goal of mediation of transcendence is not limited to the current context. The goal is to place children on a projectory and to help them see the direction in which they are going. It is basically the skill that helps students go into the future. Teachers know it has occurred when students are able to answer the question, "What of this task can become meaningful in other situations?"
- *In mediation of the feeling of competence, learning tasks become more difficult*—from simple to complex and concrete to abstract—and help the students grow in confidence and self-reliance. Teachers should fade out as a mediator when students become stronger learners. Teachers can think about the level of intensity children have when competing in the games they play. Most games challenge students to higher levels of difficulty, and they are generally up for the challenge or commit the time to move toward their goal of success.
- *Sharing behavior is didactic.* Learning how to communicate with others creates ways to communicate the internal self. The major element of sharing is to have students fuse with or vibrate with one another. Despite cultural differences, the need for sharing is important in order to form an extension of self with others. No child is an island. Students need to believe they are a part of something.
- *The bottom line is to have students finish a task.* In mediation of goal planning, planning behavior becomes a habit, instead of just "do it." Through goal planning, impulsivity is reduced.
- *Self-regulation and control of behavior asks students to take responsibility for their behavior and become internally motivated.* Teachers can benefit most by

mediating how students self-regulate their own thinking and problem solving. As students gain control over their thinking, they become more reflective and less impulsive. With the academic successes this brings to children, teachers can then mediate the application of self-regulation to other behaviors that involve interactions with peers by increasing student choices and mediating the consequences of these choices.

- *Parents have been heard to ask, "So if your friend jumps off the bridge, are you going to jump too?"* That is a parent's way of asking children if they can think for themselves. Helping children learn to think for themselves involves the mediation of individuation. "What have I learned?" "How does what I just learned apply to me?"

- *Self-change occurs within the individual.* It is internal motivation versus external motivation. The changes are subtle, so teachers have to be the ears and eyes to show the children the evidence of the change. The teacher as mediator of self-change can help the children see how they have taken advantage of the other mediations. A giant wall rubric listing the mediations as criteria for self-change will help guide the students in seeing the changes they are making in how they think and act.

- *The operational aspects of the theory of Instrumental Enrichment include wisdom for every classroom.*
  1. *Human beings are changeable and modifiable, regardless of heredity, chromosomes, organic conditions, or metabolic errors,* no matter how serious the differences. Just think of the common perceptions held only 30 years ago regarding Down syndrome. These children and adults were all seen as "retarded," with IQs in the 70s range. Today, data are showing that "chromosomes do not have the last word" (Feuerstein). Down syndrome individuals are poets, actors, writers, and painters as well as caregivers for the elderly and soldiers in the Israeli army.
  2. *Etiology should not become an ultimate barrier.* No matter how severe a child's learning challenges, teachers should never give up; there is something to be done for every child.
  3. *Some students have weak or deficient learning functions.* They are mistakenly diagnosed and labeled as "retarded" individuals. By mediating, a teacher can create the conditions that help students with weak cognitive functions to overcome their barriers to learning successfully.
  4. *Change is a departure from a predictable path of development.* With mediation, the changes in how a student thinks are structural. For example, think about having a heap of nuts. Move one and the structure of the pile changes, but the pile is still made of nuts.

- *Mediation cannot be standardized.* It is the ultimate act of individualized learning.

- *When engaged with Instrumental Enrichment, students are more verbal,* asking questions, volunteering answers, responding to questions, and sharing ideas spontaneously. The amount of time on task is improved, and they are more focused for longer periods of time. They are willing to take risks and say, "I don't know." Their self-images improve and they use alternative ways of solving conflict. One of the best outcomes is their ability to be more aware of cause-effect behaviors, knowing the consequences of their actions. We want students to explore during learning versus coverage of material.

- *Start from the students' experiences in order to prepare them to understand and to transfer what they learn.* Teachers teach the skills but do not leave the activity as the end point of the exercise. After the students have practiced the skills, mediating teachers have to bring up questions so that students reflect on what they have learned. Without the reflection, what students may have learned is not yet in their minds. Without guided reflection, the teacher did not teach anything. If the teachers tell the students what they learned, the teachers' telling the principles defeat the purpose. The questions asked by the teachers guide the reflection and enable the students to understand the principles. The principles have to come from the child. The greatest shift that has to occur is that the children's learning, not the teachers' teaching, is what gets the attention.

- *With mediated learning, the meaning will derive only from reflecting with the help of a mediator to make the meaning come out.* The goal of teaching is to help the child understand "why." The faster teachers get to the why questions, the better. Don't qualify the answer; try to remain as neutral as possible. The art of asking questions is the art of teaching. In other words, do not micromanage the thinking of the child.

- *Keep children away from the "just do it" way of thinking.* This mentality leads to an increase in impulsivity. Impulsivity, one of the most devastating and antilearning behaviors in children, is due to a variety of factors, including not taking the time for the task or using the processes of cognitive or metacognitive controls before acting. Students have to learn to take their time to analyze and plan before doing the task. They must stop and think in order to achieve.

- *Look for well-thought-out responses.* It is best for teachers to discourage quick thinking and fast answers. Fewer questions are better than many.

MULTIPLE INTELLIGENCES

In the 1980s, Harvard cognitive psychologist Howard Gardner (1983) reinforced Feuerstein's position that intelligence was flexible by advancing the theory of multiple intelligences. Like Feuerstein, Gardner challenged the traditional belief that intelligence was fixed and immutable. Gardner's theory has very powerful implications for instruction in urban classrooms, especially for those many students whose ways of knowing differ from the conventional approaches to learning.

Multiple intelligences theory brightens the possibilities for what is understood to be a classroom. Instead of thinking of the classroom as a 35' × 35' room where a teacher guides 30 students, all places that are rich learning environments become learning centers. Thus in Gardner's eyes, a children's museum is not a place limited to field trips—it becomes a classroom rich in learning opportunity. A botanical garden is not simply a place to visit and observe—it is a classroom where children can dig their hands into the dirt. A classroom is not a place to visit for 40 minutes of a day—it is an environment rich with materials and tools for making, doing, and expanding many intelligences.

Gardner's theory of multiple intelligences does not occur by happenstance. He supports his theory by choosing rigorous criteria for proposing the existence of his proposed intelligences. Beginning with his definition of intelligence as "the human intellectual competence [that] must entail a set of skills for problem solving—enabling the individual to resolve genuine problems or difficulties he or she encounters, and when appropriate to create an effective product" (Gardner, 1983), Gardner expanded his theory and described a multiplicity of intelligences that met his criteria.

For any classroom that contains a child with a special challenge as easy to include as mild dyslexia or as difficult to include as advanced multiple sclerosis, Gardner's theory rips down the barriers to learning that protect the belief that there is one right way to teach all children. Instead, he provides a strong foundation for the development of classroom environments and instructional strategies that take teachers and students well beyond traditional limits. Freed from perceived constraints on instruction, teachers can apply the theory in an endless array of learning opportunities that challenge students well beyond traditional expectations.

One of the largest benefits of Gardner's theory is its allowance for more authentic ways to promote student learning. Its largest weakness is that it leaves out the decisions on how to do that, especially when the teachers are working to promote achievement for those student populations that have the greatest learning needs.

In the years since Gardner first released his theory of multiple intelligences, research on effective instructional strategies has helped by clarifying which instructional strategies have the most effect on student learning. This research has helped educators target their selection of strategies so that they do not have to go by guess or by golly or follow the whims of the local education professor's pet theory. With these "high-effect" strategies identified, teachers can more easily design lessons aligned with multiple intelligences theory and, at the same time, better instruct those students who are most ready to benefit from the targeted strategies.

In the context of high-expectations instruction, the strategies identified in the following chapters align well with multiple intelligences theory. They provide the practical tools teachers need to put theory into practice. Cooperative learning, asking questions, and graphic organizers stand out as best examples for raising student achievement (Marzano, Pickering & Pollack, 2001).

AUTHENTIC ASSESSMENT

Conventional assessment methods, spurred by the use of Scantron marking machines, favor short-answer responses to questions of fact. The students' ability to answer many questions in a short time period becomes the chief measure of their ability to learn. Under the pressures of accountability, teachers mold instruction to fit the short-answer test. Students, knowing the game well, decide how much time and effort they will expend in memorizing facts and figures. Obviously, those with the fastest recall have the least difficulty with rote work; many others, seeing no value in rote work, refuse to play the game.

> Teachers can apply an array of learning opportunities that challenge students well beyond traditional expectations.

In the past few years, the focus on student evaluation has switched from short-answer tests and single-score grades to multiple sources of information about what a student knows and does to demonstrate learning, performance standards, and the alignment of classroom instruction with district, state, and national standards. In almost every content field, national commissions work on defining the content and process standards for that discipline. In other areas such as staff development, national associations lead the way in defining standards. Most recently, recognition has begun to be given to the teacher's role in assessing students in multiple ways.

When assessment goes beyond the limits of the #2 pencil standardized test and examines authentic learning with authentic assessments, multiple views emerge regarding what a student knows and is able to do. Thus in writing, teachers return to assessing how well the student actually prepares a persuasive or an expository essay. The standardized test may show what students know about grammar usage, but it is in writing an authentic essay that students show how well they can use grammar. In social studies, the short-answer test may show the students' knowledge of the facts in the course; the completion of a service project or the application of key course ideas in a debate shows their ability to use the knowledge. By forming standards and criteria for success and by using new tools that challenge the multiple intelligences in a class-room, the teacher can assess both the knowledge and the students' ability to use the knowledge in meaningful ways. When students learn by using knowledge, they are learning by "authentic means"; when the teachers use the standards, the criteria, and the tools to assess that authentic learning, they are performing "authentic assessment."

By its very nature, authentic assessment creates higher expectations than does the simple short-answer test that allows students to escape the responsibility of significant learning. In the high-expectations classroom, where students know from day-to-day experience that there is no hiding from the teacher's adherence to high-engagement learning tasks, they know they are accountable to higher standards to demonstrate what they know and can do.

The Benefits of Authentic Assessment

There are several ways that authentic assessment benefits students' learning.

- It allows teachers to assess what a student can do with new, standards-aligned knowledge. Assessment is not limited to knowledge alone.
- It allows teachers to identify analysis errors in how students are thinking and doing. These analysis errors are a rich source of information that helps teachers correct the underlying misconceptions once and for all (Ben-Hur, 1994).
- It allows teachers to focus on process as well as product. Teachers can better assess how well students know the "why" of their knowledge and skill and challenge the students to go beyond learning by rote memory.

> Authentic assessment creates higher expectations than does the simple short-answer test.

- It allows teachers to define "higher expectations" not just as "more work" but as work that requires more complex thinking and problem solving. This counters the low-level expectations foisted on many poor and minority students, which limit assessment by quantifying "how much" a student has learned without considering the intellectual rigor of the tasks.

TWO DECADES OF RESEARCH

In the past two decades, researchers have provided ample evidence that the tools exist to put the words of high expectations into practice. Standards have provided a framework for ensuring that all students have access to an equally rigorous curriculum. Curricular content aligned with the standards ensures that equal attention is given in every classroom to the most important concepts. High-effects instructional practices, differentiated by individual student needs, can provide teachers with the necessary tools to help even the most reluctant learners. To help the teachers learn how to use the tools, research-strong professional development practices can aid teachers in learning what they need to know and how to use that knowledge with low-performing students. When it comes to raising the academic performance of all students, the tools exist.

Research: Always Necessary but Never Sufficient

The fact that researchers have identified which of these high-expectation practices will best lead to closing achievement gaps by producing the strongest gains for the lowest performers is only a start. It is a necessary start, but insufficient for making the needed gains.

Educational researchers have identified which tools belong on the store shelf. They have analyzed the data on how various programs, approaches, and strategies impact student learning. This has produced, as it were, a rank order of those effects on learning that most correlate with student success.

With this necessary information in hand, the job of educational leaders and classroom teachers is made easier. No longer do those in the trenches have to guess which tool will work best with the students in their classrooms. Nor do they have to rely on mythology. With research, they now have the opportunity to make informed choices. So what else is needed?

Where There Is a Will, There Is a Way

Effective schools pioneer Ron Edmunds told educators more than three decades ago that they had more than enough information on how to raise achievement. His question was, Did they have a sufficient desire to use these tools? Since Edmunds threw down his glove to challenge educators' will to help all children, many districts have made significant strides. Others have done little other than rely on teachers to make the difference without giving them the needed resources. The will to change the quality of learning cannot spring solely from teachers. Will starts with public policy and funding, followed by district and site leadership, in providing teachers with access to the tools and the money to buy.

Professional development is the obligation of district leadership. It is professional development that provides teachers with the shopping cart for gathering the tools they need from the store shelves.

To gather the tools, teachers do not need the worn-out, battered carts that they used in the days of "inservice" filled with one-shot workshops and hot topics. What they need are carts that have all the up-to-date features that will ensure they get their selections of best practices home. For this, classroom follow-up to support application of new ideas and peer support are essential.

HIGH EXPECTATIONS AND PROFESSIONAL DEVELOPMENT

In addition to its pioneering work to identify which teaching tactics had the largest impact on student achievement, TESA identified the ingredients needed in professional development to ensure that teachers did more than attend a workshop, say "been there, done that," and continue with their established ways of teaching. TESA showed the importance of multifaceted professional development wherein workshops were reinforced with peer coaching and strong supervisory support.

TESA: The Professional Development Component

1. A Community of Learners

2. Research Reviews With Guided Workshop Practice

3. Classroom Follow-Up With Demonstrations and Feedback

4. Peer Coaching and Support Groups

5. Site Leadership and Support

6. Assessment of Results

Individual teachers working on individual projects to use the tools from the shelf will have a mild effect on student achievement. However, as a school community, with teachers and principals working together with the will power to put in the time and energy to make a large impact on the achievement gap, it is important that they establish a shared achievement goal and shared methods selected from the tools that research has identified for making the greatest impact. Team effort with a shared intention will produce more than solo efforts.

Getting Started With High-Expectation Practices

The first steps a school can take to end low performances are to make a goal and complete a first-year plan. What it selects to do will depend on what the current data say about the students' current performance.

If large numbers of students above the fifth grade are more than two years below grade-level expectations, it is essential that teachers not dump more information into their supersaturated brains. Having come this far without assimilating the required curriculum content is a strong indicator that these students have not yet developed the prerequisites of learning. They lack sufficient development of the basic thinking skills to make sense of the information they are taking into their heads. Thus it seems piled like garbage in a giant dump. Nothing connects. More content will only enlarge the pile.

To help these students, teachers will have to start with the prerequisites of learning. They will need to strengthen these students' cognitive processes so that these students can make sense of what they are learning.

Teachers who see the achievement gap widening with these students who need to gather the prerequisites can take the following steps:

1. Start an instrumental enrichment program in the school. Institute it in Grades 5–7 or 6–8 for all students.

2. Prepare to use the TESA methods. The proven format is to introduce three of the teaching behaviors per workshop, followed by three to five weeks of classroom implementation, peer support, and feedback. TESA methods are the heart of the high-effects strategy: asking questions.

3. After teachers are using question-asking tactics well and are adept at asking "why" questions with wait time distributed to all students, especially the low performers, they can prepare to use high-effects cognitive learning tools such as the graphic organizers, cooperative learning, hypothesizing, and summarizing in all content areas on a regular basis. This may be a two- to three-year professional development project.

4. Prepare to use concept-rich instruction that focuses on the key concepts in each curricular area, error analysis, problem solving, and the advanced use of the cognitive tools provided in instrumental enrichment.

This road map for closing the achievement gap encourages teachers and administrators to attend directly to the needs of the lowest performers. By raising the performance levels of these students with the excellent instruction that will follow the above recommendations, teachers will achieve the greatest gains in student performance and close the gap. Although it is important in this plan to start with the prerequisites for learning, it is not necessary to wait until all students are engaged in these basic learning-to-learn skills. Teachers' question asking, cooperative learning, and other high-effect strategy development can parallel this task.

Less Is More

When planning to reduce the achievement gap with significant gains, school teams want to establish a measurable goal in one or two content areas. This will provide focus for a three- to five-year effort. With the goal in place, each school will set up its professional development structures and concentrate all effort and funds. Least desirable is each teacher or administrator walking an individualistic path with graduate course work or conference attendance that does not align tightly with this goal. By maintaining this "less is more" stance, the school increases its chances of achieving the result it desires.

To achieve the outcome or achievement results desired for the long-range plan, the teams can start with a first-year goal. To ensure that the goal is attained, the team can set up the structures that will develop the learning community and support the efforts of the teachers implementing the changes. What are these essential structures?

1. The Site Leadership Team. This team, selected and led by the principal, best includes (a) a union or professional association representative, (b) a second administrator, (c) 3–5 grade-level team leaders or department chairs, and (d) a parent or community leader. District personnel, external consultants, and the evaluation consultants will advise. The team's responsibilities include oversight of the plan, scheduling of logistics, data analysis, communication with the district and consultants, assessment of the process and the results, and problem-solving implementation obstacles.

2. Peer Coaching and Support Teams. Since Joyce and Showers (1983) published their studies, many researchers have added support to the unequivocal power and potential of peer support teams as an essential tool in making achievement gains. Scheduled weekly, these teams meet to plan, review, and assess weekly application of project activities in the classroom. Any issues they cannot solve, they refer to the site leadership team and attending consultants for assistance.

3. Grade-Level Teams. Once a month, grade-level or departmental teams meet to assess the progress toward the schoolwide change goal. At this meeting, often facilitated by a school-based mentor, peer support teams identify issues needing input from others, identify process obstacles, share and celebrate successes, and provide interactive encouragement that builds the community of learners.

4. Expert Advice. However a school team gathers its information for making the changes, it is often necessary that an external expert provide implementation advice. This is essential when the methods of the implementation are new to the teaching staff. Experts who come to classrooms to demonstrate application methods, to observe teachers' first use of new ideas or strategies, to confer with teachers about the difficulties they encounter, to facilitate problem solving with the leadership team, to help grade-level teams refine their applications, and so on, streamline the implementation and assist the teams through the difficult challenges in the change process. At least one day a month in the first year of a project, teams will benefit from a site visit by an external expert who is well versed in the strategy or program being implemented.

5. Assessment and Evaluation. Although some schools have internal resources to gather and assess data from the project, many need an external evaluator. Even when there are internal resources, it is beneficial if an external evaluator sets up the assessment and evaluation process and does the analysis of results for reporting to the school team and the district.

6. District Coordination Team. When several schools in a district are implementing projects, even though each may have a different focus, these schools' principals and the associate superintendent for curriculum and instruction or chief academic officer should meet at least once per quarter to assess progress and provide mutual support. In the first year, this team will help most as a problem solver with contractual and budgetary issues.

Who's in Charge?

With the structures in place, school teams can begin their information-gathering process framed by the targeted goal. This may occur in action study teams, through consultant-led workshops, or by action research. Because it is imperative that all information gathering end with action plans that require, at least on a pilot basis, all teachers to implement what they have learned from the information, expertise and leadership are key in setting up and maintaining the processes that the team will use as they investigate new ideas. The principal, as research has identified over and over, is the key person. If principals are well trained in a particular action study process or certified in a program such as Feuerstein's Instrumental Enrichment or TESA, and have the time and inclination, they should lead the change process. At a minimum, the principal may hire an external, certified expert to guide the project and report to the site leadership team. When it comes to leading a major change effort for improving student performance, there is no room for the laissez-faire principal who just says, "Whatever the teachers want is fine with me."

Just What Is It About Me You Can't Teach?

When students ask, "What is it about me you can't teach?," they are asking a question that should have only one response: "Nothing. There is nothing about you that we cannot teach." This means that the entire school community has assessed the particular learning needs and developed a plan for high-expectations instruction. A powerful way for a school team to deliver such instruction begins with Feuerstein's criteria for a mediated learning experience. In the following 11 chapters, teams can study each of the criteria, gather information about strategies and tactics with a strong research base, review sample lessons that integrate the strategies into the curriculum, and make plans for trying out new ideas they can integrate into their repertoires.

Over a three- to four-year period, there is sufficient material for a school team to spend one quarter of the school year on the study and implementation of a chapter in this book. In the first week of the quarter, the team would study the information and develop weekly lesson plans for use in the classroom during the ensuing weeks. During these middle weeks, they meet in their peer teams weekly and in their grade-level teams once per month. In the final week of the quarter, they would review formal test data and informal teacher data to assess student progress.

KEY POINTS TO REMEMBER

- With the help of Reuven Feuerstein (Instrumental Enrichment), Samuel Kermin (TESA), and Howard Gardner (multiple intelligences), educators have been provided with (a) the means to develop the prerequisite skills for learning in students who come to school unprepared for today's rigorous standards, (b) the research on those instructional behaviors that most make a difference in student performance, and (c) a case for more authentic ways to promote student learning.
- Proper utilization of Instrumental Enrichment, TESA, and the multiple intelligences will result in strong, measurable, and significant outcomes in the achievement level of students often claimed to be "unmotivated" or "not teachable."
- TESA study results showed the negative impact on instruction when educators thought about students from poor families and children of color as "less

capable." Through the research, it became clear that high-expectations behaviors often contrasted with teachers' perceptions and beliefs that these children could not perform academically. Teachers properly prepared to use the high-expectations behaviors learned how well these students could learn when properly taught.

- There are school skills and survival skills that students possess. What does a teacher do to help students survive in school? Teachers must recognize that a major issue is how they communicate with these students. Teacher vocabulary may mean different things to different communities. It is important that teachers adjust their words so that all students receive the high-expectation message.
- Metacognition requires students to ask the question, "Do I have the necessary data to answer the question?"
- Trial and error is not an effective way for students to learn. Students must learn to think before they answer. Reflection inhibits and controls impulsivity and accelerates student understanding in all areas of the curriculum.
- Most teachers were never prepared in their preservice to use the emerging theories and best practices. To learn how to use these powerful tools to raise student achievement, especially with students who lack the prerequisites of learning, teachers need the support of intense and systematic professional development over time.

SAMPLE LESSONS

Should primary grade teachers take the high road or the low road? When it comes to expectations, the answer may seem obvious. However, practices don't always match the words. For instance, many primary teachers are forced to read from phonics scripts. The students are forced to recite sounds over and over in unison, whether they know the sounds already or not. There is no room for allowing students who "get it" to go ahead.

All are slowed to an average pace. Other primary teachers go by the "readiness" motto. They wait and wait for mysterious signs that a student is ready to grasp a pencil, sound out words, and so on. Between these extremes, there is a need to put high expectations into practice. On one hand, teachers need lessons that excite the children about reading and interest them in reading for meaning. Although it is important that they learn the word sounds, it is equally important that they are challenged to think as they learn. Nor should teachers just wait for "developmentally appropriate" readiness. Students are best helped by being challenged to "go the next step" and try tasks that may seem difficult. This is especially important in the early grades.

In the first sample lesson, primary students are introduced to the structure of a story. Through the elements, which teachers can reinforce as they introduce at least one story read to the students each week, students can begin to build a "heuristic" about stories. Such heuristics are cognitive road maps. Researcher Barak Rosenshine (1997) noted that these road maps are critical to students' enjoyment and understanding of reading, not as a collection of sounds, but as a mental act that transports them from learning to read to reading to learn in a lifelong learning task that is fundamental to success in all content areas.

ELEMENTARY LESSON

Create a Story

Standard
To understand the parts of
a story

Multiple Intelligences Focus
Verbal/Linguistic

Supporting Intelligences
Visual/Spatial, Intrapersonal,
Psychomotor

Mediation Emphasis
Meaning

CHECKING PRIOR KNOWLEDGE

On the blackboard or butcher paper, outline a K-W-L graphic organizer (see Chapter 4). Write in the words for the initials, pronounce them for the students, and guide a choral repetition (Know, Want to Know, and Learned). Ask for ideas on what each header means. Once the framework is established (keep it available for later stories), ask the students what they know (K) about "telling a story." Encourage them to use favorite TV shows. You may want to give an example to model, for instance, "Every story has a person who is a main character. In *The Little Engine That Could,* who was the main character?" Proceed to find out and identify "the problem faced by the little engine," how he solved the problem, and what the result was. Use other stories to reinforce the pattern or heuristic.

STRUCTURING THE TASK

Place students in groups of three. Put a strong reader, an OK reader, and a not-yet reader in each group.

1. Ask each group to think about a TV show that has a story, a character, and a problem.

2. Show the following graphic for all to see. Ask each group to figure out what it will say in each column.

Character	Problem	Solution	Result

SOURCE: Courtesy of Bob Kapheim, Thinking Kap, Inc.

3. Fill in the words on the chart for all to see. Practice sounding out the words.

4. Give each group one of the following strips to read. Help as needed when you circulate among the groups. Each group will search for the character, the problem, the solution, and the result in the story it is assigned (you may duplicate strips among the groups).

a. Juan has lost his money for lunch. What will he do for lunch? Make a story that ends happily for Juan.

b. Carla's mom forgot to pick her up after school. How can you help Carla get home?

c. Jo called her best friend, Tony, a bad name. Now he is mad at her.

d. Robin's friend wants to steal doll clothes at the store. How can you help Robin?

e. Jamie lost his new jacket. He thinks someone stole it. How can you help him find it?

LOOKING BACK AND REFLECTING

After all groups have come up with a solution, review the four elements. After the entire chart is full, ask students to think of other stories they know and fill in the chart. Select one or two TESA behaviors to practice as you guide the discussion.

BRIDGING FORWARD

Pick a story to read to the class. Review the four elements for the story. Stop at the appropriate places to allow students to identify the elements.

Assessing Student Performance

1. Check each student's ability to pronounce the four key words.

2. When students are reading silently during Sustained Silent Reading, ask them to identify the elements in the story.

3. Fill in the K-L chart (see Checking Prior Knowledge above) by asking students what they have learned about the elements of a story.

Materials

Story strips, butcher paper, story books

Variations

1. Substitute stories for the strips as reading material for older children.

2. Read big-book stories to the class. At the end of each story, fill in the chart.

MIDDLE GRADES LESSON

Rainy Days

Standard
Problem solving in environmental science

Focus Intelligence
Naturalistic

Supporting Intelligences
Intrapersonal, Verbal/Linguistic

Mediation Emphasis
Transcendence

CHECKING PRIOR KNOWLEDGE

Read an article from a science journal about acid rain. Ask your students what they know about acid rain. Chart responses for all to see.

STRUCTURING THE TASK

1. Explain to your students that in our high-tech world, there are many environmental problems. In some sections of the country, acid rain is a persistent problem. Tell them that the purpose of this lesson is to teach them how to investigate a problem.

2. Form the class into heterogeneous groups of five. Help each group select a lead scientist, a recorder, a reporter, and associate scientists.

3. Select a film about acid rain. Show the students how to make a cognitive map of the ideas they will see. After the viewing, let each group complete its map, starting with the identification of the problem.

4. Assign the groups to complete research on the topic by reviewing articles they find in the library or online. They will use the information they gather to substantiate or extend their map. Be sure to show them how to make a note card for each article read so they can quote the sources used. The note card should include the title of the article, the author, the source with dates and pages, and key words selected. Groups can divide up the work task as they see fit, with the assurance that each person makes an equal contribution.

5. Each group will select the solution it deems best and based on the research it completed.

6. Call on each group to share its map and explain why they made the solution plan they did.

LOOKING BACK AND REFLECTING

Acknowledge that there are a variety of solutions. However, in this study, the groups were learning a pattern for solving a problem. This pattern included (1) a hypothesis, (2) gathering information, (3) evaluating information, and (4) drawing a conclusion that they could defend. Ask them to look back at this example study and assess how they did with each of the four steps. Ask each group to report on its assessment. Use your TESA tactics to amplify each group's report.

BRIDGING FORWARD

Identify at least one environmental problem per quarter to which the students will be asked to apply the four elements in arriving at a possible solution. Let them know that your expectation at the end of the year is for all students to demonstrate how they can use this sequence with an environmental problem they have not analyzed in the school year.

Assessing Student Performance

1. See Looking Back and Reflecting, above.

2. Ask each group to brainstorm what it learned about the problem-solving sequence. Assign each to apply this sequence in an essay on a current environmental issue you select.

Materials

1. Film/video on acid rain

2. Markers and chart paper for each group

Variations

1. Substitute a local environmental problem.

2. Give each group a different problem to solve after they have understood the heuristic with its four elements.

SECONDARY LESSON

Death of a Salesman: A Character Analysis

Standard
Analyzing principal characters' motivations in fiction

Focus Intelligence
Verbal/Linguistic

Supporting Intelligences
Intrapersonal, Visual/Spatial

Mediation Emphasis
Meaning

CHECKING PRIOR KNOWLEDGE

Conduct an all-class discussion about forming opinions about why people act as they do and sometimes wreak havoc on each other. Invite the students to share examples from personal experience, TV, or their own reading. Use your TESA tactics to help students amplify their ideas.

STRUCTURING THE TASK

1. Assign students to read Miller's *Death of a Salesman* in a reader's theater format. Begin by dividing all the roles among all the class. This may mean you have several for each role. Divide the class so that you have several groups with all the characters (if needed, some students will read more than one minor role).

2. After the reading of the first act is done, put all the same characters in a character group (e.g., a Willy group, a Biff group). In these groups, the students will look for clues (what the character said or did or what others said about the character) that are clues to character. They will make a concept map for their character and predict which will be the key characteristics.

3. Invite each group to select, by drawing straws, a person to report the group's findings. Others in the group will defend the choices by responding to your questions (use TESA tactics). Repeat this cycle after each act.

4. After the final act, each group will look back over its data to see how well the group made its predictions.

LOOKING BACK AND REFLECTING

1. Conduct a discussion with the entire class.

   a. Which characters acted most as predicted? What is the evidence?
   b. Which did not? Why?
   c. Consider that Biff might be your brother. How would you have treated him differently than Willy did?
   d. What did you learn about analyzing characters in a play?

2. Ask the students to explore why they think the play was named *Death of a Salesman*.

BRIDGING FORWARD

Review with the students how to best analyze a character from what the character says or does or what others say about the character. What other ways does the author give clues to character? Make a chart to hang on the wall and for students to keep in their notebooks. For each fiction story read, take them through this heuristic. Continue to use TESA tactics to guide these discussions.

Assessing Student Performance

1. Assign each student to use the heuristic with a short story, making a concept map for the main character.

2. Assign the students to write an essay about the character they studied by incorporating the key elements of this analysis.

Materials

1. Student copies of the play

2. Butcher paper, markers

Variations

1. Show the movie of the play before the reading.

2. Select a different play, such as *Raisin in the Sun* or *My Fair Lady.*

3

Intentionality and Reciprocity

One writes out of one thing only—one's own experience. Everything depends on how relentlessly one forces from this experience the last drop, sweet or bitter, it can possibly give. This is the only real concern of the artist, to recreate out of the disorder of life that order which is art.

—James Baldwin (Riley, 1993)

In our modern, high-tech society, we are all bombarded with stimuli. Events occur rapidly and forcefully; TV ads deliver pictures at a super-fast rate with high volume sound; fast-food signs flash ads for new, quicker meals; and school curricula are jam-packed with facts and details that teachers must cover at an ever-quickening pace.

More than ever, it is important for children to have mediators who can instill the ability to filter out stimuli that distract them from learning and prevent them from making important distinctions among stimuli. If the children lack impulse control, or if they have physical, mental, or emotional challenges that limit their ability to process information with precision and accuracy, they need a system for processing information in an orderly way.

INTENTIONALITY: A FILTER WITH A PURPOSE

In the early stages of every mediation, the caring mediator isolates and interprets the various stimuli and presents the filtered stimuli in a way that encourages the student to respond positively. This act of purposeful mediation is called intentionality.

The mediator's work at intentionality, as a filter of concrete experiences, is much like a medical doctor's putting a slide under the microscope and highlighting selected tissue with a colored dye. The doctor does this to point out more easily what he or she wants other staff to look at. Because the dye makes the special tissue stand out, the others more easily focus on what the doctor has targeted for them. As soon as they focus their attention on examining the colored tissue, they are aroused to a state of vigilance. This responsive state of vigilance is called reciprocity.

> The teacher-mediator is concerned about the quality of interaction.

No Holds Barred

Whether helping students learn how to compare two objects, complete a mathematics problem, or memorize science vocabulary, teacher-mediators are concerned with the quality of interaction. They begin by helping the student filter out distracting and inappropriate information. If students' feelings of inadequacy arise as excuses, the teacher-mediators keep them on track by use of encouragement ("You can do it, I know you can"). If the students are distracted by an overabundance of factual information, mediators microscope the key points with cuing ("I want you to start here") and focusing ("Look right here at these two examples"). In large classrooms, teacher-mediators target those students who are especially resistive. They do not allow hiding. Their tone is firm, respectful, and direct. As students perform the assigned task, the mediators recognize their success with warm, enthusiastic, and specific feedback: "Good for you! I knew that you could find at least five items for comparing the characters in the story—you found seven! Bravissimo!"

There is nothing wishy-washy about the intention to secure the student's responses. The skilled mediator may go so far as to force eye contact from the student: "Look at me. Read my lips. Follow my finger as it points the way. Your tiredness and your interest in doing something else don't count at this moment. Focus on what I'm showing you. Stay with me."

Before they can have success with intentionality, many mediator candidates must first unlearn the laissez-faire "be sweet" and "oh, he's so cute!" models on which they have built a lifetime of low-quality interaction with students: "Don't push. Don't embarrass. Don't confront. Don't persist with your high expectations for change by the students. Let them construct their own meaning."

Feuerstein teaches the opposite. He knows from his own experience as a survivor of the Holocaust how resilient students are. He also knows that student reciprocity is not enriched when the adult rescues the student from responsibility for learning. He also knows from his work with the children of the Holocaust and with troubled youth from all over the world that unless the parent or teacher expects these youngsters to change how they think and behave, unless the mediator persists in demanding the changes, most students will form low expectations for themselves and stay trapped in the inability to learn.

> Unless the mediator persists in demanding the changes, most students will form low expectations for themselves.

Mediating With Respect and Care

Feuerstein also differentiates mediation with respect and care from mean, verbal abuse. Any observer of his intentional mediation with young people will see the bond of caring that he creates. He is firm and pressing while being gentle. One observer called him a pied piper whose interactions with children attracted them to him like magic. The magic he uses starts with his willful insistence that they not engage in escapist behaviors, some as extreme as a child hiding her face behind her hands, a child climbing under a table, or a child burying his head in his arms or clasping his ears. His soft but firm voice urges, empathizes, encourages, and commands; it never whines or begs. And when he notices the first movement that shows his voice is getting through, he applauds, he reaffirms, he whispers his delight, and he strengthens the connection until he has full, willful attention from the child. "Bravo!" is his favorite salute to success.

Mediational Strategies That Promote Intentionality

Intentionality suggests purposeful direction. Mediators have two levels of intention when they begin an interaction. First, they want to engage the student in the lesson or task at hand. They recognize and strategize to overcome the student's natural resistances and distractions. They build on the student's interests and needs.

In addition to the verbal interactions mentioned, intentional mediators use visual signs and verbal statements that tell the students the direction they propose.

Mediational Strategies That Promote Intentionality

- Posted goals and objectives for a lesson
- Posted agenda with expected tasks
- Posted criteria for assessing student performance
- Verbal review and clarification of terms used for goals, agenda, and criteria at the start of a lesson
- Verbal questions that ask students to connect tasks in progress with goals and criteria
- Map of yearly goals posted in classroom in a sequence
- Stories and examples of questions to examine the value and rationale of a lesson or task

Mediational Strategies That Promote Reciprocity

Feuerstein's insistence on respect building and interaction does not absolve the mediator from amassing a repertoire of inviting strategies that facilitate student reciprocity, especially with resistant or academically challenged students. These are the nets that the mediator uses to snare students and draw them into the learning act. Beyond drawing students into the lesson, the mediating teacher will want the students to go beyond the specifics of the lesson and make more generalized connections. The immediate intention may ask students to learn how to add whole numbers or to name the state capitals. An intention that goes beyond the use of a skill or the recall of a fact may ask students to explain why the information or skill is important, to identify uses, or even to make a use or demonstrate an application. These are the transcendent goals that connect the details of learning with the principles of knowing, understanding, and using knowledge.

> Four major elements invite students to engage in the lesson: checking prior knowledge, task structure, metacognitive reflection, and bridging.

Obviously, the mediation of intentionality and reciprocity is needed throughout a lesson or unit. As the mediators work through the lessons, they return time and again to the task of pulling their students, physically and mentally, into what they are teaching. The more their intentionality enables students to engage and reengage themselves in the learning task, the richer the result.

Mediational Strategies That Promote Reciprocity

- Using printed words, symbols, and pictures drawn in color on newsprint or whiteboard to reinforce lesson objectives, instructions, or rubrics
- Designing tasks that move students from concrete manipulatives to abstract symbols
- Using a variety of instructional materials at different reading levels to accommodate individual reading readiness
- Standing in a single place while addressing the class to lower distraction for students with low focus tolerance
- Using graphic organizers such as sequence charts or mind maps to help students see relationships
- Teaching vocabulary before starting a lesson
- Shortening length of tasks
- Visually checking for understanding with hand signals

- Honoring all answers to questions by noting what part of the answer was correct and asking other students to add to the correct part
- Using the "wraparound" with the pass rule to structure responses to questions
- Asking a question before saying a student's name
- Daily use of "Today I learned . . ." wraparounds
- Starting each class period with a pair review
- Using the bulletin board for a connection map
- Using a buddy system so that each academically challenged child has a specific partner but isn't singled out
- Allowing students to substitute a tape-recorded answer
- Providing special materials such as lapboard, felt pens, taped paper, page holders, and turners to assist students with physical challenges

DESIGNING INTENTIONALITY AND RECIPROCITY IN EVERY LESSON

In addition to using mediational strategies throughout instruction, the mediator will weave intentionality and reciprocity through each lesson's design. High-quality design will contain four major elements that invite students to engage in the lesson: checking prior knowledge, structuring the task, looking back and reflecting, and bridging forward.

Checking Prior Knowledge

A strong lesson begins with a check of what the students already know about the topic. This provides a context as well as a motivating connection to past learning. In many lessons, there is neither context nor linkage to the student's past knowledge. The teacher not adept at using intentional strategies may introduce a new set of words or a new semantic technique. The teacher makes no attempt to link words found in one chapter to their occurrence in other chapters. These practices reinforce learning as an incidental, isolated, or episodic series of words or events.

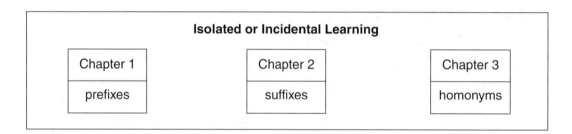

When those urban students who have dispositions to impulsive and episodic learning are reinforced by disconnected and episodic instruction, the results are doubly damaging. The students miss the material and find no way to make sense of how to learn. However, when teachers mediate these students for intentionality by using a prior knowledge check to start the construction of connections, the teachers not only learn what students may know, but they also learn how well the students see a topic's relationship to previous topics. For instance, do the students see how prefixes and suffixes are both important to changing a word's use? If this is noted, it prepares the mediator to point out the connection and use examples from the previous lesson on prefixes to explain suffixes in the new lesson. As the teacher helps provide these connections, the episodic students' discovery of the relationship leads to their increased interest.

By checking prior knowledge, the teacher builds a bridge for the students and mediates their understanding of the relationships between new ideas and past experience, as well as between intentionality and reciprocity. The teacher is strengthening the students' knowledge of how to learn. Having clarified their existing knowledge of the subject, the teacher has invited the students into a task that will expand the universe of knowing.

The best known tool for checking prior knowledge is Donna Ogle's (1986) easy-to-use K-W-L chart. Using a newsprint chart or whiteboard, the teacher outlines the chart:

Topic		
K What We **K**now	**W** What We **W**ant to Know	**L** What We **L**earned

Small groups or the entire class work together to fill in the first column about the topic. When all ideas known to the class are listed, the students generate questions about the topic. At the lesson's conclusion, they complete the final column, with the teacher making explicit those connections that the students miss.

> By checking prior knowledge, the teacher builds a bridge for the students.

Structuring the Task

Because the curricula in many American schools are badly disjointed, teachers routinely say, "It's 10:00 a.m., time for spelling," then at 10:30 a.m., they announce, "It's time for mathematics," and so on. One piece is piled atop another, and students who are already episodic are lost in the swirl of the day's events.

In contrast to those teachers who present students with bits of unconnected information and ask them to do tasks, even fun and engaging tasks, without helping the students make sense of the information, the mediating teacher selects those instructional strategies that help students understand what they are learning.

Most helpful lessons begin with the teachers' check of prior knowledge: "What do my students already know about this topic?" Once teachers have checked prior knowledge, they can best help students with a lesson design that structures the gathering and exploration of new information as they facilitate students' understanding of what they are learning now. Following the check of prior knowledge, it is helpful for teachers to include the design elements of practice, "meaning development," connection making, and transfer.

Each of these elements lends itself to teacher creativity by helping the students make sense of what they are learning. First, it helps teachers identify how they are going to ask students to gather new information to add to their prior knowledge. It enables teachers to select and adapt those learning strategies and cognitive tools that will engage students in gathering the required information and in understanding how the pieces are connected. It also prepares students for the reflective process that will lead them into transfer.

Take, for instance, a lesson from geometry. The lesson is presented in their textbook to help them compare geometric shapes and to discover the attributes of each figure.

The teacher provides the students with colored sheets of paper, scissors, and tape. She shows a picture of each shape to the class and asks the students to identify the critical attributes of each. Following instructions from the teacher guide, she structures the students into cooperative groups with each group assigned a different figure. (Practice)

After each group has identified the attributes of the assigned shape, they share their ideas with the class. The teacher reinforces or corrects as needed. When all have reported, she instructs the groups to use the colored paper to cut out each shape and label it. In addition, she instructs the students to draw each shape in their journals. After checking for understanding of the task, the students complete these tasks.

The students go to work fully engaged in what the teacher asked. When she notices that most are finished, she signals the class to finish up the drawings so that they can now discuss what they did and why they did it, before identifying what they learned from this series of tasks. To facilitate their understanding, the teacher asks questions that cue their thinking. These include, "What are the distinguishing marks of the square?" "The triangle?" "The rectangle?" "The rhombus." "Why is it important that you know these marks?" "What do they add to your understanding of each shape?" "As you distinguish one shape from another, what rule can you make that will apply to all the figures?" "What are some helpful ways that you can take advantage of this rule?"

These questions, each followed by other probes to clarify and expand the students' thinking about what they understand about what and how they learned, enable the teacher to take the students beyond the normal "doing" of the pre-scribed task to the mathematical thinking that is the essence of the lesson. In this instance, the teacher's mediation facilitates that understanding, which will then allow her to move them into transferring the knowledge in a variety of different situations. Without the mediation, the students are left with having fun with the task and identifying attributes to memorize. No more. With the mediation, they not only had the fun reaped from engaging tasks that used multiple representations to make clear the respective attributes and a knowledge of the attributes of each shape, but they worked together to understand why the attributes are important for each shape, and they responded to her questions that led them to frame generalized rules about geometric shapes. Throughout, she stuck with her intention of using their intellectual engagement in understanding the geometry they were "doing."

Looking Back and Reflecting

At the conclusion of a well-structured lesson, time needs to be allotted for episodic learners to reflect on what they have learned and how they have learned. The reflection will start with a strategic review of the content learned in the lesson. It may also call for an assessment of how the students learned and the applications they can make. In essence, this review forces the making of key connections so that students not only see the immediate relationships but also learn how to establish the connections themselves. It is important that the students have time to consider what they have learned and how, so that they can learn the process of their learning as well as know the product.

> Checking for understanding is the most important "connection-making" tool the teacher has.

Bridging Forward

This establishment of connections in the learning process is advanced in a lesson design under the heading Bridging Forward. The behaviorists' notion of transfer (S-R) says, "It doesn't happen." The mediator's notion is that transfer does occur when it is "shepherded" (Fogarty, Perkins, & Barell, 1992). A "good shepherd" is one who takes time to structure the purposeful transfer of learning. This occurs when the mediator bridges key lesson concepts into other content areas to be studied or into appropriate life situations.

Note in the following sample lesson how the design includes the four elements described:

- Checking prior knowledge
- Structuring the task
- Looking back and reflecting
- Bridging forward

A Sample Lesson Design

Each sample lesson used in this book follows the four-element model above. In addition, the lesson will tell for which grade level it is designed, a standard alignment, a multiple intelligence alignment, and the mediational connection. These alignments are found in the box in the upper right corner of the lesson page. When teachers go to design lessons, they will find a template that uses this format.

ELEMENTARY LESSON

Mapping Tanzania

Standard
Identifying geographic regions

Focus Intelligence
Verbal/Linguistic

Supporting Intelligences
Bodily/Kinesthetic,
Visual/Spatial

Mediation Emphasis
Intentionality and Reciprocity

CHECKING PRIOR KNOWLEDGE

Invite one student from the class to locate on a map or globe (a) Africa, (b) Tanzania, (c) Mt. Kilimanjaro, (d) the Serengeti Plain, and (e) the Ngorongoro Crater. On newsprint, blackboard, or overhead, show this chart. How can we find the differences among these geographic regions?

	Plain	**Mountain**	**Crater**
Know			

Ask the students to volunteer what they know about each word. Fill in the responses. When there are no more responses, draw a dotted line across. Next, identify the geographic areas and an explanation of the three terms: *plain, mountain, crater.* Let the students know that by the end of this lesson, each will know (a) three distinguishing features of a geographic region (plain, mountain, crater), (b) how these features are found in one region (Tanzania), and (c) how to create an imaginary country with three similar features on another continent.

STRUCTURING THE TASK

Divide the class into heterogeneous base groups of three each. Assign roles (mapmaker, scribe, materials manager/timekeeper) and provide materials (newsprint, markers, print, or visual materials regarding Tanzania, plains, craters, and mountains) and three questions for each group member to answer about the assigned geographic features.

Mt. Kilimanjaro

Serengeti Plain

Ngorongoro Crater

1. What is the Serengeti Plain? Ngorongoro Crater? Mt. Kilimanjaro?

2. In what ways is it a plain? crater? mountain?

3. How is it a unique place (i.e., how is the Serengeti Plain different from other plains on this continent or in other parts of the world)?

After each student in a group has answered the three questions (allow 30 minutes), each student will group with two others with the same topic. Allow 20 minutes to share answers and agree on a common answer before returning to the base group. Back in the base group, each will share the questions-responses (15 minutes) followed by the outlining of Tanzania on newsprint and by entering pictures or symbols to depict the principal traits of the region. Every member of the group needs to be prepared to explain the picture or symbol selection. Identify three different mapmakers to describe their group selections (five minutes). Ask the other students to listen for areas of agreement. Discuss these briefly before checking for understanding (five minutes). Check for understanding by asking students at random to explain a term. Ask for thumbs-up (agree) or thumbs-down (disagree) votes. Where there is disagreement, ask others to describe their understanding until there is agreement on each definition. Write the "official" definition of each term on the board or overhead. Instruct each group to select a continent (excluding Antarctica). (You can use a box for a random draw.) The group is to use what it knows about each region's common characteristics to create a country on that continent with the features and characteristics learned in the lesson. Show a sample you have made and point out how each group should label regions and characteristics. Use newsprint for two-dimensional maps or provide materials for a three-dimensional diorama (50–90 minutes).

LOOKING BACK AND REFLECTING

After the groups post the complete products and view each others' work, conduct an all-class discussion.

1. What have the students learned about each of Tanzania's three regions?

2. What have they learned about the general terms *plain, mountain,* and *crater*?

3. If they were to go to the moon, how would they identify plains, craters, and mountains there?

4. When identifying the similarities and differences of regions, what thinking processes would they use?

BRIDGING FORWARD

For student journal entries, select one or more of these tasks:

1. You find yourself lost on what you recognize as a plain. How do you know it's a plain? Tell what resources of the plain will help you survive and why?

2. Select another country with at least three different geographic regions. Explain how you will distinguish each region.

TACTICS TO PROMOTE INTENTIONALITY AND RECIPROCITY

In addition to the four elements of lesson design, teachers can enrich a lesson with additional tactics that facilitate learning and promote achievement.

1. A Problem-Centered Focus. Problem-centered lessons sit on a continuum from well defined to ill defined. Well-defined problems such as, "Determine how long it took a train to cover the 236 miles between Stations A and B if it traveled the distance at 92 m.p.h." are close-ended with set answers. Ill-defined problems are those such as, "Investigate the possible causes of this accident." By structuring a lesson in a problem format, the mediator sets up learning as a process of inquiry, as opposed to rote coverage of information. Mediative teachers present the problem visually on the board, check for vocabulary understanding, and ask the students to predict the lesson content. They will then connect the problem to the standard by which they will evaluate the students' performance. Again, they will write the standard and clarify vocabulary for the students.

2. Engaging Tasks. After inviting students into a lesson with the check for prior knowledge, the mediator is ready with an engaging and challenging task (such as mapmaking in the geography lesson) that will deepen their understanding or extend their skills. To heighten active engagement, collaborative investigations that promote sharing behavior (see Chapter 8) will in turn promote student reciprocity. Graphic organizers, highest on the list of engaging tools, invite student mental engagement (Lyman & McTighe, 1988).

Each graphic organizer amplifies intention. The mediator selects the organizer as a tool to help students "see" the structure of their thinking about a topic. For instance, the question web shows students how to ask a sequence of questions that apply in like situations. The web helps them identify characteristics of a person, place, event, or concept. When used in a cooperative task, the visual organizer may help students engage print content in a way that promotes comprehension. They can see readily how pieces of information connect one to the other in the form of a thinking pattern that promotes complex thinking.

> The mediator selects the organizer as a tool to help students "see" the structure of their thinking.

3. Checking for Understanding. In its most simple form, teachers check for understanding by asking students to signal that they can explain an idea. Elementary teachers use a thumbs-up, -sideways, or -down signal in response to the questions, "Who can repeat my instructions?" or "Who can explain what you must do now?" By the middle grades, students can signal with color-marked cards (red, yellow, green) in response to more thought-engaging questions. "Who can explain why . . . ?" or "Who is ready to give me a reason for . . . ?" By secondary school, students can raise hands in response to questions of prediction, hypothesis formation, and summation. Of course, in all cases, the signal is only the start. After waiting for everyone to signal, teachers select who will respond. When teachers receive a partial response, they can ask, "Who can add to what _____ said?" or "Who has additional or different ideas?" The best teachers distribute the chance to respond so that all students have the expectation to answer all questions. Finally, when the check is not producing the information and understanding needed, teachers can fill in the blanks by reteaching before rechecking.

4. Project-Centered Lessons and Units. Projects, especially those carried out in collaborative pairs and trios, are a third tool for challenging students to high mental engagement. Notice how the design in this project ends a unit on insects by elevating the content (insects) with a project to transform the information learned into a thought-provoking experience.

Create a Creature

	A	B	C	D	E	F
	Body Symmetry	Segmentation	Form of Locomotion	Sensory Organs	Support Structures	Body Covering
1	bilateral	none	none	eyes, ears, & nostrils	bony skeleton	skin-hair
2	radial	2 body segments	2 or 4 walking legs	paired antennae	cartilaginous skeleton	scales
3	bilateral	3 body segments	legs & wings	compound eye & antennae	exoskeleton	skin-hair
4	bilateral	multiple segments	6 or 8 legs	tentacles	soft bodied	feathers
5	radial	2 body segments	fins	eyes, ears, & nostrils	shell hinged	scales
6	bilateral	none	multiple walking legs	compound eye & antennae	shell carried	skin-hair

Courtesy of Bob Kapheim, York High School, Elmhurst, IL

When a total lesson includes all of these engaging elements in a design that invites students to respond to the curriculum, the teacher can more easily focus on mediating the other interactions that heighten student involvement and result in increased achievement. Note how all the elements mark the design of the following sample of a problem-based lesson.

MIDDLE GRADES LESSON

Cultures and Continents

Standard
How to understand the ways an ecosystem influences the world we live in

Focus Intelligence
Visual/Spatial

Supporting Intelligences
Interpersonal, Naturalist, Verbal/Linguistic

Mediation Emphasis
Intentionality and Reciprocity

CHECKING PRIOR KNOWLEDGE

1. Invite students to identify the nations or regions from which their families came to the United States. Make a 3" × 8" sign for each student to wear.

2. Ask the students, each wearing one sign, to assemble under one of these signs hung in the room: (a) North America, (b) South America, (c) Central America, (d) Europe, (e) Asia, (f) Africa, (g) Australia. Read the signs to the class and use choral response to teach pronunciation.

3. Tell the students they are going to learn some ways the environment (explain the word) influences how people in these places live. Show a chart with an example to illustrate how weather impacts natural materials and how natural materials are used to protect against weather. You may want to select three to seven words to teach new vocabulary in the lesson context.

STRUCTURING THE TASK

1. Using pictures on a bulletin board or a slide show, show examples of housing from many cultures. Be sure to include samples that relate to students in the class. Here are some starters:
   a. Native American/First Nation
   b. Inuit
   c. Mexican-Indian
   d. Mexico City
   e. East Africa-Masai Herders
   f. Virgin Islands
   g. England
   h. South Pacific Island

2. Ask the students to explain how and why they think the shelters are so different and how and why the shelters are alike.

3. From heterogeneous groups of three, give each group the materials they'll need to research, sketch, and build a model house from a culture different from their own. After the model is made, the students will (a) label the feature shared with their current homes and (b) prepare to explain how the environmental conditions influenced the special features (e.g., the igloo derived from cold weather, snow).

4. Display the finished products for all to see.

LOOKING BACK AND REFLECTING

1. Ask each group to share what it has learned about the influence of environment on the culture studied. Use the completed works to illustrate.

2. Construct a large matrix to display on the bulletin board. Across the top, list the cultures studied in this lesson. After you demonstrate one example, invite the groups to fill in the chart. (You may have to do the writing, or you may allow sketches on cards to fit each block.)

Culture ▶					
House Shape					
Number of Rooms					
Raw Materials					
Uses					
Special Features					
Weather					

3. Use a wraparound so that each student in turn can respond to this lead-in: "In our study of different houses from different lands, I learned . . ." ("I pass" is allowed.)

4. Summarize the students' statements.

BRIDGING FORWARD

For student journal entries, select one or more of the following tasks:

1. Make a list of how the environment in our town or city has influenced our shelters.

2. Make a sketch that matches the environmental factors (e.g., snow) with the elements (e.g., heater) that are in your house.

Assessing Student Performance

To what degree can the student (using an example from a nonlocal ecosystem):

1. Explain the connection between key environmental factors and the elements of design and construction in a common shelter?

2. Identify the environmental factors that influence the design and construction of shelters in a selected ecosystem?

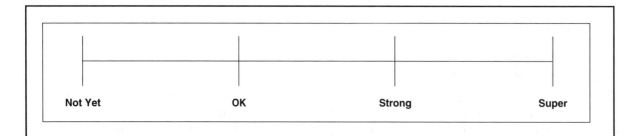

Not Yet	OK	Strong	Super

Materials

Globe or world map, sign for each continent, pictures of climate conditions in a variety of ecosystems, pictures of homes from 6 to 12 cultures around the world, art or model-making supplies, and student journals

Variations

1. Select one ecosystem with unique housing. As a class, build a life-size model of the shelter with representative geology and plant life.

2. Select an ecosystem with unique housing and create a representational mural.

TWO SIDES OF A COIN

Intentionality and reciprocity are two sides of a coin. Effective teachers will plan how they will engage students from the beginning of a lesson until the end by making sure the students are clear about what it is they are to learn and why they are learning it. They will design every lesson using the most research-proven tactics and strategies for making students want to learn and will excite the students' interest in working hard in the lesson because the students enjoy being engaged.

When using intentionality and reciprocity, the teacher invites students to a learning party. For some students, a single mailed invitation is sufficient. Others need a follow-up phone call or a special "don't forget tonight" reminder. Some may turn down even the most glamorous invitation. The skilled mediator understands that a single invitation may not work for all and instead makes allowances for the different needs of students with their different readiness to learn by adjusting, repeating, modifying, preventing, intervening, and repeating the invitation until each student shows up at the party.

KEY POINTS TO REMEMBER

- Intentionality, like a laser focus, is equivalent to saying that things are done on purpose or by design, not by accident or happenstance; it is purposeful direction.
- Share professional decisions with the students (i.e., teachers want to engage the children in discussions in order to make them aware of what the teachers

are doing and why.) There will be less episodic behavior and the students will buy in.

- Students not only need to know what they are to learn but why they are learning it.
- As with this chapter and all that follow, four main elements of a lesson design are included in each of the grade-level sample lessons: checking prior knowledge, structuring the task, looking back and reflecting, and bridging forward. Each of these elements requires active student involvement in the process so they know what the teacher is doing and why.
- Every lesson includes intentionality and reciprocity, transcendence and meaning.
- No student is given a pass from learning; students have to construct their own meaning.
- Students' prior knowledge is the starting point of every lesson, and the teacher builds upon the knowledge and skills the students bring to the class.
- Graphic organizers give students a visual of their work and amplify intention.
- Students need to share in the learning experience. Teachers must offer mediation to the children based on the desired changes in how the children are thinking by using their state of mind

SAMPLE LESSONS

Before beginning a review of the model lessons on the following pages, it is best to review the major points made in this chapter.

Examine the lesson that is most age appropriate for your students. As you go through the lesson, make note of what tactics and strategies you want to use that will most remind students of the lesson's intention or purpose and promote their reciprocity.

ELEMENTARY LESSON

Right Angles From Any Angle

Standard
Understanding the attributes of right angles

Focus Intelligence
Mathematical/Logical

Supporting Intelligence
Visual/Spatial

Mediation Emphasis
Intentionality and Reciprocity

CHECKING PRIOR KNOWLEDGE

Show your students a picture of a right angle. Check to see who can identify it by name. Ask other students to identify other examples in the room (e.g., desk corners, chair legs, door and window frames).

STRUCTURING THE TASK

1. Check to see if any student can identify the attributes (name them) of a right angle (e.g., 90 degrees, two lines). Spell out the words and ask each student to copy the words on a 3" × 5" index card. When all have finished, give a piece of tape to attach the card to a right angle they see in the classroom. Check for accuracy, and ask students to explain why the angle is a right angle.

2. Show a reverse right angle and an upside-down right angle for all to see. Ask for volunteers to identify each sample. All should respond "right angle," although many may say "left" or "upside down." Correct this error by reviewing the attributes of a right angle. Direction doesn't matter.

3. Pair the students. Present a worksheet with at least eight right angles seen from different points of view. Invite the pairs to agree on the label of each.

4. Ask students to share why they think it is important to pick out right angles.

LOOKING BACK AND REFLECTING

Ask students to look around the room and notice the right angles marked earlier. Ask for volunteers to tell why they are right angles.

BRIDGING FORWARD

Give each student five copies of the "right angle" index cards. Ask them to think of places outside school where they will find right angles.
After listing these for all to see, ask each to look for right angles on the way home from school or around their homes. Draw a picture of the object on the card.

Assessing Student Performance

1. Prepare a multiple-choice test showing a variety of angles. In each test item, include one right angle at a different perspective.

2. Ask students to draw a right angle and label the critical elements.

Variations

1. Take students on a city walk. Ask each student to identify and draw three right angles seen and label with its location.

2. Provide students with construction paper and scissors to practice cutting right angles.

MIDDLE GRADES LESSON

Subways and Buses

Standard
Read, comprehend, and critique literary works

Focus Intelligence
Verbal/Linguistic

Supporting Intelligences
Interpersonal, Intrapersonal

Mediation Emphasis
Intentionality and Reciprocity

CHECKING PRIOR KNOWLEDGE

Place the students into heterogeneous (mixed-ability) groups of three. Ask each group to make a sketch of the perfect subway car or city bus (no limits on comfort!). Call upon groups to show their sketches and explain the design. In the process, record on the board the words they use to identify what they know about subways and buses.

STRUCTURING THE TASK

1. Provide each group with a poem or song from the collection *Poetry in Motion: 100 Poems From Subways and Buses* (Parchen, Peacock, & Neches, 1996).

2. Ask each group to study its poem.

   • What does the poem say about subways or buses? About the city and its people?
   • What feelings does the poem evoke? How does it do so?
   • What do you like or dislike about the poem? Why?

LOOKING BACK AND REFLECTING

Ask each group to read its poem to the class and discuss the responses to the questions. Hold a summary discussion on the elements that promoted enjoyment.

BRIDGING FORWARD

Invite each group to compose its own poem about a bus or the subway.

Assessing Student Performance

To what degree:
1. Does the poem capture the feeling of urban life?

Not Yet   OK   Strong   Super

2. Does the poem use poetic forms?

3. Does the poem deliver a message about urban life?

Materials

Copies of the poems

Variations

1. Select other examples of urban poems or urban-based short stories.

2. Allow groups to represent buses or the subway in different media such as videos, songs, mobiles, sketches, and so on.

SECONDARY LESSON

The Right to Vote

Standard
How the Bill of Rights applies to current social problems

Focus Intelligence
Visual/Spatial, Interpersonal

Supporting Intelligences
Mathematical/Logical, Interpersonal, Intrapersonal, Verbal/Linguistic

Mediation Emphasis
Intentionality and Reciprocity

CHECKING PRIOR KNOWLEDGE

Ask each student to complete this agree/disagree chart. After students have completed their charts, invite random responses to each statement. Because many of the items are controversial and you want the students to explore multiple points of view, you are encouraged to mediate student thinking by asking such questions as, "Why do you think that?" "What is your evidence or rationale?" and so on. Encourage students to defend their points of view with good logic and valid evidence. After each question, show on the overhead the statement from the Bill of Rights that each case statement is related to. Highlight instances from the above discussion that touched on the Bill of Rights.

Possible Rights	Agree	Disagree
1. The Bill of Rights says women have a right to vote.		
2. A high school diploma is a right.		
3. Every citizen has a right to own a shotgun.		
4. U.S. citizens have a right to life, liberty, and the pursuit of happiness.		

STRUCTURING THE TASK

Explain the purpose of the problem-centered task. Give each group a copy of the Bill of Rights and one of the four case statements. Using the Bill of Rights, each group is to make a ruling on the constitutionality of the case and develop its rationale in a written essay. Rotate the papers so that one other group gives feedback on each team's essay. (You may also want to read and give feedback.) When all feedback is given, conduct an all-class discussion on the disagreements.

LOOKING BACK AND REFLECTING

Instruct each group to examine the steps it took in completing the task. Post these questions as a guide:

1. What steps in problem solving did you use to connect the case to the Bill of Rights?

2. In your discussions, what were the areas of most agreement? Disagreement?

3. How did you resolve the disagreements?

4. How did you monitor your own behavior during the hot moments of discussion?

5. If you were to do a second case, what changes would you make in your process?

After the group discussions, sample the responses with a classwide discussion.

BRIDGING FORWARD

In journals, invite students to write

1. What they learned about the Bill of Rights.

2. How they might react in the future to a personal challenge that posed a threat to their constitutional rights.

Assessing Student Performance

To what degree can the student

1. Explain why the Bill of Rights is an important document?

2. Identify the rights contained in the Bill of Rights?

3. Describe how the Bill of Rights is used in ruling on the constitutionality of a court case?

Not Yet	OK	Strong	Super

Materials

Agree/disagree charts, copies of the Bill of Rights and case statements

Variations

1. Substitute other parts of the Constitution as the tool for judging a problem.

2. Invite students to create real-life legal cases from their own experiences. Are these cases resolvable by the Supreme Court?

3. Enact a mock trial around a significant case. Assign student teams as prosecutors, defense, judicial panel, and so on.

4. Conclude with a final discussion of the agree/disagree chart.

4

Meaning

Don't take another mouthful before you have swallowed what is in your mouth.

—Madagascan proverb

Very often parents and teachers are faced with the question "Why?" from an inquisitive child. For the insecure parent or the inexperienced teacher, the quick defense is, "Because I said so, that's why!" What is missed in such instances, though, is the child's need to understand the purpose, rationale, or compelling "why" that will make clear the task's or activity's significance. Most often, that answer is best found within the values and beliefs of the family's culture. Rather than give a quick "I said so," the parent or teacher helps the child by providing a patient mediation of meaning.

THE MEDIATION OF MEANING

The mediation of meaning occurs when the parent or teacher connects children's wonder to a value-rich understanding of purpose and significance at both the cognitive and affective levels. At the cognitive level, the mediator communicates important values and beliefs; at the affective level, the mediator transmits enthusiasm for the belief. Children thus receive compelling and energetic explanations to match their compelling questions of why. In this way, the mediator, a significant guide, moves the interaction to a more profound level of mental and emotional engagement than was provided by the mediation of intentionality. In the mediation of intentionality, mediators broke down the students' resistance and invited them to consider the possibility of learning something of importance: they captured attention, and the students agreed to listen. In the mediation of meaning, though, mediators charge the learning experience with value and energy, inviting students to understand the compelling "why."

For Feuerstein, the mediation of meaning has special import. Because the value he speaks about is grounded in the student's culture, it is the mediator's task to connect students to the inherent power of their culture. The mediator can accomplish this by interpreting and explaining at ever-deepening levels of understanding the significance of students' heritage. In essence, the mediator is the translator, celebrator, and transmitter of cultural heritage, with all of its knowledge, traditions, values, and beliefs, to the next generation.

> In the mediation of meaning, mediators charge the learning experience with value and energy.

For most youngsters growing up in a family able to mediate its culture's meaning, the parents are the first mediators. For those whose family is destroyed or disabled by poverty, racism, war, or other causes, there is a great chance that the children will miss the mediation that sets the foundation for successful learning, thinking, and problem solving.

History is replete with examples of cultures destroyed and disabled: in Canada, there was the institutionalization of the First Nations peoples; in America, the creation of slave quarters for the Africans, of reservations for Native Americans, and of prison camps for American citizens of Japanese descent; in Germany, there was the Holocaust; and in Bosnia and Rwanda, we have witnessed ethnic cleansing. In all of these cases, and in the abundant number of cases like them, many children who survived did so with their cultural identity severely impaired or irretrievably lost.

Combating the Destruction of Culture

First Nations' advocate Lorna Williams was a child who survived in the face of grave difficulties. Taken from her family and sent to boarding school by the Canadian government, Lorna was taught to forget her family and her heritage. Achievement tests administered by the provincial government indicated that she and 45 of the 47 young people from her village were "retarded." Hoping to eradicate beliefs they labeled as "primitive," her teachers ridiculed her family, debunked her customs and beliefs, raised self-doubt about her abilities to learn, and frightened her into giving up "the old ways." The school's low expectations and destructive instruction practices almost worked. It was not long before the traditional ways of knowing and acting—which taught her how and why to control her behavior, show respect for her elders, and learn from the examples of the natural world—were beginning to appear stupid, foolish, and superstitious.

Confused, Lorna returned home for summer vacation. Happily, a relative, strong in her own cultural beliefs, intervened. Through story, song, and parental talk, her aunt returned Lorna to the roots of her culture and restored her beliefs in herself, in her people, and in their traditions. From that experience, and other experiences that Feuerstein would label as the true mediation of meaning in her life, Lorna grew as a student, vowing that she too would find ways to

> The mediation of meaning is a necessary and powerful learning tool for all children.

help her peers maintain the integrity of their culture. Today, Lorna leads the First Nations Project for the Vancouver Public Schools and consults with school districts across the United States and Canada.

Lorna's commitment to finding the best ways to help the children of the First Nations survive in the modern world, and yet retain their traditional ways of "making sense," brought her to the work of Reuven Feuerstein. She quickly connected his teachings about "meaning" to her own travails and triumphs. More important, she recognized that his approach, the mediation of learning within the cultural context, would help larger numbers of children than would the tutorial approach her aunt had used to help her recover from what the government school had tried to force upon her.

The Cultural Roots of Meaning

The assimilation of meaning begins with what we learn as children. What a child learns is rooted in the culture and values of the family. If the culture and the values of a family are systematically discounted, as in Lorna's case, or destroyed, as in the case of the Holocaust children, or if the family is uprooted from its environment, as in the case of the Africans brought to America, it becomes extremely difficult for the children to extract meaning from the world around them. Without the mediation that starts in the family, the child is left to learn in episodic and impulsive fits and starts.

Feuerstein's successful work with the children of the Holocaust demonstrated that there is hope for young learners approaching adolescence with cognitive levels lower than their ability; Lorna's work with the First Nations' children and similar projects around the world reinforces the message. The mediation of meaning is a necessary and powerful learning tool for all children who have experienced damage to their cultural roots.

STRATEGIES FOR THE MEDIATION OF MEANING

In the classroom, a teacher can mediate meaning in a variety of simple but powerful ways. This mediation can start with an enthusiastic explanation of the value of the subjects or topics that the curriculum introduces. The teacher's facial expressions, hand motions, and tone of voice communicate in subtle ways how the topics have value not only in the classroom but in applications to life as well. In addition, the explanation of reasons for classroom rules, modeling behavior for appropriate inter-actions with other students, and discussions of classroom procedures add to the mediation of meaning. When the teacher makes explicit the strategies, skills, and procedures needed for a learning task (such as solving a mathematics problem or writing an expository essay) and asks questions that engage the students in examining the why of such procedures, meaning is successfully mediated. When teachers illuminate the curriculum to examine the underlying significance of themes and issues as they relate to the values and beliefs of the students, they mediate meaning at the deepest level.

The daily curriculum provides many opportunities for mediating meaning with the students. With curricula typically being overloaded, the meaning-mediating teacher does not want to add additional material for students to cover superficially. The concept of "less is more" comes into play here. For the mediation of meaning, it is helpful to students if the teacher judiciously and selectively abandons material that is removed from student interests and focuses instead on material that is relevant to the students in each class. By building on their relevant prior knowledge or familiarity with each topic, such material will help the students construct a deeper understanding of the content they are being presented with.

The construction of meaning is what goes on in the head of a student. It is the mediator's job to make curriculum and instruction decisions that help each student make sense of daily lessons. The more the student is responsible for actual sense making, the deeper will be the student's understanding; the

> Mediation can start with an enthusiastic explanation of the value of the subjects that the curriculum introduces.

more the teacher has to tell the student what sense to make of a lesson or of lesson material, the less the student will develop. The mediator, the person who intervenes between the student and the new material, plays a critical role in active facilitation of the sense-making processes.

Links With Prior Knowledge

A variety of strategies lend themselves to the mediation of meaning. As introduced earlier (see Chapter 3), sense making begins with the classroom teacher's linkage to the students' prior knowledge or familiarity with a new topic or concept. Donna Ogle (1986) devised the K-W-L strategy as a visual, easy-to-use prior knowledge check. After asking the class to list all that they think they know (K) on a topic, she prompts them to list what they think they want (W) to know; at the end of the unit, she will help the students check back on what they learned (L) as a review and closure. For instance, here is a sample K-W-L chart completed by a fifth-grade class for the unit covering ancient Egypt.

Topic: Ancient Egypt		
K What We **K**now	**W** What We **W**ant to Know	**L** What We **L**earned
the Pyramids the Sphinx King Tut Moses and the Red Sea they liked cats the desert	Why did they embalm the pharoahs? Where is modern Egypt? How did they build their monuments? Why did they build them?	the religion of the Egyptians their modern government how archeology is handled in Egypt Egypt's place in Africa

The K-W-L format has several advantages as a learning tool. First, it helps students recall knowledge about a topic they have studied in other classes, seen videos of on TV, or read about in books. This list helps the teacher know what the students already know so as not to spend time reworking the curriculum and prompting moans of "We did that already!" It also gives the teacher quick insight into what they do not know on the topic. Finally, it gives a framework for checking the depth of their understanding and for evaluating which specific parts of the planned unit need amendment or deletion.

The most important benefit of this strategy, however, is that it provides students with a solid foundation on which they can build new knowledge. This foundation provides a readily understandable rationale for studying the topic. It also creates the bridges that enable the student to extend or to deepen knowledge through writing, discussion, and other modes of expression that help with the elaboration processes.

When students are challenged to start with what they already know of a topic, their level of interest rises (teacher educator Madeline Hunter ranked interest as one of the preeminent motivational factors). As students call up what they have learned, they are asked to think about what else they would like to learn on the topic. Although this is a difficult challenge for students who have always let the teacher do all the talking, cuing and delving strategies soon bring them around. Once they begin posing questions that they know will get answered, students' willingness to ask questions on the topic increases as the lesson, project, or unit unfolds.

> When students are challenged to start with what they know, their level of interest rises.

Explicit Thinking Across the Curricula

The second strategy that helps students make sense of subjects in the curriculum is their learning how to use higher-order thinking skills. The literature on metacognition—that is, thinking about thinking—reveals the importance of this strategy in improving student achievement. This particular kind of questioning speeds the process of student inquiry and leads to student readiness to read and listen more critically.

Thinking About Thinking

The first way to help students learn how to think more skillfully is to make explicit the key "thinking processes" implicit in most curricula. For instance, "prediction" is a key reading skill that is introduced by at least the third grade. Most standardized tests show how well students can use this skill. A few students are natural predictors. Most others can benefit from direct instruction that helps them develop the skill and use it to improve their reading comprehension and test scores. The lessons on the following pages and at the end of this chapter provide models to help all students develop this thinking ability.

Along with the skill of predicting, there are many other embedded thinking skills across the curriculum (e.g., classification in biology and chemistry, attribution in social studies and language arts, and summarization throughout the curriculum).

MIDDLE GRADES LESSON

Learning About Predictions

Standard
How to make predictions in fiction and problem solving

Focus Intelligence
Verbal/Linguistic

Supporting Intelligence
Mathematical/Logical

Mediation Emphasis
Meaning

BACKGROUND

One of the conclusions we have reached about skillful thinkers is that they are risk takers who use data to make sound predictions. The better they are as thoughtful students of data, the more successful they are as predictors. In essence, they do not need to make wild guesses; they take calculated risks based on careful study. Their bets are usually safe bets. Studies also show that the skill to make predictions in reading correlates strongly with the skill to make predictions in critical thinking.

CHECKING PRIOR KNOWLEDGE

1. Invite one student to the front of the classroom. Show a coin and predict whether it will come up heads or tails.

2. Have the student flip the coin and tell you whether you were correct or not. Ask the class to guess how many times out of a hundred flips it will come up heads, how many times out of a thousand flips.

STRUCTURING THE TASK

1. Using the board or overhead, provide the students with this information:
   A definition of "prediction": anticipating what will occur with a high degree of success (at least 80 percent of the time).
   Identify when prediction is important in reading fiction, in scientific experiments, in detective work, in a surgical operation, and in math problem solving.

2. On the World Wide Web, locate the story *The Dinner Party* by Mona Gardner. Print out a copy and draw lines to divide the story into five segments. Then make copies and distribute them to your students. Prefold the sheets on the lines.

3. Post the BET strategy and explain why it is helpful for this lesson:

   *B*ase on facts.

   *E*xamine clues for probability and possibility.

   *T*ender your bet and make a guess.

4. Invite the students to silently read the first segment. When they are ready, tell them to use BET to predict what will happen next. Elicit responses by identifying the facts, discussing the clues, and making solid guesses.

5. Continue through each segment.

LOOKING BACK AND REFLECTING

Invite students to answer the following:

1. Explain BET in your own words.

2. What are some times that you might use BET (in and out of school)? Explain and clarify.

3. How is this method of reading different from what you ordinarily have done?

4. What would happen if you were to use BET in preparing for your next major test?

5. What are the advantages and disadvantages of using BET? (Make a chart.)

BRIDGING FORWARD

1. Instruct the students to write a telegram to the president or a member of Congress. In the telegram, make a prediction, based on known facts, of what will happen if a specific policy is followed, OR

2. Write a telegram to the student government and make a prediction what will happen if . . . Collect the telegrams and read samples.

Variations

1. For K–3 use of BET, draw from this list of books or stories that help with prediction:

Verna Aardema, *Who's in Rabbit's House? A Masai Tale.* Retold by Verna Aardema, illustrated by Leo and Diane Dillon. Dial Press, 1977.

P. C. Asbjornsen and J. E. Moe, *The Three Billy Goats Gruff.* Illustrated by Marcia Brown. Harcourt Brace Jovanovich, 1957.

Carol Blackburn and Libby Handy, *The Thing From Somewhere.* Ashton Scholastic, 1975.

Franz Brandenberg, *Nice New Neighbors.* Illustrated by Aliki. Greenwillow, 1977.

Margaret Wise Brown, *Where Have You Been?* Illustrated by Leo and Diane Dillon. HarperCollins, 2004.

Remy Charlip, *Fortunately.* Four Winds Press, 1986.

Ed Emberley, *The Wing on a Flea.* Little, Brown, 2001.

Norma Farber, *As I Was Crossing Boston Common.* E. P. Dutton, 1973.

Wanda Gág, *Millions of Cats.* Coward, McCann & Geoghegan, 1977.

Nonny Hogrogian, *One Fine Day.* Aladdin, 2005.

Pat Hutchins, *Don't Forget the Bacon.* Greenwillow, 1976.

Arlene Mosel, *Tikki Tikki Tembo.* Holt, Rinehart, & Winston, 1968.

Uri Shulevitz, *One Monday Morning.* Farrar, Straus, & Giroux, 2003.

Taro Yashima, *Umbrella.* Puffin, 1977.

2. Select other short stories for the practice of predicting with older students.

Harry Allard, *Miss Nelson Is Missing*

Eugenia Collier, *Marigolds*

Richard Connell, *The Most Dangerous Game*

Carson McCullers, *Like That*

Sylvia Plath, *Imitation*

E. A. Poe, *The Pit and the Pendulum*

E. A. Poe, *The Cask of Amontillado*

Judith Viorst, *Alexander and the Terrible, Horrible No Good Very Bad Day*

Inquiry

A second way to develop students' thinking about thinking is to use an inquiry approach. Inquiry will focus students' attention on skills needed to master curricular content. For instance, in biology, as students prepare to categorize, they must be prepared to make logical comparisons. Note how the teacher in the following example uses only questions to mediate meaning in the making of predictions.

A Sample Scenario: What Does the Mediation of Meaning Sound Like?

Teacher: Who would like to draw a comparison between Page 3, which we shall deal with today, and Pages 1 and 2. Yes, Jasmine?

Jasmine: Here, like on Pages 1 and 2, we have to write down what is similar and what is different, but this time we're presented with words rather than pictures.

Teacher: Very true, Jasmine. Could you tell us, in a few words, what the pages have in common?

Jasmine: The kind of exercise, or activity.

Teacher: Right, they have the activity in common. And in what way are they different? Try to use one word.

Jasmine: How can I use one word to say that instead of pictures, we have words?

Teacher: Pictures, words, numbers, drawings, and symbols [writes on the black-board] all have a common use. What is the function of all of these? Please, Nyere.

Nyere: They tell us something or give us a message.

Teacher: Very good, Nyere. Every one of these forms of telling us something or giving us a message is called a language or a modality [writes on the board]. So how can we sum up our comparison of the pages? Yes, Lupe?

Lupe: They have the activity in common, but they differ in modality.

Teacher: Excellent. Let us now take the first pair of words. What do a church and a factory have in common? Juan?

Juan: They are both buildings.

Teacher: Very true. But is the fact that they are buildings their most important and most essential common attribute?

Juan: Yes, I think it is.

Teacher: You know, class, near my neighborhood there is a factory that manu-factures bricks. It has a big sign that reads Benedict Brown's Brick Factory. However, all the activity in this factory takes place in a big yard, in the open air, and not even the smallest building is present. Should this not be considered a factory? Roberto?

Roberto: Yes, but most factories are in buildings.

Teacher: This is true, Roberto. But if factories that are not in buildings are also considered factories, then perhaps factories have some other common attribute that is more critical or essential. Yes, Francisco?

Francisco: Perhaps they should be called places where people manufacture things.

Teacher: Excellent, Francisco. This is indeed a more essential attribute. Except that we can't relate this attribute to churches also. Let's take a look at the list of words I'm writing on the whiteboard: *church, factory, school, public library, sports center, youth club, municipal center, hospital*—how can we refer to all of these with just one word, one concept? Yes, Maria?

Maria: I think I know what you mean, but I can't say it.

Teacher: Well, we can refer to all these things as organizations or institutions [writes on the whiteboard]. Now, who can help me by describing how we came to this conclusion? What were the steps in our thinking that made this a successful comparison? Juan?

Helping Students Connect Culture With Academic Work

A third strategy for developing meaning is in classroom strategies that encour-age students to connect their own worlds and cultures to their academic work. Tasks and assignments that help students investigate the worlds they know best, as a means to achieving academic goals in the basic subject areas, are powerful motivators. In the middle grades, a writing assignment that can help students expand knowledge of their heritage while improving their writing or speaking skills is a meaningful learning tool.

Curriculum Materials and Life Experiences

The fourth strategy, the one with the most potential for engaging urban students in the making of meaning, but also the most underused, is the selection of curriculum materials closely connected to their life experiences. If advancement in learning starts with prior knowledge and experience, why don't urban students see more science experiments that relate to urban life? Why don't math problems deal with items the urban students know about? Why can't they hear of the African American and Hispanic American history makers who contributed to the growth of the American nation? Most especially, why don't urban students have more chances to study the literature of high-caliber writers who describe the pains and joys of American city life?

The lack of curricular materials that provide examples drawn from urban life is clearly attributable to the prevailing practice of the textbook industry. Urban school districts buy what the textbook publishers produce. To find a high-quality science program that features urban settings or a language arts program that devotes as much space to the poems of Gwendolyn Brooks, Maya Angelou, Langston Hughes, Nikki Giovanni, or Rita Dove as it does to those by Chaucer, John Donne, Lord Byron, or Edgar Allan Poe is extremely difficult. The books that most schools use in their curricula place the urban student at a distinct disadvantage. Most urban students' prior knowledge comes up blank when they start with the moors of England, sea adventures, castles, or characters that wear funny metal suits. On the other hand, when what they are asked to read begins with the streets of a city, with characters like the people they see each day, the prior knowledge foundation is there to start the meaning-making process that is central to interest and to learning.

In most cases today, it's up to the individual teacher to select curriculum materials, if the system allows it, that connect urban students more directly to the worlds they already know and experience day to day. This means that the teacher will have to adjust science experiments, select literature, and find social studies materials that make the direct connections. With this material in hand, teachers will need to adapt the lessons and units so that the students meet the same curricular goals but get there by a different pathway.

ADAPTING THE STANDARD CURRICULUM

Consider the three sample lessons that follow, which illustrate different ways of adapting a standard curriculum for the benefit of urban students.

This primary-grade mathematics lesson, Cows and Chickens, requires only a small change to adapt it to the urban experience. Instead of starting with cows and chickens, which many of the urban students might never have seen, the teacher can substitute familiar objects such as dogs and pigeons. The problem then reads, "There are four dogs and three pigeons. How many feet and tails are there altogether?," and meaning making is speeded up for the urban child.

It is important not only for students to obtain information, especially when that information has a connection to their prior knowledge and experience, but also for students to use that information. The more stimulating and creative the opportunity for use, the more likely it is that students will make sense of the raw information. By transforming print information into another medium, the students will have a richer opportunity to develop a second or third intelligence, lock the information into short-term memory, and build a sense of pride in their work. In essence, as Feuerstein points out, the teacher structures a meaningful task. In addition, the task provides multiple opportunities for the teacher-mediator to mediate for meaning as the project unfolds. Note that the Substance Abuse Prevention lesson for middle grade students that follows is high in urban interest as well as rich with opportunity for mediation work. Note as well that it requires less adaptation for urban students than does Cows and Chickens.

The third sample lesson calls for a more complex adaptation. At the secondary level, it's as easy to substitute a quality urban novel or autobiography in the English curriculum as it is to select an important work from Merry Olde England or Puritan America. For instance, instead of studying the trials and tribulations of Hester Prynne in *The Scarlet Letter,* the English teacher in the urban classroom might introduce her students to *Bigger in Black Boy.* To replace Boswell's *Life of Johnson,* the urban teacher might substitute *The Autobiography of Malcolm X.* Better yet, the teacher might pair two novels such as Toni Morrison's *Beloved* and Crane's *Red Badge of Courage* to compare characters against a common theme.

KEY POINTS TO REMEMBER

- The question "why" from the child should be mediated.
- You've heard a student say, "Why I gotta do this . . . ?" In addition to the 6 W and H questions—who, what, when, where, why, and how—it's essential for meaning to occur to include "so what?" "now what?" and "what next?" as metacognitve questions to help students buy into and understand the learning; these questions help students relate the learning to their own personal experiences.
- The child's culture and beliefs are the focus; the mediator serves as the translator, celebrator, and transmitter of culture, using lots of affect.
- If you are trying to help students connect their culture with academic work, connect the teaching with the experiences children bring to school, as opposed to assuming that because students have been exposed to the vocabulary, they have prior knowledge and experience with it as well (i.e., octagon and stop sign).
- Identify supplemental materials and adapt the curriculum for use with diverse student populations in mind until publishing companies meet the cultural and experience-related needs of the children we serve.
- The process is as important as the finished product; students need to understand how to transfer (process) information to other settings; if the information is important only in the setting it was taught, it is a waste of time.

SAMPLE LESSONS

As you review these sample lessons, reflect on the making of meaning. What have you learned in this chapter that might enrich this lesson?

Meaning is inherent to every lesson in the curriculum. If curricula or instructional practices leave the impression with students that learning is a piecemeal task or a series of discrete tasks ("Why do we have to use correct grammar in a history paper? Isn't grammar for language arts?"), students need to see meaning in what they are learning. If they are episodic learners already, the damage is double. Therefore, it is doubly important for teachers to double their efforts as they mediate for meaning in the urban classroom with adaptations in lesson design, materials, and units of learning. There are a multitude of other strategies and methods that facilitate the mediation of meaning. These strategies and methods are less important than the mediator's intentionality in making sure that students are in a position to take advantage of understanding the meanings. With this intention, the selection of helpful tools will make the task easier.

ELEMENTARY LESSON

Cows and Chickens: A Math Lesson

Standard
How to solve an addition math problem

Focus Intelligence
Mathematical/Logical

Supporting Intelligences
Verbal/Linguistic, Visual/Spatial, Interpersonal

Mediation Emphasis
Meaning

CHECKING PRIOR KNOWLEDGE

1. Ask the class to tell you what they know about cows and chickens.
2. Sketch each animal as they reply.

STRUCTURING THE TASK

1. Write on the board: "There are four cows and three chickens. How many feet and tails are there altogether?"

2. Put students into pairs and give each pair one pencil and one piece of paper. Invite them to agree on one answer to the question. They can do work on the paper to figure out the answer. Invite them to make their notations large enough for others to see from the class circle.

3. Check for understanding of the task.

4. Circulate among the pairs and observe how they work together to solve the problem.

LOOKING BACK AND REFLECTING

1. Assemble the pairs in the class circle. Ask a number of the pairs to share what they did to solve the problem. Ask them to save their answers. Invite all to use their listening skills when they are not speaking.

2. Comment on each strategy with positive feedback.

BRIDGING FORWARD

1. Ask random pairs to tell what they learned about problem solving.

2. Identify the answers.

MIDDLE GRADES LESSON

Substance Abuse Prevention

Standard
Use relevant details to support main ideas such as facts, statistics, quotations, information from interviews and surveys, and pertinent information discovered during research.

Focus Intelligence
Interpersonal

Supporting Intelligence
Verbal/Linguistic

Mediation Emphasis
Meaning

CHECKING PRIOR KNOWLEDGE

Ask the class to answer these questions by raising hands for each "yes":

- How many have ever seen a political campaign?
- How many have seen the TV ads against drugs?
- How many have ever marched in a parade?

STRUCTURING THE TASK

1. Brainstorm with the class all the ways it could use to advertise the goal of having a drug-free school (e.g., bumper stickers, TV ads, school parade). Select the best five or six.

2. Divide the class into work teams. Each team will select one of the brainstormed ways to advertise for a drug-free school.

3. Each team will go to work so that everyone has a different job, but everyone contributes. Set a schedule or timeline. Indicate how much class time they can use for planning, working, practicing, and so on.

4. As a first task, each team will write out an action plan for your approval. Each plan will describe the team's goal, the benefits, the tasks that need to be completed, the timeline, and the materials needed. (This is a low-budget campaign, so encourage the teams to be creative and cheap!)

5. Help the teams work. When the products are ready, have the entire class discuss the coordination of the campaign. Be sure to involve the principal!

LOOKING BACK AND REFLECTING

Ask the class to respond to these questions:

- What did we do well to communicate our message?
- What could we improve if we did it again?
- What did we learn?

BRIDGING FORWARD

Have the students tabulate the data collected from the other classes. On the basis of the data, ask the class to reevaluate its campaign with the three questions and with a discussion of what they learned (a) about designing a campaign for a drug-free school and (b) about teamwork.

SECONDARY LESSON

Literature: Understanding Malcolm X

Standard
How to identify, compare, and contrast characteristics or traits of people

Focus Intelligence
Verbal/Linguistic

Supporting Intelligences
Interpersonal, Intrapersonal, Visual/Spatial

Mediation Emphasis
Meaning, Sharing

CHECKING PRIOR KNOWLEDGE

After students have read *Malcolm X*, assign groups of three to make a concept map of Malcolm X's character. Let each group take specific scene(s) as the information source. Using what he says, what he does, and what others say about him, they will determine which characteristics or traits are most evident. After each group charts its section, assemble the all-class chart showing what they know about Malcolm X.

STRUCTURING THE TASK

Begin by creating a class list that best describes those traits of Malcolm X's that led to his death. Brainstorm to generate the list and then keep only those traits that get 60 percent or more of the vote. Next, use the trios (above) to pick the traits that, if changed, might have led to a different ending. Have each group select one of these and identify where in the autobiography it would appear, what Malcolm X or others would say or do to reflect the trait, and how the autobiography would end as a result. Discuss all the variations before asking each trio to create the lines and act out the final scene.

LOOKING BACK AND REFLECTING

Ask each student to make a journal entry describing five things they learned about Malcolm X. Match student pairs and have each student talk for one minute about one learning. Do not repeat. Form a new match of pairs. Give each 30 seconds to share a new learning. Make a third pairing and allow 15 seconds for each.

BRIDGING FORWARD

1. Ask each student to make a journal entry that summarizes what was learned from Malcolm X and that describes the applicability to his life. Do a wraparound closure, or

2. Ask each student to write a five-paragraph essay describing the character of Malcolm X and/or the lessons to be learned from the decisions he made.

Assessing Student Performance

1. Identify three to five attributes of the main character and explain why each is unique to this person.

2. Describe the process used for analyzing a literary character.

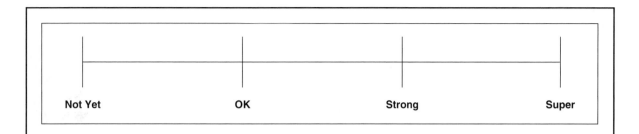

Not Yet   OK   Strong   Super

Materials

A copy of the text of *The Autobiography of Malcolm X* for each student and student journals

Variations

1. Substitute any short story, drama, novel, biography, or autobiography from the curriculum with a focus on the main character.

2. Show the Malcolm X video and assign groups to contrast various elements with the autobiography.

3. Use magazine stories about current public figures.

4. Use original historical documents and textbook entries about a public figure.

5. Conduct student interviews with local officials, prominent community leaders, family, or friends.

6. Cite supporting characters in a story. Assign one character to a group. Contrast the characters.

7. Do a comparative study of Boswell's *Life of Samuel Johnson* with the Malcolm X autobiography.

5

Transcendence

Children have never been very good at listening to their elders, but they have never failed to imitate them.

—James Baldwin (Riley, 1993)

The third mediation, transcendence, in addition to intentionality/reciprocity and meaning, is equally essential to all instructional interactions. An interaction that meets this criterion enables the learner to bridge from a here-and-now learning experience to a grasp of the experience's underlying principles and value. When tied to intentionality, a transcendent mediation facilitates the learner's making connections with higher-order goals and purposes.

GETTING TO THE HEART OF THE THOUGHT

In the mediated classroom, teachers provide multiple opportunities for the students to go beyond or "transcend" learning how to perform a task. They are more interested in the students making generalizations or grasping the underlying principles about what they are doing. Preferably, the teachers set up a hands-on, laboratory-like situation that will provide a set of common experiences that will lead to the needed generalization. Take the concept of ratio, for instance. Rather than begin a lesson by giving a textbook definition of ratio, followed by many problem examples and corrective feedback for mistakes, the teacher mediating transcendence will start the lesson by implanting the expectation of transfer and by providing a hands-on ratio experiment. In this case the teachers' immediate hands-on intention is for the students to understand how to perform this experiment; their transcendent intention is for the students to learn how to apply the principle of ratio when solving other problems in science, mathematics, or even social studies. How do teachers do this?

SEEKING THE TRANSCENDING IDEA

To transcend means "to go above." Among Feuerstein's criteria for Mediated Learning Experiences, transcendence refers to the act of "going above" facts and details to form an overarching generalization or concept. It is one of the three, along with intentionality and reciprocity and meaning, that Feuerstein teaches is essential to every lesson. Whether in mathematics, where students practice many variations of fractions, or social studies, where students study many migrations, Feuerstein wants the teacher to take the students above the fraction problems or the individual migrations to form a general statement that shows the students' understanding of the meaning in more universal terms. "What is always true about this type of fraction?" "What is the general principle that is true of all migrations?" In this chapter, you delve into the how to and the why for bringing transcendent instruction to the classroom.

First, teachers give each pair of students a cardboard tube from a roll of paper towels, a crayon, a tape measure, a pair of scissors, and a 12-inch piece of string. They show the pairs how to mark off the roll into thirds. At this point, they make explicit transfer back to check prior knowledge of "fractions." Next, they invite each pair to use all hands to wrap the string around the tube and cut a piece of string of the measured length. Next, they ask the students, "If you now stretch the string along the length of the tube, which line marked on the tube will the string reach?" After the students test their guesses, the teacher shows them that the circumference (distance around the tube) is almost three times the distance across (diameter) and has them check this out once again with their strings.

After the pairs agree on this principle by checking out their own measurements, the teacher gives them other circular objects (glasses, cups, wooden dowels, plant pots, metal pipes, cans, etc.) to see if the principle holds. After the students have charted different examples, the teacher asks explicit questions to be sure they can explain why, with a variety of different circular objects they can visualize at home or in their community, the principle of ratio applies. If there are doubts, the teacher will challenge them to test out the theory on other objects. Finally, using what they have observed in the experiments, the teacher will help them form a generalized or "superordinant" concept called "ratio." At this point, the students are prepared to do ratio problem solving with round objects. Although some might understand the principle well enough to solve a ratio problem with a square or rectangular object of different sizes, most would struggle with such a transfer challenge. To ensure success for all, teachers must devise enough additional concrete experiments with ratio that the students can strengthen the generalization that allows them to see how ratio works, regardless of size or shape. When these understandings are in place, the teacher is then ready to cement the transcendent definition of ratio and to move the students to pencil-and-paper word problems.

A teacher of mathematics who feels forced to race through chapter after chapter in a textbook can argue, "I don't have time for all of these shenanigans. I have two days to teach ratio. I cover the text. They do the assignments. We move on. My job is to get those who can perform the tasks ready for the test. They either have the smarts to use what I taught or not. The time is not there for anything 'transcendent.'" Such arguments strike right to the heart of the issue of transcendence. Time is important. However, if time is not allotted to develop deep understanding, the coverage of

> If time is not allotted to develop deep understanding, the coverage of material does little more than hide success from students.

material in the textbook does little more than hide success from most students. They may memorize the formula; they may understand the problems given, but without understanding the concept, future applications of the principle are iffy, especially when students are the episodic learners that many urban students seem to be. Ultimately, use of the textbook approach alone ensures that many students will leave school with a diploma but without the ability to connect ideas or events. To ensure that this doesn't happen, it is imperative that teachers selectively abandon the extraneous topics that force superficial coverage of the curriculum and take time to mediate in-depth understanding of the most critical concepts that are needed across the curriculum and in the world of work.

Reciprocal Teaching

There are a variety of methods that promote transcendence. One of the most notable is a well-researched tool called reciprocal teaching. This method works in all disciplines that rely heavily on reading comprehension. Whether students must read from a math, science, or social studies text, decipher written instructions on a computer screen, or study a short story, the strategies learned in this approach will improve their comprehension and promote their ability to transfer new concepts through every discipline.

Reciprocal teaching starts with the teacher's introducing students to four reading comprehension strategies that help them read with the lesson's focus in mind and that are especially good at helping students remember what they have read. For each reading passage, whether it is instructional, expositional, or narrative, the students will learn how to ask a generalizing question, how to summarize, how to clarify meaning, and how to make predictions.

A generalizing question is one that focuses on the main idea of a paragraph or story. It is the opposite of a detail question that focuses on the facts. For instance, the question, "What mark does a cheetah have under its eyes?" is a detail question—the student can point to one sentence in the paragraph as the answer. On the other hand, a question such as, "What kind of animal is the cheetah?" is a generalizing question— it requires several sentences as clues that point to the paragraph's main idea.

A summary is a concise explanation that captures all the details related to the main idea. For instance, a complete summary about how the cheetah protects her young would include several details such as "by whistling when danger is near," "by hiding them in the tall grass," and "by walking away alone from where they are hidden." Clarification of meaning occurs when unclear referents, complex concepts, and abstract ideas are identified or when poorly organized material is explained. For instance, if a paragraph has overused the pronoun *she,* the teacher might substitute, where necessary, "the mother cheetah."

The ability to make predictions demonstrates that students read texts with precision, draw correct inferences, and can anticipate what will happen next in a story or other selection. In a cheetah story, with students already aware of how the mother protects the cubs, students should be able to predict what will happen next in the passage when they learn that the cubs are threatened by the arrival of a lioness.

Implementing the Four Tactics

After introducing the four comprehension strategies with examples to the students, teachers inform them that the teachers are going to model the use of the strategies when reading a short story. First, they invite each student to read the first paragraph. When all are done, they ask detail questions about the paragraph and point out differences between the main idea and detail questions. Finally, teachers summarize the first paragraph and show the students in detail how they made the summary.

As teachers model the use of the generalizing question and summarizing, they are careful to engage all the students in the discussion (see the discussion of TESA, Chapter 2). Teachers are especially careful to seek out random responses by calling upon students from all around the room. When an answer is given, whether it is correct or not, teachers respect the response. At the minimum, they say, "That was an interesting response, LaMont. Show me how you found it." Better yet, they listen for the part of the answer that was correct and point that out before calling for another student to complete the answer or give a different response. "I like the part of your answer that said . . . Who can help LaMont with the other part?" When students are confused by unclear ideas, unusual and abstract words, or poor sentence structure, teachers take time to invite students to seek further summary or clarification, or simply to ask more questions. Once the summary is completed and the students seem clear on the main idea and the details, teachers model prediction making. They ask the students to tell what they think will happen next in the story and ask them to explain the prediction based on what they have just read.

Once the first paragraph is done, teachers return to the definitions and ask the students to recall samples of each strategy that they used in understanding the first paragraph. After reminding students that reading in this manner is a group effort and that all are expected to work together in a respectful way, teachers ask for a volunteer student to take the teachers' place in leading the discussion of the next paragraph. Teachers continue this cycle for each paragraph; each time a new volunteer leads, teachers assist and review the four strategies at the end of each discussion. For each new paragraph, teachers fade more into the background, saving their input for the end when the class reviews the strategies.

As mediators of transcendence, teachers direct the thinking processes in a supportive way. They are not telling students how or what to think. Instead, as mediators, they provide the structure that refines the thinking process so that students are using the process in an appropriate and logical manner. For instance, if the student creates a generalizing question for the paragraph, the teacher can provide support by asking, "Can you finish this question about the paragraph: 'What are the different ways that cheetahs _____?'" (e.g., protect their young). After the student responds with the organizing idea, the teacher mediates by asking, "Why do you think that is the generalizing question?" (main idea). If the student gives a detail statement ("She hides them in the brush") instead of a summary sentence ("She protects her young in several ways"), the teacher might say in a respectful tone, "Maria, you have selected a very interesting fact. Let's see what we can add to the sentence so that we have a more complete picture of the main idea. What else can you add from the paragraph? What do these sentences add up to mean?"

When students are having difficulty with words, the mediator may ask, "Are there some words in the third sentence that might give students of your age difficulty?" "What words are not clear to you?" or "Whose name would you put in

> As mediators of transcendence, teachers direct the thinking processes in a supportive way.

place of this pronoun in the third sentence?" Such questions help students clarify the ideas and untangle confusions created by unclear syntax.

Finally, it is helpful for the mediator to ask questions that provide students with a pattern for making predictions in what they are reading. Research on reading comprehension has shown the importance of helping students become explicit predictors, noting that the strongest readers make predictions a natural part of their reading tasks—less able readers seem to lack a systematic way to do this. As discussed in the "mediation of meaning" sample lesson on making predictions (see Chapter 4, Learning About Predictions lesson), the mediating teacher increases all students' functionality as predictors. As more student-readers learn to improve their predictive ability, their reading comprehension will improve not only in their daily work but on district, state, and national standardized tests as well.

To develop predicting skills for reading comprehension, the teacher-mediator models a systematic method that the students can practice with each other in reciprocal situations; they will be able to go on to use this method on their own in any reading task in the curriculum (see the lists of reading materials from the Learning About Predictions sample lesson in Chapter 4). Instead of providing a complete text, the teacher begins by doling out the text to the students one paragraph at a time. After the students have read a paragraph, the teacher asks them one of two questions: "What do you think will happen next?" (for selections of fiction) or "What do you think the author will say next?" (for passages of nonfiction). After a number of students have declared their guesses (a guess is an unsubstantiated prediction), the teacher has the class pick the most likely predictions and then asks them to explain why. The teacher cautions the students to limit their explanations to information provided in the paragraph just read. After hearing a number of rationales, the teacher distributes the next paragraph and repeats the question sequence. As the teacher listen to the responses, he or she will not comment or judge. However, the teacher will insist that all rationales come from the text, not from prior experience.

After the entire story or article is read, the mediating teacher asks students to focus on the system that the teacher used and to say what they may have learned about the system itself (the "system" is simply the two questions of "what do you predict?" and "why?"). The students have learned the systematic method of predicting from what they have read and how making predictions increases their attention to detail and main ideas and holds their attention in the reading process. After the first practice story has been modeled, the teacher can initiate the reciprocal process with pairs of students. Students use other readings to ask each other the questions to make their predictions and to assess the prediction process. It is important that the teacher continues guiding practice of the process over several months until students show that they can use it without direction in a variety of academic disciplines.

> The teacher continues guiding practice until students show that they can use it without direction.

Fostering Communities of Learners

After teachers feel comfortable with students' use of reciprocal teaching, they may want to carry the strategy to the next step with an approach called "fostering communities of learners." With this technique (advanced by Anne Brown, the researcher who devised reciprocal teaching), the teacher divides students into research teams. Using classroom materials or Internet resources, they seek information on a question posed to the entire class. Information is shared by using Aronson's cooperative learning strategy called the "jigsaw." In the jigsaw, once the groups have begun to gather information, group members disperse to other groups and share their information. After the cross-group sharing, the class discusses the question using the reciprocal strategies of clarifying, summarizing, generalizing statements, and predicting with the mediating teacher's guidance. In pilot classrooms in San Francisco, Brown's research showed large and significant increases in comprehension, problem-solving ability, and reading performance.

To ensure bridging the reciprocal teaching techniques and processes, it is important that teachers remember that the goal is student self-direction in using techniques to increase comprehension. Beginning with a direct instruction of the method, teachers guide student use of the questioning strategies. When there is evidence that the students understand the process, teachers move them to more independent practice in cooperative pairs. Ultimately, teachers set up a challenge for all students to practice the reciprocal process. At this point, teacher-mediators take time to guide students to an understanding of the process and to explore other uses across the curriculum. As the school year progresses, the teachers will provide explicit opportunities for students to practice and refine the reciprocal process. This last step ensures a high degree of transcendence. For students who are used to teacher-only direction of the reading process (i.e., only the teacher asks clarifying questions, predicting questions, etc.), it may be difficult to assume responsibility for asking peers these questions and becoming autonomous enough to ask themselves these questions when doing independent reading. For the transfer from teacher-centered questions to learner-centered questions to occur, teacher-mediators must model and remodel, coach, and firmly support the students' efforts to master the strategies. It should not be surprising if students resist taking on this responsibility ("It's so hard to remember!" or "We didn't have to do this in Mrs. Smithson's class!" or "It's the teacher's job to ask questions!" are some of the whiny avoidance strategies teachers may hear; pouting, goofing off in the pairs, or acting out in other ways are some of the "you can't make me" power strategies students will use). It's important that mediators encourage students to work through their insecurities and live up to this high

> It is important that teachers remember that the goal is student self-direction.

expectation for learning the process as well as the content of the reading task. The content gives them information; the process enables them to make connections for a lifetime.

The experienced mediator can encourage students to stay focused on the reading strategies by preparing a bulletin board or providing a handout that lists the four reciprocal strategies with their definitions and patterns for asking each type of question. When students get stuck, the mediator can point them to the printed material for review. As students become more skilled in the use of reciprocal strategies, the mediator can increase the length or the complexity of the reading assignments. After each assignment, teachers allow time to discuss the process with the entire class and for self-reflective journal entries that challenge the students to think about their use of the skills, how they are progressing, and the difficulties and concerns they are having. Eventually, with continued practice and support, the students are able to bridge the reciprocal strategies to complete fiction and nonfiction assignments in many different subject areas.

RECOGNIZING PATTERNS

For the primary grades, learning about mathematical shapes is an important topic. Many workbooks end the lesson by asking students to match a shape with a word.

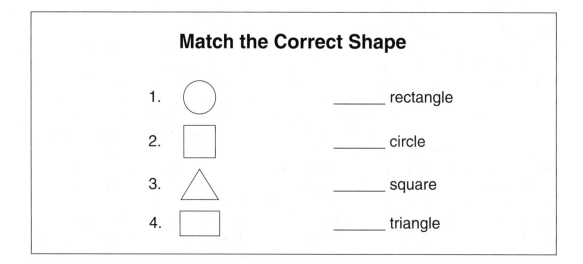

A lesson designed to mediate transcendence goes beyond simple recognition of isolated shapes. It instead enables children to recognize each shape wherever it may be located. Notice how the lesson calls for explanations of the definition as the transcendence promotion method.

FORMULATING PRINCIPLES

In the middle grades sample lesson that follows, mediation for transcendence appears at two levels. First, the lesson asks the teacher to bridge from the poet's concrete description to other related experiences. Second, the lesson uses the reciprocal teaching model with this poem as a model. In addition, it asks the teacher to bridge forward the students' use of the model into other experiences. From this, the students are asked to formulate a principle for use of the model.

LEARNING FOR A LIFETIME

In the secondary sample lesson, a single skill for improving reading comprehension is the focus. Without the mediation of transcendence, the lesson would end with the students bridging examples of what they had learned. Note how the lesson leads up to Bridging Forward, where the emphasis is placed on identifying transfers for the purpose of formulating a principle that will transcend all appropriate situations. Here the emphasis is on learning a principle that will hold true for a lifetime.

The mediation of transcendence, coupled as it always is with intentionality/ reciprocity and meaning, is the theoretical explanation for the proverb, "Give me a fish, I will eat for a day; teach me how to fish, I will eat for a lifetime." When teachers mediate transcendence for urban children whose learning is often episodic and incidental, they provide those children with a powerful tool for the development of their understanding. As children learn to form principles that bind experiences, they learn why it is important to avoid life-threatening situations, why it is valuable to take advantage of schooling, and why ideas generated in school are part of a connected universe.

This element is critical for students in urban classrooms where there are large gaps in achievement. If students are not challenged and enabled to transcend factual details, they will continue to fall behind. Having students memorize facts without being led to the generalization that binds the facts condemns students to the low expectation that all they have to do is "get the facts, just the facts." Never will they have to meet the high expectation of thinking in transcendent terms.

KEY POINTS TO REMEMBER

- The transcendence interaction that strongly promotes transfer of learning looks like the proverb, "Give me a fish and I will eat for a day; teach me how to fish, and I will eat for a lifetime."
- Moving students from concrete to abstract and simple to complex gets students unstuck from lower tracks with lower expectations. It takes time to develop a deep understanding. The goal is uncoverage of knowledge, not coverage of material.
- Don't leave the bus stop with an empty bus; reflections and journal writings will give an idea of what the students are thinking, perceiving, and understanding.
- Make it a habit to incorporate the four comprehension strategies of asking a generalizing question: how to summarize, how to clarify meaning, and how to make predictions for each reading passage.
- Ask students what reading strategies they use to complete tasks. Have them take ownership and understand the process.
- If comprehension, problem solving, and reading performance are your challenges, focus on mediating transcendence.
- A triangle is a triangle is a triangle; isolated shapes, facts, and base words should be identified by students in any form, wherever they are found, once they are mediated for transcendence.
- No more "sage on the stage"; students decide how and what they think, not others.

ELEMENTARY LESSON

Shapes

Standard
How to describe shapes in the world around us

Focus Intelligence
Naturalist

Supporting Intelligences
Mathematical/Logical, Visual/Spatial, Interpersonal, Bodily/Kinesthetic

Mediation Emphasis
Transcendence

CHECKING PRIOR KNOWLEDGE

On the board, draw a circle, a square, a rectangle, and a triangle. Ask each student to think where he or she might have seen these shapes. Allow pairs to discuss the sightings before you ask individuals to share. Under each shape, list the appropriate responses.

STRUCTURING THE TASK

1. Divide the class into four to six groups. Invite each group to form the shape you specify.

2. Invite the class to label each shape as you point to each example on the board. Ask, "What makes this shape special?"

3. Give each group a worksheet with the four shapes. The groups will search throughout the room to find objects in which each shape is found. Let them write the object's name or sketch it.

4. Conduct a round-robin and invite explanations/reasons for each selection.

LOOKING BACK AND REFLECTING

Invite each group to add an example to each list on the board. Conduct a round-robin until all lists are complete.

BRIDGING FORWARD

Instruct each child to take a shape worksheet home so that he or she can find at least three items that contain each shape. Use the reciprocal model to check for understanding.

Assessing Student Performance

Each child can identify and name the shape within an object and can explain why each example is reflective of the definition.

Variation

Give each child a page of shapes to cut out and make a simple picture. Ask the child to explain why the picture is a specific shape.

MIDDLE GRADES LESSON

"To the Young . . .": A Poem

Standard
How to transfer the meaning of a poem

Focus Intelligence
Verbal/Linguistic

Supporting Intelligences
Intrapersonal, Interpersonal

Mediation Emphasis
Transcendence

CHECKING PRIOR KNOWLEDGE

1. Pair students together to read the Gwendolyn Brooks poem, "To the Young Who Want to Die."

2. Use a think-pair-share strategy to guide the discussion: "What do you think the poet is saying?" Use TESA skills to guide the discussion (see Chapter 2).

STRUCTURING THE TASK

1. After several pairs have shared their responses, explain to the students how to summarize the poem. (Do not model this poem. If you must model a complete summary, pick a different, easier example.)

2. Ask each pair to make a summary before you ask three to five different pairs to share. Give positive comments.

3. Write the word *clarify* on the board. Explain how the concept works with several samples from the poem. Invite the pairs to review the poem and ask about items that require clarification. Help the class respond and clarify.

4. Return to the whole poem and ask for students who want to change the summary to do so. Ask why and get their new ideas.

LOOKING BACK AND REFLECTING

Ask the pairs to respond to the poet. Do they agree or disagree with the final sentence? Why? Encourage listening to each other.

BRIDGING FORWARD

Review the strategies of summarizing and clarifying. If need be, repeat the process above with another poem for guided practice. When students demonstrate a heightened ability to summarize and clarify, make an independent practice assignment. Conclude your review by asking students to identify other opportunities to use these skills in school or at home and to form a generalized principle for their appropriate use.

Assessing Student Performance

1. Students can make an accurate summary of a short poem without assistance.

2. Students can clarify ambiguous items and weak associations in a poem.

Variations

1. Use a different medium, such as a short story, editorial, news clip, or short topic from the Internet.

2. Select a different poem.

3. Model both processes before using the selection.

SECONDARY LESSON

What Is Next?

Standard
How to develop predicting skills as a tool that promotes advanced reading comprehension

Focus Intelligence
Verbal/Linguistic

Supporting Intelligence
Intrapersonal

Mediation Emphasis
Transcendence

CHECKING PRIOR KNOWLEDGE

1. Select a novel or drama for an all-class study. Authors such as Lorraine Hansberry, James Baldwin, and Langston Hughes provide strong literature adaptable to this strategy.

2. Present the title of the work selected. Ask a variety of students to predict what they think the work is about. Probe for why and honor all ideas.

STRUCTURING THE TASK

Make the first reading assignment. Let the class know that after completing the first chapter assignment, you will ask only two questions (show on board).

1. What do you think will happen in Chapter 2? Why do you think so? (Some of the responses will draw upon students' generalized past experiences with structure: "The first act introduces the conflict. The second . . ." These are appropriate, but remind students that you are seeking specific evidence from the chapter just read that points to specific predictions about what's next.)

2. Solicit as many ideas as time allows. Assign each chapter, one at a time, followed by the two questions. As students make more accurate predictions, they will read more carefully to prepare for the next chapter and to see if they understand it!

LOOKING BACK AND REFLECTING

1. As the work advances, call for chapter summaries. (You may need to review "how to.") At the end of the novel, call for a one-page summary of the novel or drama and review ideas from students.

2. Discuss how the two questions helped with reading comprehension.

BRIDGING FORWARD

1. Invite students to describe opportunities in school, at work, or at home in which they might benefit from making accurate predictions. Mediate why so that they will form a principle appropriate for use of this approach.

2. After the final summary, invite students to share lessons learned from the characters and how these lessons might benefit them at home, at school, or at work. Again, mediate why so that they can formulate the principle.

Assessing Student Performance

1. Each student will demonstrate how to ask the predicting questions in a piece of literature.

2. Each student will demonstrate how to respond to the predicting questions.

3. Each student will demonstrate the ability to apply the use of the questions in three different situations.

Variations

1. Use a video of a play. Stop at key breaks and use the two-question process.

2. Begin with a short story to model the process.

3. Instruct students to write individual essays as the bridging task.

6

Self-Regulation and Control of Behavior

The man who never submitted to anything will soon submit to a burial mat.

—Nigerian proverb

For several decades, national surveys have shown that the public is most concerned about school discipline. In spite of a multitude of proposed solutions, ranging from the systemic approach of the effective schools movement to make the school a safe and secure place for all, to the more teacher-directed approaches of Driekurs, London, Jones, Burke, Denny, and other advocates of sound classroom management, the concerns have escalated.

Self-Regulation and Control of Behavior: The First in Line

After the first three criteria that Feuerstein uses for each lesson, the remaining criteria require teachers to select those that apply to their students. Among these, self-regulation and control of behavior is most often selected. For those who wish to mediate self-regulation and control of behavior, it is important that they not misconstrue Feuerstein's cognitive approach with the behaviorists'. When Feuerstein speaks of "behavior," he is talking about how the mind behaves as it seeks to take charge of thinking and learning. Eventually, the mind, mediated by the parent or teacher, learns to govern all behaviors. This is not the stimulus-response pattern of the behaviorists. It is the mediator stepping in to help the students learn how to make sense of the world and then to develop the intrinsic motivation to control how they interact. As students develop their self-regulation, they become less impulsive in their thinking, more systematic in their problem solving, and more willing to impose restraint on all the ways they interact with the world around them.

DISCIPLINE AND INTRINSIC MOTIVATION

Alfie Kohn (1993) attributes the failure (or the perceived failure) to correct the "discipline problem" to a misguided behaviorist belief that "rewards and punishments" will change students. Supposedly, the stimulus imposed by outside forces over and over builds a pattern of good behaviors. As he notes in his writings, all of the most popular approaches to managing student behavior not only have a very low success rate (as evidenced by both the persistence and the growth of disruptive behavior) but also are not beneficial to students. In place of the common reward-and-punishment systems derived from the long-term influence of Skinner's behavioristic theory, Kohn advocates the development of systems and strategies that foster students' intrinsic motivation.

Kohn's advocacy of intrinsic motivation complements Feuerstein's belief in the importance of self-regulation and control of behavior. According to Feuerstein, only self-regulation leads students to take responsibility for their own behaving, learning, and thinking. Like other cognitive psychologists such as Ellis, London, and Dinkmeyer, as well as cognitive instructional strategists such as Costa, Brown, Barell, Musial, Hammerman, and Perkins, Feuerstein grounds self-regulation and control of behavior within the individual's mind. As individuals "think about thinking" (metacognition), they construct new ways of acting that lead to control of impulsive behavior, learn to break complex problems into small parts, and move away from guessing how to behave toward a more systematic approach of self-discipline. In Feuerstein's systemic approach, it is the teacher's responsibility to mediate the development of this self-regulation, not to impose punishment, dole out rewards, and ignore attention-getting misbehavior. When it comes to helping children develop positive learning habits and raise their achievement, Feuerstein finds rewards and punishments to be ineffective and ludicrous tools that weaken a child's desire to behave well, work hard, or achieve more, even as these short-term answers get some quick responses.

INTERRUPTING IMPULSIVE BEHAVIOR

Mediation of self-regulation and control of behavior occurs when the mediator interrupts impulsive and unsystematic behavior by asking students to "stop and think." This makes students conscious of the need to monitor and adjust what they are doing or thinking. As students are rushing helter-skelter through a task or impulsively reacting to a situation, the mediator waves a stop sign in front of their eyes. This signals, "Stop your uncontrolled response. Look both ways. Recall the proper ways to react. Think about what you're doing. Proceed with caution." With this mediation of self-control, the mediator then can continue to other mediation such as the mediation of challenge or the feeling of competence to help the student build success and the intrinsic motivation that goes with success. More important, this approach gives students the confidence to control their own learning not just for that instance but for the future.

Consider these two cases for a common challenge. The challenge is the standardized test performance and a growing trend for students to ignore their value. The first principal, a 150 percent behaviorist, goes to his discretionary budget and draws out several hundred dollars to buy prizes that his less-than-wealthy students will covet: a racing bike, a lunch at the local fast-food restaurant, two passes to a movie, an iPod, several CDs. He calls the eighth graders together and tells them, "Last year, a lot of your friends blew off this test. This test is very important for you and the school. I don't want you not to try your best. Therefore, I am going to give these prizes to the students who . . ." Stimulus and response.

The second principal believes in intrinsic motivation. Throughout the year, the eighth-grade teachers mediated students' self-regulation. They taught them test-taking skills, and on the sample tests they stressed impulse control techniques. In addition, the teachers gave many minitests so that students could try out their new methods and see immediate success. Using metacognitive reflections, students assessed what they did well in preparing for the test and in thinking through their answers, what they didn't do so well, and what they needed to improve. As students progressed through the year, they built a repertoire of strategies to stay focused on the most important information they were learning in each subject. Teachers emphasized "self-pride" in doing well on all tests.

INSTRUMENTAL ENRICHMENT

In urban classrooms where there are large numbers of students labeled "at-risk," attention-deficit/hyperactivity disorder (ADHD), "learning disabled," "behavior disordered," "emotionally disturbed," "left behind" (and all the other excuses listed in Chapter 1), the most advantageous way to introduce impulse control is through an intense, long-term program of Feuerstein's Instrumental Enrichment. This gives teacher-mediators the opportunity to establish a foundation of self-regulation without the distraction of course content. As many studies have shown, the most challenged students are no different from their high-performing peers: all students find it difficult to "think about thinking" when course content and subject matter are "what they are used to doing." In a high-action culture such as in the United States, reflection is not a highly prized way of learning. Feuerstein's Instrumental Enrichment requires that students learn to reflect, to stop and think, to plan and monitor what they are learning and doing, and to take responsibility for how they think and act. Mediation of this reflective behavior comes faster and easier without the added complexity of content. It also makes the ability to transfer across the curriculum and into other aspects of the students' lives much stronger.

There can be no question that an intense, structured program such as Feuerstein's Instrumental Enrichment changes how students think and behave—more than 1,400 studies from nations around the world document that students can learn to regulate their own behavior. As this change occurs, attendance increases, referrals to the principal's office, fights, and other acting-out behaviors decrease, while achievement test scores, critical thinking test scores, and teacher-parent satisfaction increase. Two cases in point:

In Taunton, Massachusetts, middle school teachers in the small urban system used Feuerstein's Instrumental Enrichment with all students in an inclusive setting. In Grades 6 to 8, each day started with a full period of mediation. During the other class periods, teachers helped students transfer what they had learned about self-control, systemic planning, and problem solving into each subject area. In addition, each subject area teacher mediated transfer of appropriate thinking skills into the various content areas, such as comparison and contrast in mathematics and categorization in science.

In Cleveland, Ohio, Chief Academic Officer Mryna Lewis used Feuerstein's Instrumental Enrichment to make significant gains in state-mandated mathematics test results. In two of the lowest-performing high schools, where as many as 90 percent failed the math graduation requirement on this high-stakes test, the 9th- and 10th-grade math teachers gave half of their two-period block for math to Feuerstein's Instrumental Enrichment. Within five months, the numbers passing jumped above 30 percent. After 16 months, the schools were showing an effect size gain above 75 percent (Musial, 2002). In contrast, students in these schools who were in the control group that received two full periods of math and no Instrumental Enrichment showed no gains at all.

Schools in Alaska, scattered from the top of the state to the bottom, in small villages and large cities, have introduced preschool children to the BASIC instruments. Originally not believing that these young children could even hold a pencil to do the tasks, teachers have transformed their teaching. Once they saw demonstrations and the children asking for more "clouds" (organization of dots and unit to group), they tackled this new form of active instruction with relish. Out went their preconception that they should "wait" until each child was ready to move from random play to the structure of the instruments. In came the daily work with the instruments and the teachers' mediation. Within seven months, the first test results showed that these young students had made as much as two years of gain on their standardized tests.

Feuerstein's STANDARD Instrumental Enrichment program is now being implemented around the world, from Madrid, Spain, to New Delhi, India, from Budapest, Hungary, to São Paulo, Brazil, from Israel to the Netherlands, from the United Kingdom to Mexico. It has more than 50 years of success in Grades 4 through adult, with a complete range of student populations in gifted, challenged, ELL, and regular classrooms. The BASIC Instrumental Enrichment program, released in 2003, is experiencing like success with young children (preK–3). The most important start-up project in the United States is occurring in Alaska. From large urban centers such as Fairbanks and Anchorage to the smallest of isolated villages in the Artic, trained teachers are using Instrumental Enrichment as the core of Alaska's early childhood program.

Each of the 14 instruments in Feuerstein's STANDARD set and the nine in his BASIC set focuses development of a specific cognitive prerequisite for learning. In addition, the continuous and intentional mediation of self-regulation enables the learners to decrease impulsivity and increase internal motivation for learning tasks even as they are learning how to learn more efficiently. These instruments, aligned with Mediated Learning Experience, enable teachers to reach those students whom even the best of conventional instruction has not. This occurs because mediated and transferred Instrumental Enrichment teaches the students how to think more efficiently and builds in cognitive structures that many have not developed.

There are 14 instruments in Feuerstein's STANDARD version:

1. Organization of Dots
2. Orientation in Space
3. Comparisons
4. Analytic Perceptions
5. Categorization
6. Family Relations
7. Temporal Relations
8. Numerical Progressions
9. Instructions
10. Illustrations
11. Orientation in Space II
12. Syllogisms
13. Transitive Relations
14. Representational Stencil Design

There are nine instruments in the BASIC version:

1. Organization of Dots
2. From Units to Group
3. Orientation in Space
4. Identifying Emotions
5. From Empathy to Action
6. Comparisons
7. Trichannel Assessment
8. Reading Comprehension
9. Controlling Violent Reactions

Research Results

The use of Feuerstein's Instrumental Enrichment on a daily basis produces numerous results, including cognitive improvement and academic achievement. The results are measurable in a number of ways. The first measurable effects, however, come only after structural changes in the brain. These are not superficial. Nor are they merely changes in external behavior. These structural changes, validated by studies conducted by brain researchers, impact the students' cognitive capabilities as well as their propensity to intrinsic motivation (Tribus, 2004). When mediators help students improve self-regulation, they change their learning habits for a lifetime.

STOP, THINK, ACHIEVE

Teachers want students to stop and think before they act. In a high-expectation classroom, this stopping to think is the first brick in the large house of self-control. Ultimately, as students build their reflective dispositions by stopping and thinking as they face a learning challenge, the disposition pays off in higher achievement.

Imagine that high achievement is a large house. The house has many ingredients: bricks, mortar, lumber, window frames and glass, shingles, wallboard, and so on. Each piece has a place, and there is a place for every piece.

The pieces interconnect to make the whole. Putting the pieces together as called for in the architect's plan requires precision, accuracy, patience, and hard work. So too does high achievement.

Slapdash construction and slapdash thinking do not result in a quality product. Tradespeople require several years of instruction, guided practice, and internalization to develop their skills so they can move from being apprentices to licensed journeypeople. Just as the bricklayers learn how to place the bricks one at a time according to a plan and a pattern so that the house is strong and attractive, so too must students learn how to think with precision, care, and skill. Although there are a variety of means for teachers to help students learn how to think with greater efficiency, precision, and accuracy, like the master tradespeople who instruct the apprentices, they must have mastery over the best available tools themselves.

Certainly, teachers can use their own homegrown tool sets to develop students as more efficient thinkers. There are two drawbacks to this approach for most teachers. First, they lack the formal training themselves that best prepares them to develop students' thinking capabilities. Second, they usually don't have the time or resources to invent their own tools and research their effectiveness. If they do have any time, they are likely to have less than they need to create all the tools needed. Thus they end up relying on a very small and inadequate tool kit.

Feuerstein's Instrumental Enrichment gives teachers the tools they need to expedite the task. Each of the instruments has a precise function. As students work with each instrument, they build the habits that make them into sharper thinkers who have the attributes to be highly successful. There are no shortcuts in this task. As with any trade or professional preparation, the students need time and feedback to build their skills. Feuerstein used considerable resources and time to develop the complex and complete array of tools called "instruments" and the systematic use of mediated learning experiences. Together, these tools, used by teachers who receive training to use them, produce the results in well-regulated thinking and achievement.

Some have attempted to take pieces of the system of teaching and learning that Feuerstein built. Of these, some have had a positive impact on student learning.

For instance, take the strategy of asking questions. There is no doubt that a teacher who becomes more skilled in asking higher-order questions can impact student achievement. However, asking questions is only one of the techniques used in mediated learning. It does not meet all the criteria. Asking questions helps students think about what they are learning in deeper ways, but it does not teach them how to think. If teachers recall the proverb, "Give me a fish, I will eat for a day; teach me how to fish, I will eat for a lifetime," they will have a clear understanding of the distinction between asking questions of students and teaching the students how to regulate their own thinking, ask their own questions, and take control of their own learning.

To understand more deeply the complexity of Feuerstein's systemic and systematic approach, it is helpful to start with a review of the tools he researched that have proven successful over the 50 years since he completed this enormous task.

THE STANDARD INSTRUMENTS DESCRIBED

1. Organization of Dots. "Connect the dots," say the ads. "Have you connected the dots?" asks the salesperson. What are they talking about? They are using a term made popular by Feuerstein's strategy of challenging students to connect a series of dots to make a recognizable figure such as a square, a triangle, or a trapezoid. The first and basic instrument in his series calls for students to work with increasingly difficult frames of "dots." After organizing the first few frames, students construct the pattern used to connect the dots. Although different students report different sequences, all begin to see that they are most successful with patterning when they use a purposeful plan. As the students identify their own personal patterns, the mediator mediates use of the learned thinking pattern for the next, more difficult instruments. Success builds intrinsic motivation and the desire to attack the more challenging task. The mediator cues the students' metacognition by encouraging the planning and assessment of the increasingly difficult

Organization of Dots

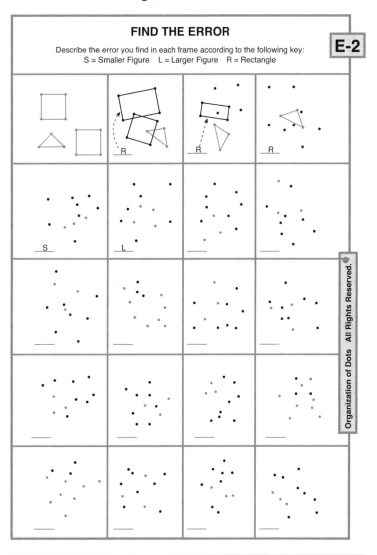

SOURCE: Feuerstein (1996).

patterning process. It is here that impulse control becomes internalized and ready for application in the remaining instruments.

Orientation in Space I

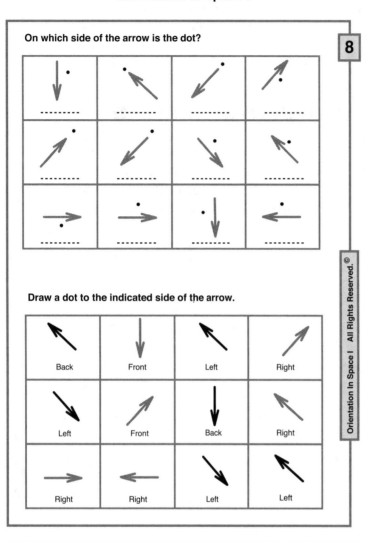

On which side of the arrow is the dot?

Draw a dot to the indicated side of the arrow.

SOURCE: Feuerstein (1996).

2. Orientation in Space. In his studies, Feuerstein noticed the difficulties that low-performing children experienced in locating their own position in relation to objects. Where is right? Left? Up? Down? North? West? He devised a series of tasks that would challenge the students to find their place in space, even when familiar landmarks disappeared. The Orientation in Space instrument helps children develop physical and abstract spatial relationships. It shows them how to use environmental clues and how to set direction. The gradation of instrument tasks from simple to complex allows the mediator to cue students on the gathering of directional information and the use of it to find their way first in concrete situations and then in conceptual problems. As the tasks increase in difficulty, frustration can also increase. Intentional mediation of self-regulation, though, reinforces habitual self-control of behavior and thinking processes.

3. Comparisons. It is popular in many classrooms to use Venn diagrams to help students note similarities and differences between characters in a story, periods of history, mathematical figures, and so on. When students lack the foundational skill for identifying attributes of similar objects and for identifying differences, it is difficult for them to make meaningful comparisons. Feuerstein's third instrument helps students start with noting observable physical characteristics that denote similarities and allow identification of concrete attributes. As they proceed, the instrument presents more and more abstract comparisons. Noting how they think about comparisons as they move from concrete examples to abstract representation, the students build the cognitive structures they will need to work in content areas. As students learn to generalize the thinking processes inherent in comparisons, the mediating teacher helps the students transfer to a variety of subjects such as language arts (e.g., two characters), mathematics (two-number sets), and social studies (two cultures). During the transfer process, students' frustration will likely intensify, since the learning transfer is taking place in unfamiliar and difficult territory. Once again, the mediator will bring the students' attention back to self-regulation as needed.

Comparisons

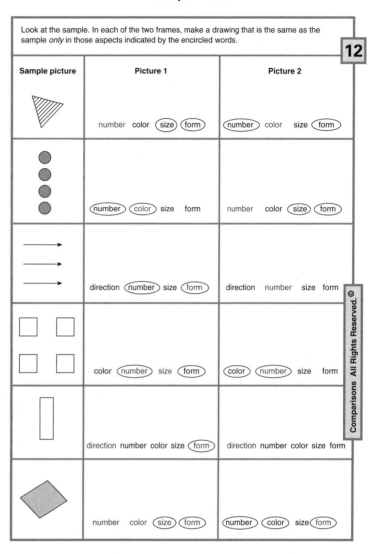

SOURCE: Feuerstein (1996).

Analytic Perceptions

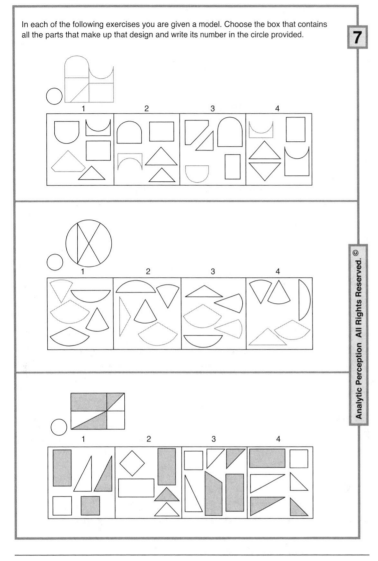

SOURCE: Feuerstein (1996).

4. Analytic Perceptions. When students weak in their ability to see the differences in geometric shapes approach their first geometry assignments in math, they encounter immediate failure. Unable to differentiate parts in the whole picture or confused by how to connect parts into a whole, the world of shapes and figures appears as a meaningless mishmash. With this instrument, the mediator helps students become proficient in recognizing geometric forms, thus freeing the students to distinguish foreground images from background shapes. As students develop multiple strategies for seeing and manipulating shapes, they become ready to perform geometric calculations in mathematics, develop systems for gathering information in completing complex tasks, eliminate trivial trial-and-error behaviors in favor of planned actions, and acquire precision and accuracy in relating parts to the whole. In addition to the obvious transfer into geometry, this instrument transfers into all situations where planning is important, including the assembling of machinery, the construction of furniture or buildings, the development of planning charts, the analysis of literature, and the drawing and reading of maps.

By this point, students have spent three to five hours a week for 30 weeks working on instruments, developing thinking patterns, applying these patterns to their daily course work, monitoring their own impulsive behaviors, and learning how to plan the completion of complex tasks. Impulsive behavior becomes more subtle and individual; this growing subtlety requires that the mediator have sharp eyes and ears, along with strong intention, in identifying students' impulsive thinking and acknowledging their ability to control their impulsiveness.

5. Categorization. This instrument helps students build on comparisons (Instrument 3) by focusing on the classification of information. Starting with items that are familiar to them (sinks, faucets, fences, flowers, trees, dogs, birds), students learn how to use precise verbal labels, gather data in an orderly fashion, compare similarities and differences, select the relevant qualities of an item, and place it in the most precise cognitive category. As students improve their ability to categorize concrete items successfully, they are presented with new items of increased abstraction. On the affect side, the mediator assists students in restraining impulsivity by encouraging systematic exploration of possible answers and precise placement of objects in well-defined categories. Transfer tasks range from helping students organize their desks to categorization tasks in science, social studies, and English grammar.

Categorization

CLASSIFICATION OF GEOMETRIC FORMS

11

Below are geometric forms, each of which is numbered.

Data Collection

Fill in the table:

Number	Form	Size	Color
1			
2			
3			
4			
5			
6			
7			
8			
9			
10			
11			
12			

SOURCE: Feuerstein (1996).

Family Relations

5

Above you see a diagram of a family.
Such a diagram is called a genealogical map. The map is blank (empty).

Place the names in the blank genealogical map, as indicated by the following sentences:

    a) Arthur is Rita's father.

    b) Simon and Jerry are brothers.

    c) Jerry is Laura's son.

Answer the following questions with the help of the map.

    a) Who is older, Rita or Laura? _____

    b) Who has two brothers? _____

    c) Who has a brother named Simon and one sister? _____

Complete:

    a) Arthur and Laura are the _____ of _____.

    b) Arthur and Laura are _____.

    c) There are more _____ than _____ in the family.

    d) There are more _____ than _____ in the family.

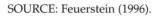

SOURCE: Feuerstein (1996).

6. Family Relations. This instrument uses the metaphor of "family" to mediate students' ability to make connections or see relationships. Feuerstein selected the family metaphor because of the wealth of emotional experiences that it provides as prior knowledge. This richness expands the possible number of valid generalizations that students can create about the thinking process of "seeing connections." Starting with a discussion of the possible ways students are related to other people, the mediator helps students form generalizations about how other objects in their world of experience are related or connected. The mediator can then move the students to apply the generalizations to academic subjects. In this way, the mediated instrument leads to the breaking down of the very common student perception that "English is not math; math is not social studies; and social studies has nothing to do with science." As the students develop their connection-making ability, they become better able to integrate what they are learning (including impulse control) across the curriculum.

7. Temporal Relations. Telling time seems like an easy task. However, when children don't have digital watches or clocks, the task becomes slightly more difficult. When time-telling problems go beyond the immediate 24 hours, children who have never mastered the mysteries of duration and intervals must struggle to know what time it is. Starting with an examination of time intervals and relationships (e.g., 60 seconds to the minute) as a hierarchical structure, the seventh instrument helps students explore other differentiated hierarchies that involve dynamic continua that require temporal orientation (e.g., the seasons, inferred events). The mediator works to facilitate student planning and thinking through goal-setting and achieving behaviors and to enhance the use of plotting tools such as the continuum, the matrix, and the chart. When students have completed this instrument, it is anticipated that each will have built a framework for diagnosing complex temporal relationships—this ability will transfer into studies of historic timelines, units of measurement, and the analysis of time-dependent information in such fields of knowledge as geology, anthropology, and literature.

Temporal Relations

> **19**
>
> Complete the sentences below using one of the following three words:
>
> time, distance, speed
>
> 1. We measure _____ with a watch.
> 2. We measure _____ with a speedometer.
> 3. We measure _____ with a tape measure.
> 4. We say "60 miles (96 km) per hour" in order to indicate _____.
> 5. We say "three hours" in order to indicate _____.
> 6. We say "50 miles (80 km)" in order to indicate _____.
>
> To the left of each sentence, indicate whether it describes time, distance, or speed.
>
> _____ A racing car can travel 200 miles (320 km) per hour.
>
> _____ In order to reach New York City, one has to travel 300 miles (480 km) from Washington, D.C.
>
> _____ In order to reach Paris from New York, one has to fly for about eight hours.
>
> Write a sentence describing the speed of a car.
>
> _____
>
> Write a sentence describing the distance between two places.
>
> _____
>
> Write a sentence describing the time that has passed.
>
> _____

SOURCE: Feuerstein (1996).

Numerical Progressions

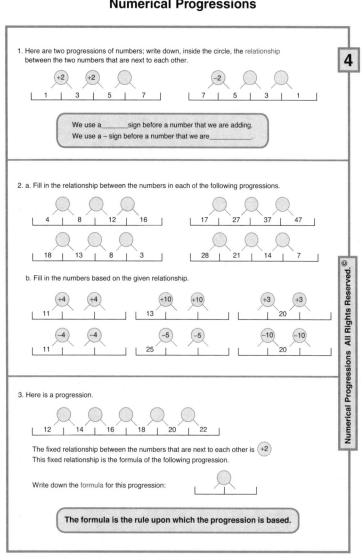

SOURCE: Feuerstein (1996).

8. Numerical Progressions. How many high school math teachers face students whose computational skills test at a third- or fourth-grade level? In spite of years of remediation, these students have not improved their basic skills; as the years pass, they stay frozen on the third-grade plateau. Such students exemplify Feuerstein's category of "retarded performers." In this case, their stymied per-formance was preceded by a glitch in the formation of the cognitive basics needed to advance mathematical per-formance. This instrument attacks the fundamental prob-lem that impedes math mastery. The glitch is called "the episodic grasp of reality." When young children do not receive the mediation that enables them to see connections between events, facts, or ideas, they may master the first math basics by rote and by guess. When faced with more com-plex number tasks, such as adding or multiplying in tens and hundreds or following a sequential number pattern, they are at a loss. Without understanding the rules and laws that govern a succession, students cannot construct new number sequences, see recurring patterns, or predict new order. In short, without this understanding, math that goes beyond children's ability to memorize is impossible. By repeating instruc-tion in the how-to of addition, subtraction, multiplication, and division without helping students understand the principles of numerical progression, the teacher has little chance of improving the students' mathematical performance.

One of the main goals of this instrument is to help students discover the connec-tions between facts and concepts. In this way, they form patterns of thinking that reduce their episodic grasp of experiences and events in everyday life and increase their ability to deduce relationships between increasingly complex items, concepts, and problem-solving tasks.

9. Instructions. One of the chief difficulties students have in school is their inability to follow instructions. The causes of this are numerous. Sometimes impulsivity and lack of planning are the culprits; in other cases, students may lack the ability to discover or coordinate the most important parts of an instruction; still others lack the ability to put instructions into a precise sequence. The instructions instrument returns the students' attention to geometric shapes. They are given written instructions to describe and construct drawings that coordinate number, size, color, location, and direction. This process requires cooperation with another student, as one works to give precise instructions and the other to follow. To complete the tasks, the students must form hypotheses and use logic as they seek alternatives for carrying out an instruction. The transfer possibilities for this instrument are obvious. The mediator's task is to help students use their increased understanding of instructions in test-taking situations, work situations, and the completion of projects.

Instructions

SOURCE: Feuerstein (1996).

10. Illustrations.

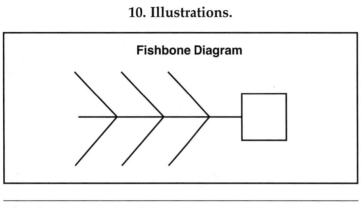

Fishbone Diagram

SOURCE: Feuerstein (1996).

10. Illustrations. A popular graphic organizer used by business teams is the fishbone diagram, developed in Japan by Ishikawa (1985) for use in analyzing cause-and-effect and for making judgments about connections between means and ends. For instance, in the auto industry, work teams searching for the causes of common car defects have used the fishbone to track down the problem; this sophisticated tool let these users arrange the relevant clues that showed the real causes of the defect rather than leaving workers to repair superficial dents and scratches on each car as it came off the assembly line.

In order to work with the fishbone diagram, the problem-solving process requires advanced and very subtle thinking skills. Most important is the need for the problem solver to have refined inferential skills. As the national data on reading comprehension reveal, making inferences is one of the most challenging and one of the least developed skills in the preadolescent and adolescent population.

Before students can succeed with a cause-and-effect thinking task, even one made easy by a fishbone diagram, they must have the capability to make simple inferences. If this capability is weak, Feuerstein's Illustrations instrument becomes a prerequisite. Using humorous illustrations, the instrument introduces the important relationships between affect and cognition. Building on skills developed in other instruments, illustrations sharpen inductive and deductive reasoning, improve decoding of information, promote divergent thinking, and teach students how to extrapolate information in order to synthesize facts into an integrated concept connecting causes with effects.

From the perspective of transfers, this instrument has multiple values. Most important, it improves students' ability to make inferences. Starting in the fourth grade, inference making is the critical skill for strengthening reading comprehension. As students experience the content-free, fun challenge of visual inference making, the mediator guides them in using the process for making inferences about literature, science, and mathematics. In addition, as the students' inference making becomes stronger, they become better at diagnosing cause-and-effect in literature, social studies, applied mathematics, and science.

11. Orientation in Space II. Orientation in Space II extends students' ability to use absolute external and stable points of reference so that they can describe their own relationships and location in different spatial dimensions. It provides intense practice with the use of compass points, coordinates, and spatial graphs, and it challenges students to see relationships in differentiated representational space. This instrument also gives the mediator the opportunity to reinforce planning behaviors for use in solving complex geometry problems.

Orientation in Space II

1. Write the directions in the rectangles.

NORTH

14

2. Where will you be?

A. You are facing west. Make 6 turns to the right and 2 left turns.
Where do you face now? _____

| 6 | – | | = | | Equal to _____ turns to the right

B. You are facing southeast. Make 6 left turns and 2 right turns.
Where do you face now? _____

| | – | | = | | Equal to _____ turns _____

C. You are facing southwest. Make 10 turns to the right and 2 left turns.
Where do you face now? _____

| | – | | = | | Equal to _____ turns _____ or a _____ circle

D. You are facing south. Make 5 left turns, 3 right turns, and 6 left turns.
Where do you face now? _____

| | – | | + | | = | | Equal to _____

E. You are facing southeast. Make 8 right turns, 2 left turns, and 3 right turns.
Where do you face now? _____

| | – | | + | | = | | Equal to _____

F. You are facing southwest. Make 3 right turns, 2 left turns, and 5 right turns.
Where do you face now? _____

| | – | | + | | = | | Equal to _____

© 1996 R. Feuerstein, HWCRI, Jerusalem. Orientation in Space II

SOURCE: Feuerstein (1996).

Syllogisms

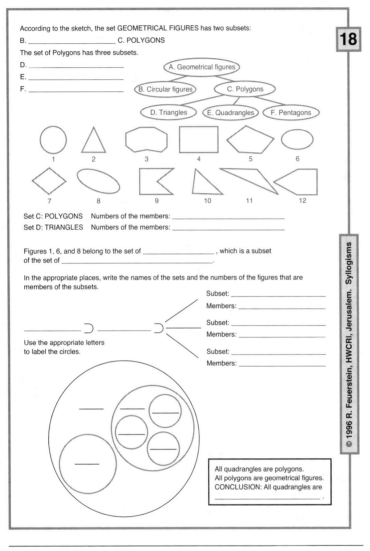

According to the sketch, the set GEOMETRICAL FIGURES has two subsets:

B. _____ C. POLYGONS

The set of Polygons has three subsets.

D. _____
E. _____
F. _____

18

Set C: POLYGONS   Numbers of the members: _____
Set D: TRIANGLES   Numbers of the members: _____

Figures 1, 6, and 8 belong to the set of _____ , which is a subset
of the set of _____ .

In the appropriate places, write the names of the sets and the numbers of the figures that are members of the subsets.

Subset: _____
Members: _____

Subset: _____
Members: _____

Subset: _____
Members: _____

Use the appropriate letters
to label the circles.

All quadrangles are polygons.
All polygons are geometrical figures.
CONCLUSION: All quadrangles are
_____ .

SOURCE: Feuerstein (1996).

12. Syllogisms. When the title of this instrument is given, many wonder how students who can't pass a basic skills test can operate in the world of logic. Logic, after all, has long been associated with the private domain of gifted thinking and philosophers. This advanced instrument relies on the cognitive foundations established with previous instruments to develop a particular type of reasoning by which students draw logical conclusions. The instrument begins by introducing the concept of "set" as a well-defined collection of items. As students proceed through the instrument, the mediator helps them learn how to define the limits of a set, to draw conclusions based on simple deductive arguments, to distinguish between universal sets and subsets, and to provide practice in drawing conclusions about the connections between sets. Finally, the mediator has the opportunity to use the Venn diagram as a tool for transfer not only in identifying sets (as done with literature, math, social studies, etc., elsewhere in the instrument) but also as a tool for establishing logical arguments.

13. Transitive Relations. Algebra is an obstacle, the gatekeeper, that keeps many students from proceeding into advanced mathematics. Unless students get past algebra, the gate to higher education is closed. This instrument extends students' ability to learn and apply the principles of logic begun in Instrument 12 (Syllogisms) and uses the new understandings so that they can learn how to form equations. This instrument introduces the concepts of "greater than" and "less than" by working with concrete examples such as the ranking of people by age, height, weight, and size and the ranking of places by area, population, age, housing units, and so on. From these examples, students form generalizations that the mediator helps them apply to day-to-day experiences. Finally, students use the instrument's tasks to learn about signs, symbols, and equations and about how to seek the information that allows them to transfer relationships in an equation.

Transitive Relations

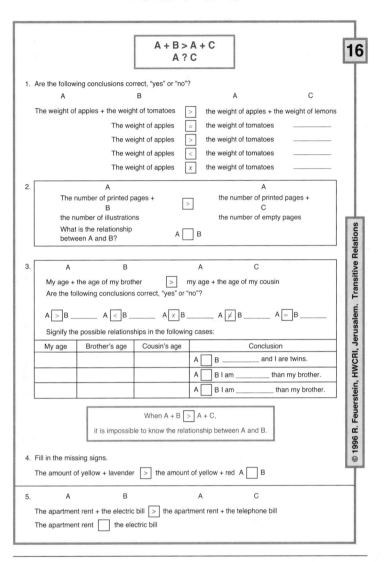

SOURCE: Feuerstein (1996).

Representational Stencil Design

1

1. Look at the poster and fill in the blanks.

Solid square ___red___   Number _____
Solid square ___white___   Number _____
Solid square _____   Number ___1___
Solid square _____   Number ___5___
Solid square ___yellow___   Number _____

The solid squares are all found _____.

2. Square number 10 is _____.
On the poster there are two more green squares which are cut out inside

a) The form which is cut out of the center of number 11 is _____.

b) The form which is cut out of the center of number _____ is _____.

3. On the poster are four white squares: one is _____ and three
_____ inside. List the number and the form of each of them.

a) Number _____   Form _____
b) Number _____   Form _____
c) Number _____   Form _____
d) Number _____   Form _____

4. List the colors and the numbers of the cut out squares.

Color: _____   _____   _____   _____

Number: _____   _____   _____   _____

Color: _____   _____   _____   _____

Number: _____   _____   _____   _____

The squares that are on the poster are called STENCILS. On the poster there are _____ stencils that
are solid, and twelve stencils that are _____.

© 1996 R. Feuerstein, HWCRI, Jerusalem. Representational Stencil Design

SOURCE: Feuerstein (1996).

14. Representational Stencil Design. One of the most complex thinking tasks that blocks students from thinking in complex ways is the forming of hypotheses. Using representational stencil designs, this instrument provides students with the skills to form and test hypotheses. As they are challenged to do "what if?" thinking in order to solve design problems, the students begin to extend the flexibility of their thinking. In order to succeed at the challenging tasks in this instrument, students must increase their comfort zone for taking conceptual risks. The mediator helps by facilitating the students' recourse to their prior knowledge of problem solving, as this knowledge was developed with the previous instruments. In addition, the mediator helps the students with hypothesis-forming tasks drawn from science, mathematics, and social studies.

GETTING TO THE BASICS

After more than 50 years of success in using Feuerstein's Instrumental Enrichment to develop the "learning propensity" of populations ranging from nonliterate Ethiopian workers, low-performing impoverished Brazilian students, high-level managers and scientists from Motorola, Down syndrome young adults in the Israeli army, second-language children in Italy, average students in Massachusetts, and many others, Feuerstein turned his attention to younger students and special needs adolescents for whom his STANDARD version was too difficult. From several years of research and study came the BASIC instruments.

The nine BASIC instruments target early childhood learners, Grades preK–4 and special needs adolescents with severe challenges.

THE BASIC INSTRUMENTS

1. Organization of Dots. BASIC engages young children in forming primary geometric forms from a collection of dots. As the spatial orientation changes, the children must project the form onto the new arrangements that become increasingly complex. As the children form rules from example by recalling the strategies they have used in the simpler task, they also must become more precise and accurate by attending carefully to the straightness and length of lines and which lines connect which dots.

2. From Units to Group facilitates the children's development of the cardinal concept of numbers. In each ever more difficult frame, they must divide an amorphous cloud of dots into equal subgroups. Gradually, they develop an understanding of the concept of group in spite of variations of color, form, and configuration and construct the operations of multiplication and addition.

3. Orientation in Space. BASIC introduces children to the vocabulary of spatial relationships. In increasingly complex scenes, children must identify positions in space using their new vocabulary with precision and clarity.

4. Identifying Emotions facilitates the children's understanding of the relationship between emotion and thought. In these prereading tasks, children examine pictures and make connections between a situation and the emotional response. As they work through the increasingly complex frames, they must call on prior frames to make the most appropriate match.

5. From Empathy to Action challenges the children to reflect on emotions and react with appropriate empathy before making a plan of action that is also appropriate to the situation. "What should I do in this situation?" is the question they must answer for each frame before examining current events with the same question.

6. Comparisons. Viewing incongruous and absurd situations, the children are mediated to compare what they see in order to find what does not make sense. With the absurd identified, they must consider alternative situations that lack the absurd elements.

7. Trichannel Assessment. With this tool, children explore the characteristics of geometric shapes in different modalities, including tactile and visual. The children then reproduce through drawing the objects touched and/or seen, being extremely accurate and careful with their new representations. This tool is designed to prevent and remediate a variety of the difficulties underlying learning disabilities and attention deficits through its heavy emphasis on impulse control and precise renderings.

8. Reading Comprehension. This instrument develops children's understanding of reading material by mediating the development of their question-asking skills. It develops the cognitive habits of comparing, analyzing, summarizing, and hypothesis making and highlights impulse control and the feeling of competence.

9. Controlling Violent Emotions. With many children growing up in a world of gratuitous violence, there is a need to develop their self-control and regulation of behavior. This instrument presents increasingly intense conflicts and asks children to apply what they learned in the Identifying Emotions and the Comparisons instruments to resolve the conflict with planning behavior.

On a daily basis, teachers mediate cognition and metacognition as the students work with the instruments. Each day students receive a new set of problems to face on the instruments. First, the teachers spend 10 minutes reviewing and reinforcing what the students have learned about their thinking. They bridge this metacognition into the students' next lesson. After the students work on the new instrument, the teachers take 10–15 minutes to mediate the thinking used and to investigate how students can bridge these processes to other subjects the students are studying in their content classes. Each bridge helps the students solidify new habits and new skills in thinking about what they are learning. The following sample lesson provides examples of bridging that focuses on students' self-regulation.

PRIMARY LESSON

Bridging Self-Regulation Into the Curriculum

Standard
How to increase self-control and avert impulsive behavior

Focus Intelligence
Intrapersonal

Supporting Intelligence
Visual/Spatial

Mediation Emphasis
Self-Control and Regulation of Behavior

CHECKING PRIOR KNOWLEDGE

1. Show the class a picture of a stop sign. Ask them to describe its purpose and its importance. ("Cars stop" and "prevents crashes," "injuries," etc.).

2. Ask the students to reflect on "invisible" stop signs that tell us to stop what we're doing. Make a class T-chart for those signs and their importance.

Signs	Importance

STRUCTURING THE TASK

1. Select one of these tasks to help groups of students illustrate one invisible "stop sign" story:
   a. Draw a cartoon story
   b. Act out a play
   c. Sketch what happens when the sign is ignored

   Assign the students into groups of three with an encourager, recorder, and checker. Set the timelines and walk among the groups to ensure that all contribute.

2. Post the completed products around the room.

LOOKING BACK AND REFLECTING

1. In the days following, select one invisible stop sign. Ask the group responsible for it to share their ideas. What is the sign? When is it important to use? Why is it important? When was a time it worked? What happened when someone ignored the sign? Ask each group to demonstrate how the stop sign helps them regulate and control their behavior.

2. Post the chart below on a bulletin board. Explain the words and record each group's responses:

	The Sign	Use	Reason	Plus	Minus
1.					
2.					
3.					
4.					
5.					

3. After each group has shared and discussed with the class its generalization, ask the following: "What does the chart tell us about stop signs? Why are they important? How do they help us?" Use extending questions to deepen understanding.

BRIDGING FORWARD

Use students' learning logs. Invite each student to select one stop sign for personal use in the next day, week, or month. (Designate the time in accordance with student readiness.) Have each student describe how he or she will use the personal stop sign. Each day allow 5 to 10 minutes for students to record successful uses of the personal stop sign (competence). Coach and encourage as needed. To further mediate competence, follow the log entries with a few public sharings. Use random selection. Celebrate each success with a "hurrah," "you go, girl," or any variety of responses that students can relate to for recognition.

Assessing Students' Self-Regulation

What can students do after working intensely on self-regulation? To assess the "do," teachers can provide spot checks.

A Sample Checkup
To what degree can the student

1. Explain why stop signs are important?

2. Name invisible stop signs?

3. Use invisible stop signs to control his or her impulsivity?

Materials

Stop sign picture, T-chart, art supplies, student journals

Variations

1. Invite students to identify situations when they can fail to control their own behavior. Have small groups role-play on the consequences of poor impulse control.

2. Create classroom PMI charts (plus-minus-interesting questions) on your modeling of various situations calling for impulse control.

P	
M	
I	

3. Make TV ads for impulse control on important situations.

PROMOTING SELF-REGULATION

In many urban schools, Feuerstein's Instrumental Enrichment has proven a powerful starting tool for teaching students how to control their own thinking behavior. However, it is not the be-all and end-all—it is one means to the end of having students develop an internal locus of control for how they regulate their cognitive behaviors and the quality of their thinking. The mediational strategies that teachers use with students in Instrumental Enrichment are valuable tools for helping the students transfer their new habits of thinking across all curricula and outside the classroom. Likewise, other strategies help teachers mediate self-regulation even without the benefit of full Instrumental Enrichment implementation. Note how these teachers mediate students' thinking by helping them develop their self-regulation.

Sample Scenario 1: What the Mediation of Self-Regulation Sounds Like

TEACHER: "Today, class, we are taking a trip to the library. Which of our rules do you think will apply? [Pause for wait time.] Margarita?"

MARGARITA: "Listen to the person in charge. She will explain what we can do."

TEACHER: "Thank you. Are there other ideas? Tomas?"

TOMAS: "Yes. We need to respect each other."

TEACHER: "Why do you think that?"

TOMAS:	"Because it helps us pay attention to each other and not distract each other."
TEACHER:	"Does the respect rule always apply?"
TOMAS:	"Yes, when we are with people."
TEACHER:	"How do we show respect? Joseph?"
JOSEPH:	"By the way we stop and think and by not interrupting or distracting each other."

Sample Scenario 2

TEACHER:	"This is a difficult math problem. How should we begin? [Pause for wait time.] Kwan?"
KWAN	"We should stop and think about our plan."
TEACHER:	"That's a good start. Who can give me a plan? Mildred?"
MILDRED:	"We have to set our goal. Next, we have to see what information is given and plan a strategy. Once we have a strategy, we pick our starting point."
TEACHER:	"A good start, Mildred. Who can carry on? Michael?"
MICHAEL:	"We have to review the rules and check our work."
TEACHER:	"I liked how we made our plan first. Now you're ready to start. What's our goal?"
KWAN:	"To solve this word problem?"
TEACHER:	"That's a good start, Kwan. Who can add to Kwan's idea, remembering what we discussed as important for every problem we solve?"
KATE:	"We want to understand how we solved it and why we did what we did.
TEACHER:	"Way to go, Kate. That's an important answer. But tell me, can you be more specific than 'did'?"
KATE:	"Yes. 'Did' means we used certain tactics to solve the problem."
TEACHER:	"OK. Now I understand. So our goal has several parts [writes on board]: to solve this problem, understand the tactics we used and why we used each tactic. Is that it? [Waits.] Fine, I agree. So now let's decide what we do after the goal. Who can help here? And let me see some new hands." [Waits.] William?"
WILLIAM:	I think we have to review the steps for problem solving and make a sequence chart of the steps we need to do."
TEACHER:	"And why is it important for you to make such a plan?
MILDRED:	"It helps us slow down and think before we act. I do better when I don't rush helter-skelter."

TACTICS FOR FOSTERING SELF-REGULATION

Many teachers have developed tactics that enable students to improve their self-regulation and control. The following list gives examples.

- Create with the class a motto (such as "think first") to guard against impulsivity.
- Create a bulletin board that celebrates step-by-step planning of school tasks.
- Create in small groups a series of poster ads to hang around the room or in the hallways. Each poster can use the class motto and show different situations where it helps to "think first."
- Model self-control by not interrupting students' answers, by using wait time, and by saying aloud, "Just a moment, I have to think about that," before answering a student question.
- When students finish a task, allow several minutes for them to review and check their work.
- Brainstorm with the class on ways and times to forestall impulsivity.
- In cooperative groups, make a T-chart of how one acts and speaks when forestalling impulsivity. Set up individual contracts with delayed impulsivity goals and self-assessment of improvement. Once a week, discuss what improvements are occurring.
- Teach students how to use graphic organizers to plan decisions and chart sequences of procedures.
- Require students to have an assignment book. Take 10 minutes at the end of each day to enter homework assignments. Use paired partners to check each other's entries.
- Make daily use of the think-pair-share strategy.
- Record on the board with a sequence chart the steps students took in solving a problem. In algebra, insist that students can show the step-by-step procedure for solving an equation.
- Each day before collecting homework, ask students to evaluate the quality of their work against a set of criteria that you keep posted in the room.
- Assign activities in which students must rank their activities by order of importance and defend the choices made.
- Provide students with blank weekly or monthly schedules and use paired partners to fill in the schedules with all out-of-school responsibilities.
- Ask students to break a complex task into its component steps and then to put those in a sequence for which they can explain the rationale.
- Use cooperative groups to construct maps showing safe alternative routes for students to take to and from school.
- Discuss the value of thinking first and postponing action.
- Acknowledge students who take the time to reflect before giving an answer.
- Use journals to ask students to write down answers to thought-provoking questions. Tell them ahead of time that they may have the opportunity to share aloud.
- Encourage students to take time out when they feel that their emotions are getting out of control.
- Use journal entries that encourage students to track how they are improving in self-control.
- With the students, develop classroom behavior guidelines that focus students on self-regulation. Post the guidelines and refer to them as needed.

BRIDGING SELF-REGULATION INTO EVERY LESSON

Self-regulation runs contrary to much of the behavior urban students see in TV crime stories and in gang outbursts. Other sights and sounds of the world in which they live reinforce impulsive actions, too. When the teacher mediates self-control, especially in conjunction with transcendence, isolated acts of planning, goal setting, and sharing take on new meaning. These new meanings enable students to understand the value of self-control, especially when learning, and transfer that value into action.

KEY POINTS TO REMEMBER

- "Stop and think!" requires reflection. The goal is to help students learn to stop, think, plan, monitor, and take responsibility for what they are learning and doing. "Just do it" is very impulsive. One of the most frequent complaints about student behavior, impulsivity, is a behavior that can be mediated through self-regulation and control of behavior.
- Please see the deep connection between the relationships of affect (children don't care how much you know until they know how much you care) and cognition; both are necessary for successful intervention.
- Some of our students come to school totally unprepared academically and socially. Acknowledge and distinguish between school behavior and home behavior, since some things are considered appropriate in some homes and not in others. Students will begin to make choices by transferring to and seeing the value of the new habit or use "code switch" behaviors based on the environment they find themselves in.
- There is a description of 14 instruments in Feuerstein's Instrumental Enrichment, with each instrument focusing on the development of a specific cognitive prerequisite for learning and behavioral change. Each instrument assignment gets progressively more challenging, just like the structure of knowledge—the shift from facts to topics to units to concepts.
- Cognitive and social improvement comes about with the mediation of self-regulation.
- Self-control and self-regulation of behavior is a big one. The goal is to have students become internally motivated to "do the right thing," as Spike Lee would say. Think about the substitute teacher day and the student behavior phenomenon—all the things that could not be done with the teacher or another adult present (the external motivators) are done. Students are able to show how creative they can become with the rules when the school police are not around.
- Remediation just has not gotten the job done. Shift toward preventing and intervening as the mediator to help students think about their behavior.
- At the completion of the self-regulation and control of behavior instrument, students will be able to do a better job of seeing relationships, have planning behavior in place, be able to identify patterns, restrain impulsive behavior, make inferences, develop reasoning skills, form hypotheses, to name a few, to eliminate their "episodic grasp of reality."
- Set the students up for success. Success builds intrinsic motivation.

SAMPLE LESSONS

The following grade-appropriate sample lessons demonstrate how to integrate the mediation of self-regulation and control of behavior into daily lessons. The more impulsive, episodic, and imprecise students are when they come to the classroom, the more important it is to embed self-regulation mediation into every daily lesson. If teachers are interested in developing students' intrinsic motivation to take control of their thinking, problem solving, and reactions to various situations in a reflective, nonimpulsive way, start first with the intense work that a program such as Instrumental Enrichment provides and then bridge to daily lessons. In this way, teachers can have greater assurance that they will close that unmentioned gap, the self-regulation and self-control of behavior, which strangles the possible success of many urban students.

ELEMENTARY LESSON

The Three Billy Goats Gruff

Standard
How to increase self-control through planning behavior

Focus Intelligence
Visual/Spatial

Supporting Intelligence
Verbal/Linguistic

Mediation Emphasis
Self-Regulation and Control of Behavior

CHECKING FOR PRIOR KNOWLEDGE

Engage the students with a web organizer. Put them in pairs and show the class a picture of a billy goat. Ask them to talk together and find out what they know about goats. Survey the ideas and put the correct ones on the web for all to see.

STRUCTURING THE TASK

1. Introduce the story by explaining that it is about billy goats, but that there are lessons to be learned from how the goats behave.

2. Gather the students in a circle so they can see the big book of this story. Read the story.

LOOKING BACK AND REFLECTING

1. Ask the pairs to come up with some ideas about how they think the billy goats used their minds to think about the dangers of crossing the bridge. How did they overcome these dangers and land safely on the other side? What was their good way of thinking?

2. Reinforce the idea that they had to make a plan and not rush across the bridge.

BRIDGING FORWARD

1. Ask the pairs to come up with ideas of when they think it is a good idea to make a plan in schoolwork. Put the ideas on a web. After one partner gives an idea, ask the other to tell why.

2. Ask the pairs to come up with ideas of when they think it is a good idea to make a plan when they are outside of school. Call on new pairs.

Assessing Student Performance

1. Ask the students to retell the story and explain how the goats could use a plan for their new life in the meadow.

2. Give the students a task and ask them to make a plan for completing the task. Review the plan-making ingredients.

Variation

Select another story such as *Little Red Riding Hood* that illustrates how planning one's actions is a good idea. Follow the pattern given above and highlight the question "why?"

MIDDLE GRADES LESSON

The Most Dangerous Game

Standard
Apply a variety of planning strategies to generate and organize ideas

Focus Intelligence
Verbal Linguistic

Supporting Intelligence
Interpersonal

Mediation Emphasis
Self-Regulation and Control of Behavior

CHECKING PRIOR KNOWLEDGE

Assign students to groups of three. Distribute the roles of leader, recorder, and presenter. Give each group a copy of a small island outline. Tell them that they are marooned and will have to use what they find on an island to get off. Instruct them to make a plan for this task. What do they have to think about to be successful? What thinking qualities do they need to make the plan a good one?

STRUCTURING THE TASK

Assign the students to read the story for homework. As they read, they should think about how the main character used his "brain" to escape. What could they learn from him? Spend one or two days in a class discussion of the story. Ask the trios to make lists of the methods used for the possible escape and what good qualities of thinking were evident. Ask several groups to present responses to each question before making an all-class list of each. Play devil's advocate to the ideas and encourage students to defend their ideas.

LOOKING BACK AND REFLECTING

Make a list on the board for all to record. How did the main character control his thinking to his advantage? What could he have done better?

BRIDGING FORWARD

Ask the students to generate what they can learn from this story about using their thinking to get out of a tough situation. Ask for specific examples that might apply.

Assessing Student Performance

1. Ask students to identify the most important decisions the main character had to make to escape with his life. In a paragraph, ask each student to write why the thinking was helpful.

2. Ask students to write an essay explaining to others how the lessons of this story would help them in their daily lives.

Variations

1. After reading this story and discussing the power of planning, assign each student another short story to read. In groups of three, students can compare the planning done by each main character to get out of a jam.

2. Ask students to come up with a plan for escaping from the island that they would use.

SECONDARY LESSON

To Kill a Mockingbird

Standard
Generate, gather, and organize ideas to plan

Focus Intelligence
Verbal/Linguistic

Supporting Intelligence
Interpersonal

Mediation Emphasis
Self-Regulation and Control of Behavior

CHECKING PRIOR KNOWLEDGE

Make a "people search" handout for each student. Use the following questions or others of your invention:

Who can find a person who

1. Can imitate the call of a mockingbird?
2. Can tell the difference between bias and prejudice?
3. Knows a lawyer?
4. Has seen the movie from this book?
5. Has been a victim of prejudice?
6. Has been called into court?

Allow the students to mill and find the persons who can answer. Students should get no more than one answer from a person. After the search is done, call upon volunteers to answer and explain.

STRUCTURING THE TASK

Assign students to cooperative groups of five. Assign each group to analyze one important character as they read. Each day allow the groups time to review what the character said or did or what others said about the character in the chapter read. The group recorder should make a list of the examples picked. After the list is made, the group can agree on the meaning derived from these examples. What do the examples tell them about the "character" of the character? Beliefs? Values? Biases? At the end of the last chapter's discussion, the group should arrive at a "master" agreement about the character. "This is a person who believes . . . values . . . acts . . ." After sharing the group ideas, ask each person to use the following rubric for their character:

To what degree was this character

1. An impulsive person?	low	medium	high
2. In control of his or her emotions?	low	medium	high
3. A planner?	low	medium	high
4. A thoughtful problem solver?	low	medium	high

In the classroom discussion, ask individuals to share their ideas and the reasons for their thinking.

LOOKING BACK AND REFLECTING

Ask students to share their ideas. In what other stories they have read or movies they have seen did the main character think first and act second or vice versa. What are the advantages gained by stopping and thinking first? Point to examples.

BRIDGING FORWARD

Ask students to share their ideas. What are places in school where they could use the good thinking demonstrated in this story? What are other places or situations outside school where they could use the good thinking shown by these characters? How and why would this help them?

Assessing Student Performance

After asking students to identify and explain examples of controlled thinking in the novel, ask them to give examples of situations in which they were able to benefit by this type of thinking.

Variation

Invite students to select a second novel to read independently. For their report, ask them to discuss the good thinking qualities of the main character.

7

The Feeling of Competence

Once I get the ball, you're at my mercy. There's nothing you can say or do about it. I own the ball, I own the game. I own the guy guarding me. I can actually play him like a puppet.

—Michael Jordan (Riley, 1993)

In the world of professional athletics, much attention is given to the feeling of confidence. Long-time pitching star from Atlanta and Chicago, Greg Maddux once said that the confidence that springs from the feeling of confidence is more responsible for success in a game than ability. Pro quarterback Peyton Manning likewise attests to the importance of this feeling.

When distinguishing the feeling of competence from "feel good" self-esteem, this feeling of competence may be the most important contributor to a child's self-esteem. Many are the examples of bright students whose lack of confidence in their academic capabilities holds them back. They often wallow in self-defeating attitudes with which they convince themselves that they "can't." Many teachers find it difficult to distinguish ability from confidence.

STRENGTHENING THE WILL TO SUCCEED

When mediating the feeling of competence, teachers and parents purposefully strengthen the students' belief about their ability to succeed. Furthermore, the mediating adults help students turn this belief into a lasting motivation to try increasingly difficult tasks. And when success occurs, they ask the students to reflect on what they have accomplished and the talents that made the victory possible. This is another way

119

of saying that mediation of the feeling of competence is intertwined with the mediation of meaning and the mediation of transcendence in each learning experience.

A Lifelong Learning Goal

A mediator of competence uses strategies that will result in long-lasting effects. These strategies enable the student to grow increasingly persistent in overcoming obstacles and succeeding against tougher and tougher odds. The competence-building strategies require that the mediator walk a fine line between establishing goals that can be attained and mediating challenges through the provision of novel and difficult tasks. This makes the mediation of competence a process of continuous improvement, based on the student's growing perception of inner growth, accomplishment, and progress. Most important, each small act of mediation for the feeling of competence is but one small seed that has the potential to grow into a giant oak tree.

The Story of Katrinka

Katrinka was the fourth child in her family. She was born 12 years after her brother. In her early days of school, Katrinka became quite ill and spent the second half of the school year in a hospital. In the following years, this experience had a major impact on her feeling of competence. She felt isolated and inadequate to complete any tasks. She continued with the reliance on others that she had developed from her sickbed.

When she returned to school, Katrinka was placed back a grade. Shy and unsure of herself, she found it difficult to defend herself against her classmates' jibes and jests. Before her illness, Katrinka had fallen behind her friends in learning to speak English. Her parents insisted that she speak their native Russian, and her teachers spoke only English and Spanish.

After school, Katrinka walked home alone and sat in her room playing with paper dolls and singing to herself. Seldom did she even take her books from her bag and do her homework.

Throughout junior high, little changed. She received several different special education diagnoses, ranging from learning disabled, behaviorally disordered, and even autistic. Although she received special assistance in the special education resource room and from classroom aides, Katrinka remained isolated and quiet.

High school was a disaster. Katrinka continued with special coaching throughout the high school years. She took up smoking and mingled with other students she met in her low-track classes. More often than not, she was disciplined for being off campus, smoking, cutting classes, and mouthing off to teachers she didn't know. For the teachers she did know, especially her tutors in the resource room, she was polite and passive. With the special assistance, Katrinka managed to graduate in the bottom 20 percent of her class.

After high school and in search of money, Katrinka took a job at the local coffee shop. A different personality emerged. Katrinka worked quickly mixing the drinks and serving the customers. Her manager, noting her organization at the coffee bar, promoted her to assistant manager and crew chief on the early morning shift. From a student who could not rise out of bed for first period class, she arrived cheerfully at her job to open the store at 5 a.m.

Within a year, Katrinka piled up a series of accolades and promotions that culminated in her selection as a regional trainer who caught the attention of the regional manager. Soon Katrinka was nominated to attend the company's management training program. When she graduated Number 1 in her class, she received a small scholarship to attend a college and seek out a management degree. Four years later, she graduated with honors.

"What made the difference for me?" Katrinka told her college adviser; "it was confidence. Confidence that I could do things. I never thought I was very smart. I learned I was smart enough to do more than most of the people I knew at the coffee shop. And when I got back to school, I found that my work habits joined my smarts and I could do the work just as well as anybody. I got lots of feedback on how well I did things, how organized I was, and how hard I worked. I just began to discover that I really was competent and that I didn't need everybody helping me out and doing stuff for me."

STUDENTS WHO FEEL INCOMPETENT

Teachers in urban classrooms are likely to encounter many students who feel incompetent, and there are many reasons why such students feel this way. In some cases, the feeling may be present because of continued low expectations. In the home, a child's parents may take a laissez-faire or hands-off attitude; they let the child sit in front of the TV, or mope around the apartment, or talk endlessly or purposelessly on the phone, or roam the streets. "So what if he doesn't read? I didn't when I was his age" or "I don't have time to check his homework" are responses typical of low parental expectation. As

> Feelings of incompetence may start with overdemanding parents who are never satisfied with their child's level of achievement.

parents model these low expectations, children frame their own low expectations. Here, the self-fulfilling prophecy starts to work, and children are soon saying to themselves, "I'm not much good at [fill in the blank], so why bother?"

The child, responding to perfection-demanding parents, brings home a report card with five A's and a B. The parent rages: "How could you get a B? You're a disgrace!" The child, ashamed but desiring to meet her parents' expectations, becomes convinced that her failure to get six A's was worse than the success she achieved in the five courses. Thus she sees herself as incompetent.

In other cases, students compare themselves to others. Sometimes the others are siblings who do especially well in school, earn high degrees, or secure high-paying jobs. These students look at their siblings and ask, "How could I ever do that?" or "Where do I fit?"

Feuerstein's Observations

Feuerstein's identification of the feeling of competence as an important target of mediation comes from his experience with children of the Holocaust. Many of these children had lost their parents, the first mediators of success. Without their parents and other important early childhood role models, these children missed receiving the feedback and support that could help them through the many traumas they experienced. Many, overwhelmed by the challenges of survival, developed the strong feelings of inadequacy that are similar to those found in children of poverty and victims of racism and bias. When these children come to school, they bring these deeply rooted feelings that block learning.

Indicators of Incompetent Feelings

The successful mediator of a feeling of competence learns to recognize the behavioral indicators that suggest strong feelings of incompetence:

- Refusing to start tasks, lack of perseverance, finding ways to avoid tasks, acting out impulsively, missing assignments, or delaying the start of a task
- Talking the "victim" language: "It's not my fault"; "She made me do it"; "I can't"; "It's too hard"
- Showing increasing anxiety: tears, shaking hands, looking at the floor, stomach pains, feigned injury, headaches
- Increased patterns of avoidance: late or missing homework, tardiness or absence, frequent requests to leave the room, acting out to force punishment or expulsion
- Perfectionism: overworking an assignment, compulsive practicing, overattention to what others think, excessive competitiveness, sleeplessness
- Undue exaggeration: bragging, bravado
- Anger and hostility

Feelings of incompetence are not an either-or phenomenon. They are best viewed on a spectrum that is balanced against actual performance.

Academic Competence: What Is Its Role?

In school, it is academic competence that needs to be the focus of attention. Within the academic arena, students may have a feeling of incompetence that coincides with a very low skill and knowledge level, or they may have a feeling that does not accurately reflect what they are able to do.

Consider these two instances:

1. Juan moved from Central America to a suburb outside a midwestern city. Although he knew only a few English phrases, the school assigned him by age to a sixth-grade class. As he sat in the classroom, he could not follow the lessons in English. Frustrated, he began arriving at the bus stop after the bus had departed.

2. Toshan's parents had very high expectations. In the early grades, she had shown a special gift for math and science. At home, her parents provided her with science kits, played math games with her on the computer, and tutored her in advanced mathematics. In the ninth grade, her mathematics teacher invited her to join the math Olympics team. Toshan's parents were thrilled, and hired a coach to tutor her in advanced algebra and geometry. Preparing for her first competition, Toshan practiced each night until 2:00 or 3:00 in the morning. She devoted her weekends to further practice.

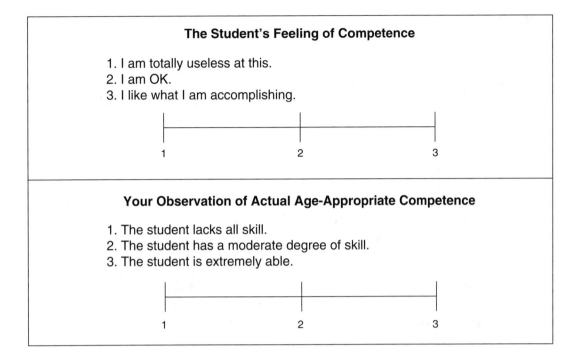

The Student's Feeling of Competence

1. I am totally useless at this.
2. I am OK.
3. I like what I am accomplishing.

Your Observation of Actual Age-Appropriate Competence

1. The student lacks all skill.
2. The student has a moderate degree of skill.
3. The student is extremely able.

Toshan's first competition was a disappointment. Because of her quickness, accuracy, and knowledge, the sponsor had placed her on the varsity team; but matched against older competitors, she froze at each question. Although she had been able to answer far more difficult questions in the team's practice, she failed to answer any in the competition.

Afterward, when the coach attempted to discuss her performance, Toshan burst into tears and blamed herself for failing to study more. She promised to rededicate herself and do a better job preparing for the next tournament.

In each of the two examples above, competence is the central issue; each case is different, however. Juan came up with an avoidance strategy, being late for the bus, as a way to handle the frustration generated by his feelings of incompetence. His feelings matched the reality of the situation. Without the language skills, he couldn't undertake the classroom tasks performed by the other students. Toshan settled on self-blame, followed by a "work harder" response. Her feelings of inadequacy were based on the wide gap between what she believed she had to do to be perfect and the high skills she already possessed.

> In spite of what self-esteem gurus advocate, there is not a magic cure-all for feelings of incompetence.

MEDIATING THE FEELING OF CONFIDENCE

In spite of what superficial self-esteem gurus advocate, there is not a magic cure-all for feelings of incompetence. As with all blocks to learning, the skilled teacher will construct mediation strategies that match individual needs.

A Both-And Challenge

Teachers must deal with both sides of the instructional coin. On the one side, they must use strategies that increase the students' academic competence; on the other, they must work to increase the students' feeling of competence. One without the other results in little or no gain and speaks loudly against those reform strategists that insist on teaching pure content. When students lack competence in a specific academic area and feel incompetent, lessons must be designed that include the most productive instructional strategies for building not only their knowledge but also the feeling of competence.

Among the tools available to teachers to develop the sense of competence are Feuerstein's Instrumental Enrichment and the Teacher Expectation Student Achievement (TESA) teaching behaviors. Instrumental Enrichment's design starts with simple tasks that allow the students to succeed immediately. Success follows success as the students learn how to use prior knowledge and skills for solving ever more challenging problems on the next instrument. With the proper feedback, these students develop their feelings of competence and a readiness to take on the next, more difficult challenge. From this success with the instruments, teachers are prepared to bridge not only knowledge but the feelings of success.

A Sample Scenario: Mediating the Feeling of Competence

TEACHER:	"Look carefully at this next page. Tell me what you see that's familiar."
MARIO:	"I see a set of instructions."
TEACHER:	"What do you think they'll ask you to do?"
SANDRA:	"The instructions will tell us how to do this puzzle."
TEACHER:	"How do you feel about that? It's a new puzzle that looks harder to do."
JUANITA:	"But I know how to do it. I did the last one in no time."
TEACHER:	"You sound confident."
JUANITA:	"I am. I plan to take my time to read the instructions and underline the most important part. Then I just have to do each step one at a time."

THE RIGHT WAY TO ASK THE RIGHT QUESTIONS: TACTICS FOR SUCCESS

In addition to Feuerstein's Instrumental Enrichment, which provides struggling students with a step-by-step sequence of tasks that take them to ever more difficult tasks, mediators use question-asking skills that help students build their feelings of competence. Among those question-asking skills are the following high-impact tactics derived from the TESA research.

1. Wait Time. After teachers ask a question, they wait three to five seconds before calling on a student. This pause allows the student to think about the answer. When teachers answer the question themselves or insist upon a quick response, they communicate, often inadvertently, that they don't value student answers. When they wait, they say to all the students, especially those who feel incompetent, "Take your time. I know you can do it."

2. Challenge Questions. Challenge questions ask students to respond with more complex thinking than they need to recall facts. When the students are asked to stop and think about a question that requires complex thinking, they experience the respect that such tougher questions engender. The most important of all questions for building student confidence in what they are saying is the challenge question "why?" asked in a respectful tone. "Why do you think that?" "Please, share your reasons," "I'm curious to hear how you came to that conclusion," asked in a respectful tone of inquiry, are among the most powerful tools for mediating the feeling of competence. The three-story intellect model (see Chapter 11) provides a visual for the types of questions to ask students.

3. Equal Distribution of Response Time. An easy way to discourage students who already feel inadequate in academic work is for a teacher to always call on the same students who have quick answers and sit in the front row. By using such tactics as the wraparound, teachers can communicate to all students that they have a fair chance to respond.

THE NO-HIDE TACTICS

Many students who feel incompetent find multiple ways to avoid participating in class or group discussions. When teachers give in and allow these students to hide, they foster these students' low competence feelings. For these students, it is far more beneficial if the teachers use tactics that encourage active participations.

The Wraparound

In a wraparound, each student gets an equal chance to respond. To ensure that all students are ready, teachers may use a think-pair-share or ask students to write their ideas in a journal from a stem starter such as, "Today, I learned . . ." After the think time, teachers ask for a volunteer to start. Teachers ask the students to listen to each other, and the teachers provide the right to pass. In addition, they note that they expect all to give an answer even if someone has "said what I have to say." All are to use their own words. After the first responder, usually the quick thinker who shoots his or her hand in the air before the question is finished, the teacher goes to the next person to the starter student's right or left. In turn, the teacher thanks each student for his or her response and then moves to the next. In this way, teachers wrap around the classroom until all have had a chance to respond. Wraparounds work best when the teacher is careful to avoid comparisons between answers, acknowledges the thinking of the reticent speakers only, and uses wraparounds at the end of a lesson or prior to beginning a task.

Encouragement and Selected Praise

Encouragement differs from praise in that teachers give their encouraging words before a task. Praise comes after. "I know that you can do this," "Take your time and think it through. You'll get it" are encouraging words. Not only does encouragement boost students' feeling of competence, but it avoids the all too common teaching error of overpraise or static praise. Such ineffectual praise happens when the teacher repeats over and over "good job," "way to go," and their derivatives, until they become meaningless static in every students' ears. Praise becomes encouraging (the building of courage) when it is meets the four super *S* criteria: selective, specific, specially deserved, and sincere.

Getting It Together

In the identification of the nine instructional strategies that make the biggest impact on student achievement, Pickering and Marzano (2001) identify cooperative learning. For students who perform poorly in urban classrooms whose teachers are strengthening the prerequisite learning skills, cooperative learning has special import as a "home for thinking." When teachers structure the groups carefully so that student members are both interdependent and accountable, cooperative groups provide the needed safety and security for these students to form their ideas and express their opinions.

Teachers who are building a sense of competence do not need to make their cooperative groups elaborate or complicated. It is best if they start with informal cooperative groups such as think-pair-share and write-pair-share to build student engagement and confidence (Bellanca & Fogarty, 2003). Afterward, they can expand the group size to groups of three with structured roles and responsibilities, a common goal, and the use of graphic organizers and projects.

SEEING IS BELIEVING

From a multiple intelligences perspective, graphic organizers, also identified by Pickering and Marzano (2001) as a Top 9 instructional strategy, are an easy tool for teachers to use with urban students who have a strong visual learning need. The graphics extend many of the left brain analytic thinking effects that Feuerstein highlights in his instruments. Most important, these visual tools help struggling students further develop their ability to connect ideas, see relationships, and leave behind their episodic tendencies. Simple graphic tools such as the web, the sequence chart, and the concept map help these students "see" the needed connections and to make sense out of information that appears at first glance to be unconnected. When teachers use these visual helpers, the students have more "ahas." With each connection comes increased belief in their own competence to make sense of the information they are receiving as they study.

When introducing struggling students who lack a strong feeling of competence to graphic organizers, teachers should do no less than a master carpenter does when introducing apprentices to a new tool. First, the teachers must show the students the purpose for the tool, demonstrate correct use, and then guide the students through easy practice. In the classroom, teachers can introduce each organizer using previously learned material. In a sense, this makes the instruction "content free." It allows the students to concentrate on the new tool. After this early success, the teachers will move the students into use of the organizer with current lessons. When they do this, it is especially important that they structure the task carefully to guarantee successful use.

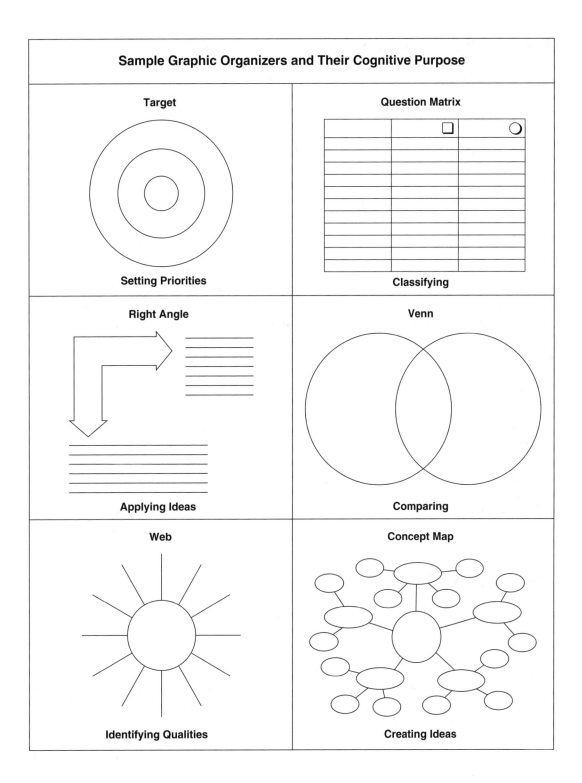

Sample Graphic Organizers and Their Cognitive Purpose

Target

Setting Priorities

Question Matrix

Classifying

Right Angle

Applying Ideas

Venn

Comparing

Web

Identifying Qualities

Concept Map

Creating Ideas

THIS ONE IS JUST LIKE THE OTHER ONE

From the earliest grades, the standards-based curriculum calls on students to make comparisons. How are these two objects alike? Similar? The same? How are they different? Not alike?

In whatever variation, success depends on a student's ability to compare. Sometimes the student is asked to do this directly by a standard: "Students can *explain how* an isosceles triangle is *like* a right triangle." At other times, the standard asks for an indirect comparison: "Students will be able to *distinguish the category* in which nouns belong" or "Students will be able to *differentiate* between . . ." The verbs indicate the process the students must use. The nouns highlight the content.

When students don't know the meaning of either the process word or the content word, they cannot do the tasks called for by the standards. Most standardized tests highlight the content with the assumption that students can do the process. As Feuerstein has pointed out, this is a false assumption and leads to much of the failure experienced by students who lack the prerequisites of learning. To counter this, not only must teachers build the prerequisites, but they must develop the students' vocabulary with these cognitive terms and embed the thinking processes in daily lessons, especially with those that are as common as the comparative family.

When teachers are told they should "ask more higher-order questions," they are being given misleading directions. The directions need to be more precise.

They need to ask more comparative questions, structure more comparative tasks, and match these with the standards. This will give students the practice they need in doing the types of thinking most called for in the curriculum so that they can "think sharply" on their tests. The more practice teachers receive in these ways of thinking, aligned with the ways of thinking that produce the strongest results in achievement, the more they will build students' feeling of competence.

KEY POINTS TO REMEMBER

- Mediation of competence, like the little engine that could, is a process of continuous improvement.
- In these days and times, touching is still important; educators simply have to make certain the touch is nonthreatening.
- Fifteen teacher behaviors are identified as TESA strategies and are used in professional development to improve expectations of teachers. Select those that draw out students who feel incompetent.
- TESA research found a strong connection between what teachers expected of students and the resulting performance. Expect all to contribute in their small groups and large class discussions.
- If you don't expect much, you won't get much; everyone easily rises to low expectations.
- Recognize those behaviors you want continued, not those you want extinguished.

ELEMENTARY LESSON

Out of the Magic Hat

Standard
How to think before we act

Focus Intelligence
Verbal/Linguistic

Supporting Intelligences
Intrapersonal, Visual/Spatial

Mediation Emphasis
Competence

CHECKING PRIOR KNOWLEDGE

Ask students to think of a time when they acted before thinking. Tell them "no hands" and to first think for a minute (wait time). After that time, use a wraparound to secure many ideas. Save praise until all have responded, and highlight the thinking done. Encourage students who have a more difficult time responding by having all write out a response to your key question.

STRUCTURING THE TASK

1. Introduce your "magic hat." Ask each child to print or write his or her name on a 3 × 5 index card, fold it over, and put it into the hat. Mix the cards up.

2. Explain the purpose of the hat: to pull the names of students so that everyone gets to answer some questions. Set the guideline "no hands to answer."

3. Ask the next think question: "Why is it best to think before acting?" Use the hat after a minute's wait. Delve and cue as needed.

4. Repeat with two other questions: "When are some important times to think before you act?" and "How are you going to become a more careful thinker?"

LOOKING BACK AND REFLECTING

On the following day (using the hat, wait time, delving, and cuing again), ask, "Yesterday, how did you stop and think before acting?"

BRIDGING FORWARD

Give pairs of students a sheet of art paper and crayons. Tell them to plan a picture showing a time or place when it is best "to stop and think." Model as needed. Post the finished work.

Assessing Student Performance

Students show increased comfort with wait time.

Variations

1. Close with a role play by trios. Each play will demonstrate a "stop and think" incident.

2. After a month or so, eliminate the hat.

MIDDLE GRADES LESSON

Who's the Leader?

Standard
Generate, gather, plan, and organize ideas for writing

Focus Intelligence
Verbal/Linguistic

Supporting Intelligences
Intrapersonal, Visual/Spatial

Mediation Emphasis
Competence

CHECKING FOR PRIOR KNOWLEDGE

Ask each student to recall a person who was a strong, positive leader. (Allow wait time.) What were their characteristics? Write their answers on the board or overhead using a web. (Distribute the opportunity to respond. Delve with "why?")

STRUCTURING THE TASK

1. Explain characteristics as personality traits or attributes, as the pieces of personality that help make each of us unique. (Give an example from history or your family life of such unique characteristics.) Note that some characteristics define personalities who become famous leaders. This unit will look at the characteristics common to leaders and examine how students can learn to develop some of these.

2. Divide the students into trios. Assign a recorder, manager, and checker in each trio. Review the jobs of each. Inform the students prior to starting the task that every student will receive both an individual and a group grade.

3. In turn, invite each trio to brainstorm the characteristics of the leader picked in the focus activity. The recorder will write down each new characteristic and put an asterisk by the duplicates.

4. Each trio will select its top three agreed-upon characteristics and develop a reason for each choice. The checker will ensure that everyone in the trio can explain the choices.

5. Instruct each trio to split into three and join new trios. Reassign the roles. Have each new trio compare its selections with the others. Identify similarities.

6. Ask recorders to report on similarities found. Record these on the board or overhead.

LOOKING BACK AND REFLECTING

Clarify in discussion the identified similarities. Seek examples of these qualities in action. Ask students to explain how the same characteristics might help them in a critical situation. (Identify TESA behaviors you will use to guide this discussion.)

Provide students with scenarios about the Reverend Dr. Martin Luther King Jr. or other leaders from the ethnic groups in your class. In their groups, the students will review the positive leadership characteristics and develop a role play. The trio will show how the characteristics helped the leader to succeed. Allow one class period for planning and practicing. On succeeding days, allow the groups five minutes each for (a) their presentations and (b) discussion of the examples as they relate to real situations.

BRIDGING FORWARD

Ask each group to identify leadership attributes found in its members. Each group will help its members make a plan for using the attributes in their daily lives. Use a wraparound so members may share the ideas generated.

Assessing Student Performance

1. Each student identifies three leadership qualities that he or she admires.

2. Each student selects one quality to develop.

Variations

1. Share one or two scenarios about leaders they know.

2. Invite each group to compose a popular song about leadership. Share these (affirm, praise).

3. Ask groups to select one of the following scenarios. How would the leader selected above use his or her traits to address the issue in the scenario?
   a. Three students are invited to a party at a good friend's house. While there, five other uninvited friends arrive and bring beer.
   b. You're at a school party. The older student who drove you gets drunk.
   c. Your teacher gives you an assignment for homework that requires library research. To get to the library, you must cross a gang's turf. Neither you nor your friends belong to the gang.
   d. On your basketball team are two players whom you overhear talking about smoking dope. As a team member who took the oath, you are bound to report what you heard.
   e. You are invited to a party after homecoming. At the party you see the team captain doing crack.
   f. On a school bus trip, a parent chaperone offers wine.
   g. Your best friend tells you that she's pregnant but doesn't want you to tell anyone.

SECONDARY LESSON

Egg Toss

Standard	Use hypothesis testing to make decisions

Standard
Use hypothesis testing to make decisions

Focus Intelligence
Bodily/Kinesthetic

Supporting Intelligences
Verbal/Linguistic, Intrapersonal

Mediation Emphasis
Competence

CHECKING PRIOR KNOWLEDGE

1. On the board, construct a T-chart titled Competence. (Practice wait time, equitable distribution, praise.)

Competence	
Looks Like	**Feels Like**

2. Ask for a number of volunteers (equal distribution) to give personal examples of what competence looks like and/or feels like. Record these.

STRUCTURING THE TASK

1. Let the class know it will play a game to test its hypotheses in the T-chart (be sure to have given advance notice: old clothes will help).

2. Take the class outside and set up two paired lines. Give each pair a water balloon. At your signal, call for the first toss and catch. Encourage partners to coach each other.

3. After each round, add another foot between the two lines. The winning team will have the most distance and be the least wet!

LOOKING BACK AND REFLECTING

Invite pairs to think about answers to these questions. (The hat described in the primary lesson will help wait time.) Practice the TESA behaviors:

How did it feel to keep dry with catches and tosses with greater distances?

How did you try to help your partner?

How did it feel when your balloon broke?

What do you think is the competence lesson here?

BRIDGING FORWARD

Discuss this question as you use your TESA skills: What lessons did this activity teach that you can use in school or in out-of-school situations?

Assessing Student Performance

Students can relate feelings of competence to their own lives.

Variations

1. Use a different game familiar to students such as Rock Paper Scissors, Frisbee toss, or Knots.

2. Conclude by asking each student to write an essay on "a competent person I know."

8

Sharing
Behavior

It wasn't necessary to kill the Indian. If we were going to steal the country, we could at least [have] shared it.

—James Baldwin (1971)

In our high-speed, high-tech world, information bombards adults and children with overwhelming intensity. Faster and more powerful computers process in a single day more new data than were generated in all of the first millennium A.D. The more the data flow, the less likely it is that the volume of information can be processed single-handedly and the more likely that individuals will feel the need to work with others. Thus emerges the increased emphasis in business, government, and other work areas for teamwork.

LOOKING BACK: THE ADVOCATES OF SHARING BEHAVIOR

Feuerstein believes that sharing behavior is "one of the foundations of our social existence" (Sharron, 1987). Sharing behavior occurs when a group of learners works together to achieve a common goal. When mediators work with students to mediate any learning goal, they model the sharing behavior that will enable them to collaborate with students so that students can develop sensitivity to others.

Feuerstein's psychological emphasis on sharing behavior parallels the work of social psychologists Roger and David Johnson, Robert Slavin, Elizabeth Cohen, and other advocates of cooperative learning. For Feuerstein, sharing relates to the intrinsic need for interdependence. The mediation of sharing behavior helps children form the friendships that facilitate communication and break down egocentric behav-

> Cooperative learning provides a powerful tool for building positive interdependence.

ior, loneliness, and emotional isolation. To accomplish this, as Feuerstein learned in his work with the children of the Holocaust, the mediator creates an environment of trust in which to strengthen students' self-concepts, promote experiences of accomplishment, listen with empathy, and clarify confused and cloudy thinking. For the Johnsons (1999), cooperative learning provides a powerful tool for building positive interdependence among individuals with a shared goal. As the Johnsons' extensive research has shown, this positive interdependence, coupled with individual accountability, taught social skills, and the assessment of teamwork in the completion of face-to-face tasks improves student achievement, self-concept, and critical thinking more successfully than other models of instruction.

SHARING BEHAVIORS IN THE HOME AND FAMILY

In a home rich with mediation, early sharing behavior is nurtured through the parents pointing at, singing to, playing with, and modeling for the child. From the parent-dominated activities in the first years of life, sharing behavior increases interactivity as the family develops give-and-take dialogues at the meal table, while watching television, when completing chores, or when shopping at the store.

When children enter school, they may have their first experience of learning to share with peers. Given the opportunity to work with a peer or complete a problem-solving task with a group, students continue to grow in their ability to show empathy and develop more complex social relationships. Most important, they learn how to work in a team to accomplish a task that they could not perform alone.

In some urban classrooms, children arrive without any notion of sharing behavior. If they have grown up as street survivors, without strong early mediation for sharing, they may come to school ready to do battle to the death. They know street survival, where "look out for yourself," "don't trust anyone," and "save your own neck" are the learned behaviors. In school this translates to "me first, last, and always," "after me, you can be first," "I'll do it my way," and "be

> Sharing behavior became the gate that could most readily admit these children to the world of learning.

reasonable, do it my way." These youngsters only know how to trust themselves. Any overture to building trust and friendship must be actively rejected.

In his work with the children of the Holocaust, Feuerstein confronted a similar set of street-survival beliefs. He had seen these children fight for scraps of food in the ghettos. He knew that many others had lost their lives through the deception of fair-weather friends. He understood the depth of pain that grew from their need to take care of themselves, and he grasped the necessity of mediating how to share. Thus sharing behavior became the gate that, once opened, could most readily admit these children to the world of learning. And just as Feuerstein succeeded with the mediation of sharing behaviors to the children of the Holocaust, he argues today for the mediation by teachers with urban children who come to school isolated and alone.

COOPERATIVE LEARNING: A STRATEGY FOR THE DEVELOPMENT OF SHARING BEHAVIORS

In the past two decades, the proponents of cooperative learning have developed a multitude of easily implemented strategies that enhance sharing behavior in the classroom. These methods are as simple as a teacher's offering encouragement to students to help and listen to each other, to be sensitive to each others' special needs, to give examples of sharing behavior, and to stop behavior that offends others in word or deed. Alternatively, sharing strategies may be as complex as use of the jigsaw (see Chapter 5), problem-based learning teams, base groups, or peer editing pairs. Consider the following examples.

Think-Pair-Share

The think-pair-share strategy is one of the easiest tools for developing shared behavior in a classroom. It has many uses. The think-pair-share strategy can be used (a) to begin a new topic or unit by having students discuss prior knowledge, (b) after a lecture, to help students summarize key points, (c) to stimulate student thinking about an important piece of information, (d) to check students' understanding of or insight into a topic, (e) to bring closure to a lesson, (f) to deepen students' short-term memories, (g) or to promote student transfer of a concept.

With each of these uses of the think-pair-share strategy, give similar instructions:

Before the task: "Today I am going to describe _____ [topic]. After I define each term, I'm going to ask you to _____ with a partner. To fill in the second blank in this statement, select one of the following: (a) summarize the key points, (b) tell what you already know about the topic, (c) pick one idea of importance and explain it, (d) tell how the information is important, or (e) tell something new you learned about the topic." After 10 to 20 seconds, sample student ideas for the whole class.

After the task: "Turn to the person on your [right/left side], and take turns _____" (see a–e above). Allow two to three minutes for each person to share.

Know Your Role

Knowing and assuming roles are important keys to successful teamwork in any group task. Roles are the first ingredients in preparing students for bonding, for being accountable for the whole group's work, and for assessing the group's performance.

Explain Why

The simple strategy of getting students to explain reasons for their answers is yet another effective means of building sharing behavior. This strategy enables students to rehearse their reasons for selecting an answer. Before a lesson, ask groups of students to discuss three to five multiple-choice questions that check prior knowledge. After each question is answered, invite several group reporters to explain why the group selected those answers. Solicit several answers to each question, write them on the board, and then discuss the merits of each answer.

Business Cards

The "business card" is another motivational rehearsal tool that involves the entire class. Give each student a 3" × 5" index card. Explain that the purpose of business cards is to present or introduce each other.

Model the following instructions on the overhead or board by giving sample answers to the following:

a. Write down your first name in the middle of the card using capital letters (e.g., TOM).
b. Write the name of your school beneath your name (e.g., Benjamin Banneker Middle School).
c. Write in the upper right-hand corner of the card a success you have had this week at school, home, or play (e.g., made a friend, got a score of 95 on a quiz).
d. Write your learning goal for this week in the lower right-hand corner (e.g., improve vocabulary quiz score, finish a paper).
e. Write a benefit of doing your homework in the upper left-hand corner (e.g., higher grades, improved self-esteem).
f. Write down a favorite book title in the lower left-hand corner (e.g., *Miss Nelson Is Missing, Freedom Songs, Who Is Carrie?*).
g. Name your best cooperative skill (e.g., listening).

After all students have completed their cards, instruct each one to find a partner. After the pairs settle, instruct them to focus on one of the corner topics (success, goal, benefit, or favorite) and explain why that topic was selected. After one or two minutes, instruct students to switch partners. Continue switching until all the students have discussed all four of the corner topics on their business cards.

We Bags

Give each pair of students a paper bag. Invite the pairs to decorate them with their own names, the names of their favorite books or foods, or the names of places they have visited. Then have the pairs fill their bags with objects that have special meaning to them. Students should prepare to introduce their partners by discussing each item that is in the bag. Match the pairs into foursomes to introduce their partners.

"I Learned" Mailgram

For rehearsal after a lesson, invite each student to complete an "I Learned" mailgram. Pass out cards with the "I learned . . ." stem. Have students fill in and sign the form. Next, match students into pairs to share the mailgrams. Rotate the pairs several times.

Vocabulary Jigsaw I

Select nine vocabulary words. Divide the class into trios. Give each group member three words and instruct each student (a) to learn the definitions of the words, (b) to draw a sketch of each word's meaning, and (c) to use the sketch to teach the other group members in a round-robin teaching. In 15 minutes, all members must know the meaning of the three words they've been given. To help, have the checker quiz the other group members after each round of three words and for the nine-word total before you quiz each student:

Get ready: review your roles and the task.

Step 1: Learn the three words and draw a picture of each word (using it to teach the other members)

Step 2: Conduct the first round of teaching and check (having each member review the definitions), coaching as needed

Step 3: Second round of teaching and checking

Step 4: Third round of teaching and checking

Step 5: Groups double-check

Step 6: Quiz

Step 7: Elicit a group list of learning strategies used (checking after each round, making and explaining a sketch, giving encouragement, etc.).

T-Chart

The T-chart consists of two columns, one column headed Looks Like (what the topic looks like is listed in this first column) and the second headed Sounds Like (with what the topic sounds like listed in the second column). Explain that the lesson at hand will now demonstrate the use of this kind of chart. The T-chart is used to help pairs of students clarify concepts or ideas and to help each other give specific examples.

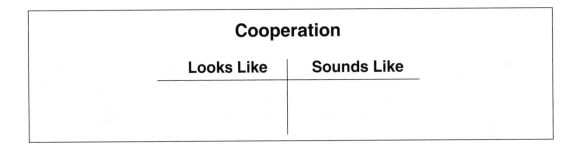

Cooperation	
Looks Like	**Sounds Like**

What? So What? Now What?

Another chart that helps develop sharing behaviors is a three-columned chart that includes What? So What? and Now What?

What?	So What?	Now What?

What?

In the What? column, students in pairs or trios organize various ideas they want to discuss at a conference and identify an accompanying artifact from their portfolio that will help them explain their points. These are listed as topics, but issues, concerns, or focal points serve as well.

So What?

So What? dictates a processing response that sheds light on why the topic or concern is included. Typical processing statements that students address as they think about the So What? column are (a) why it (the topic) seems important, (b) why it seems relevant, (c) why it seems weak or strong, or (d) what it represents or signifies.

Now What?

Now What? brings the reflection to meaningful application ideas. This is where the students project how the topic (or idea) is useful, connects to other things, can be modified, or perhaps might be of use to others.

While this is only one of many organizers, it seems particularly useful in helping students reflect and prepare for a conference, because the three questions proceed from simple information through more personal and more meaningful justification to future application.

Story Element Web

After students have read a story, provide each group with an element web. Instruct them to complete a story element web. Assign roles and review responsibilities.

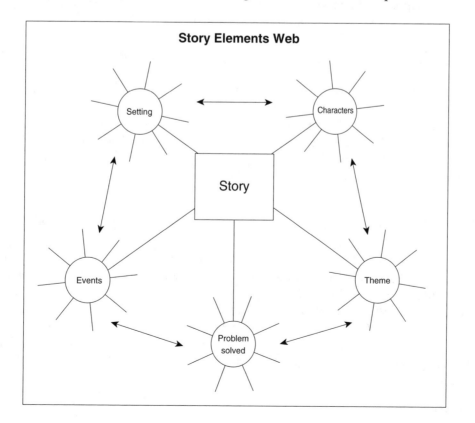

Math Practice Teams

After explaining and demonstrating a new skill (such as adding fractions), use teams of two or three students each to practice/coach through examples. Check for understanding as you monitor the groups.

COOPERATIVE TEAM SKILLS

In addition to using cooperative strategies that promote sharing behavior and student achievement, it is important also to develop students' cooperative team skills. The more skilled students become at working together, the more they will develop the sharing behaviors necessary for a learning community in which all students are respected and included.

When students come to school without the social skills that will enable them to do well, it's necessary for the mediator to set lessons that allow time for teaching the skills explicitly. After an introductory lesson, the teacher can begin to infuse what the students have learned to do and to say into subsequent lessons on a daily basis by asking students to assess their use of the new social skill. For instance, in the primary lesson that follows, the students learn how to show respect. After this lesson, the teacher can use mediating strategies such as a daily class round-robin: "I'd like each one in turn to complete this stem: 'Today, I showed respect when _____ .'"

KEY POINTS TO REMEMBER

The proponents of cooperative learning have developed a multitude of easily implemented strategies that enhance sharing behavior in the classroom. Cooperative learning strategies and cooperative teams incorporated into daily class routines are among the best practices when it comes to improving sharing behavior.

- Sharing behavior occurs when a group of learners work together to achieve a common goal.
- According to Feuerstein, sharing relates to the intrinsic need for interdependence.
- Without sharing behavior, "self-preservation is the first law of nature."
- On Edgar Dale's cone of learning, 70 percent of what is discussed with others is learned; sharing behavior is the foundation for the success of cooperative learning in the classroom.

Sharing behavior is a critical social skill. It is most easily mediated in the framework of cooperative groups. All advocates of cooperative groups do not call for explicit development of the social skills. However, all do recognize that social skill development is implicit in cooperative group tasks. Feuerstein would not only urge the use of cooperative groups but would also strongly advocate that teachers explicitly mediate the development of sharing behaviors. In the new BASIC instruments, Feuerstein goes so far as to include three instruments that attend to the development of the prerequisites of sharing behavior: emotions, empathy to action, and stopping violence. (See "The Basic Instruments" on p. 103.)

In addition to teaching explicit social skills lessons, the teacher can mediate sharing behavior by setting up classroom structures that enable students to develop interpersonal skills helpful for creating a community of learners (Senge 1990).

In a learning community where sharing behavior is the norm, achievement soars. After mastering the basics of working and sharing with each other, students can learn to use the cooperative structures and strategies in a triple agenda. First, they improve the social skills that business and industry consider essential for employment in this century. Second, they improve their cognitive skills and become problem solvers. Third, they raise their achievement level in the content areas. To build on this triple agenda, the mediator uses lessons that integrate content learning with cooperative teamwork and critical thinking in lessons that challenge students, deepen meaning, and increase sharing behavior.

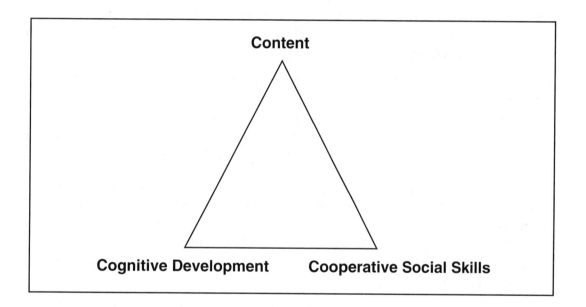

Throughout the activities and lessons that promote shared behavior, it is the mediators' responsibility to draw children's attention to ways of sharing that are helpful, ways that are not helpful, and ways to improve. The strategies and structures that mediators plan create a context for sharing behaviors. Their interventions call students' attention to understanding why they are sharing. The mediators help students construct this understanding and benefit from the positive experiences the mediators have facilitated. Their work in mediating sharing behavior is intentional. They ask, they probe, and they challenge students to see how sharing behavior benefits both their interpersonal relations and their shared academic successes.

ELEMENTARY LESSON

What's in a Name?

Standard
How to use names in schools and other settings

Focus Intelligence
Verbal/Linguistic, Interpersonal

Supporting Intelligences
Intrapersonal, Visual/Spatial

Mediation Emphasis
Sharing Behavior

CHECKING PRIOR KNOWLEDGE

Ask students, "Why do we have names?" Elicit multiple responses. Next, introduce yourself by printing your name on the board (e.g., Mrs. Patricia Cowen). Sound out your name and have the class do a choral reading with your direction. Invite them to call you by your title and last name.

STRUCTURING THE TASK

1. Explain to the class how important it is to call people by their names and that in this lesson they will learn each other's names.

2. Assign each child one third of a "people card." Each third of a people card has on it a colored dot (red, green, or yellow) and a letter. Tell the children to find the two other parts of their people card (same letter, different colors) so that they will form groups of three. (Show a model group of three and count off each child in the group: "One, two, three.") In the group of three, all must have the same letter and three different colored dots. (Show red, yellow, and green.) Signal the class to start. As groups of three are formed, instruct those groups to sit down together. Help those who are having difficulty until all groups are seated where you want them.

3. Invite the children with the red pieces to come to the materials table and pick up a sheet of newsprint and some crayons.

4. Each child is to sketch a self-portrait on the sheet. Be sure that the groups decide whether they are all going to sketch at once or take turns. They may help each other, but they may not offer any "bad talk" about each other's sketches. (Some examples of bad talk are, "That looks dumb," "That's stupid," or "Mine is nicer than yours.")

5. As they are drawing, give each child an index card (with the child's first name printed on it) and a piece of tape. If some children can't print their own names, someone else may, or else they may affix the index cards to their sketch.

6. Invite each group to stand up. As the students with the red and yellow dots hold the newsprint, the students with the green dots will introduce all three of their group members. Encourage the class to give each group applause or a hurrah after its introduction. Post the completed sketches.

LOOKING BACK AND REFLECTING

Ask class members how they felt working together on the task. Encourage a variety of students to respond. If they start to repeat each other's responses, ask for the next one to think of a different word to describe how he or she was feeling.

BRIDGING FORWARD

Give each child an index name card to wear for the rest of the day. Sit the children in a circle. Invite the children to share their names as they show their cards. After a child has shared his or her name, lead the class in a choral answer to the following:

"What is his [her] name?" "His [Her] name is _____." Emphasize that you want them to call each other by the given name.

Materials

Index cards, colored dots, newsprint, crayons, masking tape

Variation

Repeat the name circle each day until the children form the habit of calling each other by their first names. For variety, have team members introduce each other. Ask only the question, "What is his [her] name?" without modeling the response. You may want to see how many classmates each student can name. For this, have a volunteer walk behind the circle and name each child in turn. When the child misses a name, he or she sits down and another volunteer takes over.

ELEMENTARY/MIDDLE GRADES LESSON

Forming Friendship Circles

Standard
How to form friendships

Focus Intelligence
Interpersonal

Supporting Intelligences
Intrapersonal, Visual/Spatial

Mediation Emphasis
Sharing behavior

CHECKING PRIOR KNOWLEDGE

1. Place the students' chairs in a circle. Read a story or relate a personal incident about the importance of friends.

2. On the overhead screen or blackboard, build a spider map on the importance of friends. Use a wraparound (with the right to pass), inviting each student to contribute to the map. Help by clarifying and ensuring that each student is heard.

3. Invite several students to summarize the ideas.

STRUCTURING THE TASK

1. Give each student a copy of the Your Circle of Friends worksheet and invite each one to fill in the diagram privately.

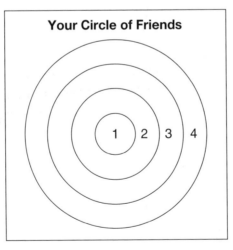

2. Circle 1 is for those closest to you, that you love and can count on the most (e.g., family).

3. Circle 2 is for those you like and can trust (e.g., school friends).

4. Circle 3 is for those with whom you like to do things (e.g., sports team).

5. Circle 4 is for those who get paid to help you (e.g., doctor, teacher).

6. Without invading their privacy, ask students to compare how it might feel to not have anyone in Circles 1 or 2 as opposed to having people absent in Circles 3 or 4.

7. Discuss what it means "to feel included."

8. Brainstorm a list of ways we can exclude a person, even by mistake.

9. Brainstorm and record ways to ensure that every student in the class is included in both in-class and out-of-class activities.

LOOKING BACK AND REFLECTING

Ask students: "Think about a time you were excluded by an important other. In your journal, describe how that incident made you feel. How can that experience help you in the future?"

BRIDGING FORWARD

Give each student a 3" × 5" index card. Have them write something they could do to help a classmate be included, and on the other side of the cards, write one thing that others might do to include them in the future. Select several at random to read to the circle.

Material

Your Circle of Friends worksheets, 3" × 5" index cards, student journals

Variation

In the Bridging Forward, (a) ask students to write about how they can strengthen the bonds of friendship in their own homes and (b) pair students who are not already friends and have them plan a project together.

9

Individuation

We live amid swarms of people, yet there is a vast distance between people, a distance that words cannot bridge.

—Richard Wright (Riley, 1993)

In the United States, every newborn child receives a Social Security number. This number is unique to the individual, different from all the other numbers that have been assigned. When individuals have to deal with the government, schools, banks, and businesses, they provide that special number so that all their documents are coded solely to them.

The Social Security number is an official recognition of the uniqueness of each individual. It is that official uniqueness that identifies how each person is different from all others, according to the records. The learning mediator fosters individuation by helping each student establish what it is that makes him or her a unique human being. Obviously, this task is more difficult and more important than merely assigning the individual a Social Security number.

THE MEDIATION OF INDIVIDUATION

In Feuerstein's system, the mediation of individuation is the process of empowering each student to establish an internal locus of control. It is this locus of control that enables people to take responsibility for their own life and to make decisions that chart their own direction. As the young child grows toward adulthood, the parent and teacher-mediators lessen their control and help the child develop independent and original ways of thinking and acting. To accomplish this, the adult mediators acknowledge the differences between this child and the others with whom the mediators work. Differences in style, intelligence, ability, past experience, and desire become the foundation for the mediator to encourage the child to chart his or her own path through life.

In some urban schools, where standardization has become an overriding burden and every teacher follows a given script with no variations allowed, mediating individuation may prove difficult, if not impossible. For some reason that has little too do with common sense or sound instructional practice, teachers in these schools are forced to make a cookie-cutter pattern that is supposed to ensure that no child is left behind. While this cookie cutter pattern may not leave any child behind, it certainly does not allow teachers to mediate the type of learning that allows any child to achieve excellence.

> Mediation of individuation is the process of empowering each student to establish an internal locus of control.

Shades of Orwell's world, where neither teacher nor child is allowed any significant decision about learning: the locus of control rests solely in the hands of some higher authority that believes in total external control.

From the time the parent encourages the infant to stand and walk without support, throughout childhood and adolescence until the day the young adult elects to leave home, the mediation of individuation is a delicate task, requiring balance and finesse. First, the parent-mediator must respect the child's natural desire to be his or her own person without taking on a completely laissez-faire approach. Second, the parent must encourage the child to take control of his or her behavior to the point that the child will not endanger himself or herself or others. Third, the parent must respect the child's right to privacy while setting clear boundaries for all family members. Fourth, the parent must encourage the development of interests and abilities without expecting the child to become a clone. Finally, the parent who wishes to develop that feeling of autonomy so critical to individuation must provide guidance in understanding the family's values and beliefs.

In the classroom, the effective teacher-mediator must walk the same fine line. On the one hand, teacher-mediators must refrain from superimposing their own values and beliefs on the students. On the other hand, it is important that teacher-mediators help students understand and respect the importance of family and community values. In the broadest sense, this means that teacher-mediators will have the most success with the mediation of individuation through a learner-centered approach.

Variety as the Spice of Teaching

Students have a variety of interests, learning styles, levels of motivation, and cultural backgrounds. Today, more than ever, teachers must have a variety of ways to meet the needs of all the students in their classrooms. Whole-class instruction (the "one size fits all" approach) has been the principal mode of instruction for decades. This method is decreasingly relevant. The students who are the most difficult to teach and the most challenging to motivate are among those we are least prepared to teach in a heterogeneous setting.

> The teacher's chief concern is the development of self-directed learners.

In a learner-centered classroom, the teacher's chief concern is the development of self-directed learners. This long-range task is not easily accomplished. Just as growing up is a process of becoming an autonomous, responsible individual within the context of family values, becoming a self-directed learner is a process of becoming an autonomous, responsible learner within the context of community values. Young people will make wrong choices; they will make mistakes; they will also make correct choices and learn from their mistakes. It is the job of the mediator to help them learn from their choices.

Guidelines for Successful Individuation

To help self-directed learners emerge from their dependence on the teacher, the teacher-mediator carefully considers the variety of students' needs, styles, and intelligences in building a curriculum that benefits all of the students assigned to the classroom. Here are eight helpful guidelines to consider:

1. Encourage each student to stand up for his or her beliefs.

2. Motivate each student to develop his or her multiple intelligences.

3. Give each student the tools to think critically about all points of view.

4. Organize the celebration of cultural diversity.

5. Welcome original ideas and creative thinking.

6. Enhance the development of each child's special abilities.

7. Respect each child's values and beliefs.

8. Differentiate instruction so children may make meaningful choices as they take charge of their own learning.

In the Urban Classroom

In the urban classroom, individuation takes on a special meaning. Today's student in the urban school comes under tremendous pressure to abandon family values and to adopt the values of the dominant gangs in the neighborhood. It is not too much to say that their very lives are at stake if they resist gang pressures. It is also not too much to assert that fear, confusion, and many other emotions dominate their thoughts in the classroom and create a major barrier to learning. Thus the guidelines for learner-centered instruction have a double import in the urban school: the guidelines also point out why the process of learning must be at least an equal partner with the content of the curriculum.

Thus it is most important that the mediator translate the guidelines into action. Howard Gardner's (1983) theory of multiple intelligences provides one of the easiest and most beneficial frameworks for making the learner-centered guidelines useful in a classroom.

Noting Student Differences—Many Ways Through the Multiple Intelligences

Gardner's theory of multiple intelligences gives teachers a new looking glass with many prisms for seeing students' individual needs. First, it is helpful to review the framework established by Gardner in his book *Frames of Mind* (1983). He wrote this book to challenge the popular notion that intelligence was a single intellectual capacity, of fixed ability, and measurable quantitatively. He declared at that time that intelligence was multiple in its capacities, changeable in its abilities, and assessable only in its multiplicity.

Gardner theorized that there are seven intelligences (in August 1995 he proposed an eighth, "the naturalist"). Relying on the accumulation of knowledge about the human brain and human cultures, Gardner (1983) has defined intelligence as "a human intellectual competence that entails a set of skills for problem solving— enabling the individual to resolve genuine problems or difficulties that he or she encounters and, when appropriate, to create an effective product." Furthermore, he describes an intelligence as "a biological and psychological potential; that potential is capable of being realized to a greater or lesser extent as a consequence of the experiential, cultural and motivational factors that affect a person." At the same time that he was arguing for intelligence as a dynamic, changing, and active process that differed radically in different cultures, Gardner was rejecting both the popular notion that intelligence was a fixed capability resulting from an a priori definition and the factoring of test scores as taught by Binet (1886) and those who value the bell curve.

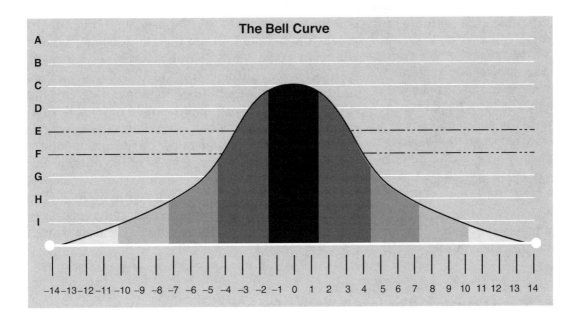

THE MULTIPLE INTELLIGENCES: MANY WAYS TO SOLVE A PROBLEM

Gardner is the first to admit that his list of multiple ways of problem solving and making products is not all-encompassing. The current list identifies those eight intelligences that up until now have met all eight criteria. Continued study by Gardner, his colleagues, and others who accept the definition and the criteria may identify 1 or 100 more intelligences.

1. Verbal/Linguistic Intelligence

The verbal/linguistic intelligence is concerned with the uses of language. People with this intelligence possess a particularly strong sensitivity to the meaning of words and a skilled aptitude with their manipulation. According to Gardner (1983), these people have "the capacity to follow rules of grammar, and, on carefully selected occasions, to violate them" (p. 77). On yet another level—the sensory level—those with a heightened verbal/linguistic intelligence are able to communicate effectively by listening, speaking, reading, writing, and linking. They also have a strong awareness of the varying functions of language or, more specifically, its power to stimulate emotions. Poets, authors, reporters, speakers, attorneys, talk-show hosts, and politicians typically exhibit verbal/linguistic intelligence.

> A godhead and a good heart are always a formidable combination, but when you add to that a literate tongue or pen, then you have something very special.
>
> —Nelson Mandela (Riley, 1993)

2. Musical/Rhythmic Intelligence

As Gardner (1983) describes it, "There are several roles that musically inclined individuals can assume ranging from the avant-garde composer who attempts to create a new idiom, to the fledgling listener who is trying to make sense of nursery rhymes (or other 'primer level' music)" (pp. 104–105). Each of us holds musical capabilities to some degree—the difference is that some people have more skill than others. No matter what range of talent, we all possess a core of abilities necessary for enjoying a musical experience. These consist of the musical elements of pitch, rhythm, and timbre (the characteristic elements of a tone). People with more highly developed musical/rhythmic intelligence are singers, composers, instrumentalists, conductors, and those who enjoy, understand, or appreciate music.

> I have to really feel a song before I'll deal with it and just about every song I do is based either on an experience I've had or an experience someone I knew had gone through.
>
> —Aretha Franklin (Riley, 1993)

3. Mathematical/Logical Intelligence

The mathematical/logical intelligence incorporates both mathematical and scientific abilities. Mathematicians are typically characterized by a love of working with abstraction and a desire for exploration. They enjoy working with problems that require a great deal of reasoning. A scientist, however, is "motivated by a desire to explain physical reality"; for scientists, mathematics serves as a tool "for building models and theories that can describe and eventually explain the operation of the world" (Gardner, 1983, p. 145). Mathematicians, engineers, physicists, astronomers, programmers, and researchers demonstrate a high degree of mathematical/logical intelligence.

> He who asks questions cannot avoid the answers.
>
> —Cameroonian proverb

4. Visual/Spatial Intelligence

Visual/spatial intelligence involves the unique ability to visually comprehend the world with accuracy. Those with visual/spatial intelligence are able to represent spatial information graphically, and have a keen gift for bringing forth and transforming mental images. Artists and designers have strong visual/spatial capabilities. They have a certain responsiveness to the visual/spatial world as well as a talent for re-creating it in producing works of art. Sailors, engineers, surgeons, sculptors, cartographers, and architects are also notable for their strong visual/spatial intelligence.

> Our eyes see something; we take a stone and aim at it. But the stone rarely succeeds like the eye in hitting the mark.
>
> —Nigerian proverb

5. Bodily/Kinesthetic Intelligence

The bodily/kinesthetic intelligence is the command of one's bodily motions and the talent to manipulate objects with deftness. It is possible for these abilities to exist separately, though most people possess both simultaneously. Those with keen bodily/kinesthetic intelligence include actors, dancers, acrobats, and athletes.

6. Intrapersonal Intelligence

The heart of intrapersonal intelligence lies in the ability to understand one's own feelings. People strong in this intelligence instinctively comprehend their own range of emotions, can label them, and can draw on them as a means of directing their own behavior. In Gardner's (1983) words, "The intrapersonal intelligence amounts to little more than the capacity to distinguish a feeling of pleasure from one of pain, and on the basis of such discrimination, to become more involved in or to withdraw from a situation" (p. 239). Examples of those with higher-than-average intrapersonal capabilities include the introspective novelist, wise elder, psychologist, or therapist—all of whom possess a deep understanding of their feelings.

> Self-progress brings its own reward.
>
> —Marcus Garvey (Riley, 1993)

7. Interpersonal Intelligence

Intrapersonal intelligence is directed inward; interpersonal intelligence, though, is directed outward to others in the environment. The most basic skill among those with a high degree of interpersonal intelligence is the talent for understanding others. Those exhibiting this intelligence have the gift for noticing and making distinctions among other individuals and more specifically among their "moods, temperaments, motivations, and intentions" (Gardner, 1983, p. 239). For example, at a very simple level, this intelligence includes the ability of children to notice and be sensitive to the moods of adults around them. A more complex interpersonal skill is that of adults being able to read the intentions of others, even when hidden. People

> A single bracelet does not jingle.
>
> —Congolese proverb

> Sticks in a bundle are unbreakable.
>
> —Kenyan proverb

typically exhibiting this intelligence include religious and political leaders, parents, teachers, therapists, and counselors.

8. Naturalist Intelligence

> Human nature will find itself only when it fully realizes that to be human it has to cease to be beastly or brutal.
>
> —Mohandas Gandhi (Riley, 1993)

The naturalist is Gardner's most recently identified intelligence. A person with a strong naturalist intelligence is distinguished by the ability to understand, relate to, and function in the natural world. Linnaeus and Darwin are examples of individuals with a highly developed naturalist intelligence.

APPLYING GARDNER'S THEORY

When Gardner first described the intelligences, he refrained from prescribing how to use his theory as instructional practice. After more than a decade of observation, he developed criteria and a set of concerns to assist educators in making quality applications of his theory to the classroom.

First, teachers can examine the guidelines that Gardner developed for assessing the quality application of his theory.

1. Does the school curriculum cultivate multiple capabilities in students? Gardner has often criticized schools for their overemphasis on the mathematical/logical and the verbal/linguistic intelligences in the curriculum. He advocates that schools develop curricula that allow for the equal development of student potential through the other intelligences. Thus instead of regarding music and the visual arts as add-ons or extracurricular activities, schools with a solid application of his theory will restructure the curricula to allow as much instruction time for the fine arts as is allowed for reading, writing, and arithmetic.

2. Does the school curriculum encourage the serious treatment of concepts, subject matter, and disciplines in a variety of ways? Gardner advocates the "selective abandonment" (Art Costa's term) of trivial and outdated material in the curriculum so that teachers can provide in-depth treatment of significant key concepts and essential questions. Given less material "to cover," teachers can work in greater depth with a greater variety of approaches that are more appropriate pedagogically for targeted lessons or units. Thus instead of listening to a teacher talk rapidly through content, students can engage in a variety of hands-on activities with time to explore, discuss, and experiment with the ideas.

3. Does the school curriculum encourage the personalization of instruction? Feuerstein's guidelines for empowering students through learner-centered instruction relate directly to Gardner's call for personalized classrooms in which curriculum, instruction, and assessment are built around individual needs in the classroom. Although uniform instruction may make teaching easier, regimented instruction's inability to benefit so many individuals, especially the diverse populations in urban schools, is well documented.

4. Does the school curriculum encourage a variety of significant assessment approaches? Although paper-and-pencil tests may make the grading of factual recall easier, it does little to show how well a student understands a topic, has mastered skills, or can demonstrate increased intellectual capability. Gardner advocates the selection of multiple means of assessment, each geared to show the range and depth of students' intellectual development. In his view, tests that call for factual answers about the history of music or about the types of paint brushes used by Renoir may grade easily on the Scantron, but they are inadequate for showing how well students can play a new score or create a landscape of their own. In the multiple intelligence framework, well-taught students not only will demonstrate how they have improved in these areas by playing the piece or completing the painting, but they will have developed the ability to explain the importance of their accomplishment.

5. Do curriculum, instruction, and assessment challenge students to develop their multiple intelligences? The key word here is *challenge*. As does Feuerstein, Gardner is concerned with the trivialization of his theory as a means to justify the continuation of trivial curricula, instruction, and assessment. In a multiple intelligences school, the system links the three tightly together in a significant way. However, in a school where assessment focuses on facts and isolated skills, instruction is low level. Thus when multiple intelligences practices are introduced into such low-level systems, the musical/rhythmic intelligence becomes mnemonics, the visual/spatial intelligence becomes "dot-to-dot" pictures, and the verbal/linguistic intelligence becomes the memorization of vocabulary, spelling, and grammar rules by catchy songs. On the other hand, significant assessments that focus students on the understanding and application of ideas that Gardner calls for raise the level of curriculum and instruction. In this milieu, multiple intelligences theory transforms key curricular ideas such as "democracy" into problem-based situations that challenge students to use different intelligences to understand the topic and to make applications relevant to their lives. Students don't give up learning how to read or write—they are asked to develop these basic skills in a real-world context, not as isolated or fragmented bits.

DIFFERENTIATING INSTRUCTION IN A MULTIPLE INTELLIGENCES FRAMEWORK

One of the most successful ways for classroom teachers to differentiate instruction using Gardner's theory as an individuation tool is to create interdisciplinary units that revolve around an important theme, concept, or question and allow students to select which intelligence they will use to anchor their study. For instance, note the multiple opportunities for studying the Constitutional Convention.

Using Different Strategies for Different Learners

A second classroom approach allows for the creation of lessons that highlight differentiation of strategies. In each of these sample lessons and the many others used throughout this book, students begin their study with a common problem. As they proceed through the lesson, each student receives ample opportunity to work in different types of groups, reflect alone on new ideas, and learn from the

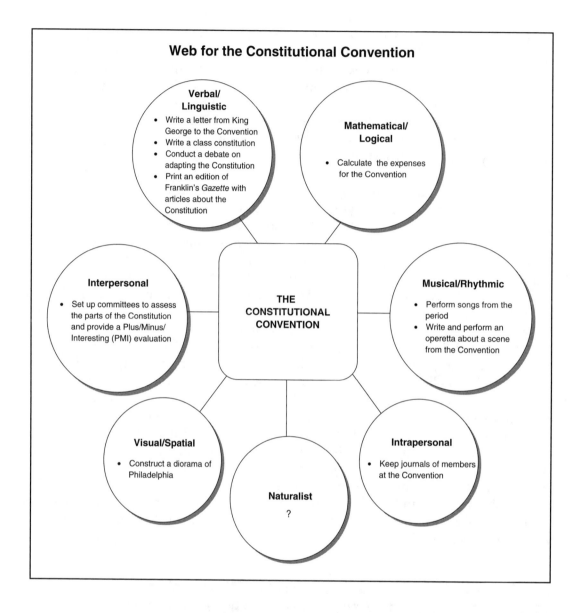

diverse experiences. At all times, the emphasis is on the students' developing their own thinking capabilities.

ELEMENTARY LESSON

Making Story Problems

Standard
How to write a story problem

Focus Intelligence
Mathematical/Logical

Supporting Intelligences
Visual/Spatial, Verbal/Linguistic

Mediation Emphasis
Individuation

CHECKING PRIOR KNOWLEDGE

1. On the board or overhead, create a sequence chart with 8 to 12 blocks. Label the first and last blocks.

Once upon a time …

The End

2. Ask students to identify stories they have heard that begin "Once upon a time . . ." List these on newsprint. After they have all contributed to the list, ask for a show of hands for those who have heard each story. Invite one youngster to share the story. (If students cannot identify one to tell, pick one or show a video such as *The Lion and the Mouse* or *How the Elephant Got His Trunk* (available from *Encyclopaedia Britannica*).

3. Chart the main events in the sequence chart for all to see, and point out that all stories have events that are arranged "start," "middle," and "end." Label these on the chart.

STRUCTURING THE TASK

1. Use the story you charted to introduce number problems. For instance, if you used the Three Billy Goats Gruff, (a) the Three Billy Goats lived here (show picture), (b) all three crossed the bridge (show picture), or (c) no Billy Goats are here now (show picture). Next show numerical operation $3 - 3 = 0$.

2. Invite a volunteer to tell you another story from the list or to invent a story. Chart the events on the board with sketches. Next, invite the class to add the number/word problem and complete the mathematics.

3. Practice additional examples each day. Select folk stories from a variety of cultures. Check for understanding of how to make a story problem:
   a. Chart story with start, middle, and end
   b. Draw the story
   c. Write story with words and numbers
   d. Solve the problem
   e. Show example

4. Form mixed groups of three. Assign roles (artist, storyteller, counter) and provide markers or crayons and paper. Review the process for creating a story problem for all to see.

5. Invite each group to make a new story problem. They may select any story not yet illustrated or invent a story to tell.

6. Work among the groups to mediate (a) how they make the story and (b) how they solve the problem.

7. Post the finished stories.

LOOKING BACK AND REFLECTING

Invite a member from each group to show the story problem and to point out how the group followed the process.

BRIDGING FORWARD

Introduce student journals so that each student can invent his or her own story problem. Encourage the group members to help each other. Work among the students to mediate their understandings. After stories are made, exchange them among the groups for solving. Mediate the thinking done to solve each problem. Collect each student's final work and individuate assessment by using the criteria below for each product.

Assessing Student Performance

To what degree can the student

1. Name the components of a story problem?

2. Sequence the components in a logical order?

3. Make a story problem using the components in a logical order?

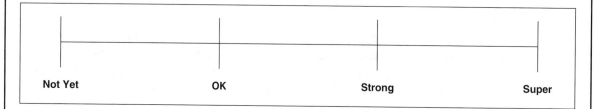

Not Yet   **OK**   **Strong**   **Super**

Materials

Newsprint, crayons, index cards, student journals

Variations

1. Show different types of story problems and have groups learn to make each type.

2. Have students show their parents how to make a story problem and then bring to class a family-made example.

Integrating Content in Projects

In a conventional classroom, mathematics is an isolated subject. Each topic and subtopic is isolated. Week by week, students work through each topic from addition, subtraction, multiplication, and division in the early grades to rational expressions, monomials, polynomials, and beyond in the secondary mathematics classroom (unless the students must repeat the basic computation until they get it!).

In the multiple intelligences classroom that uses interdisciplinary projects, mathematics can be integrated into projects that develop other intelligences simultaneously. Skills are not sequenced from simple to complex so that all students march forward (or stand still) in unison. In the context of the interdisciplinary unit, tasks requiring mathematical knowledge and skill are individuated. If a student must do mathematics and cannot, the teacher sets up a subgroup or individualized instruction mathematics module that fits the situation. If it is a complex mathematical task new to all in the project, the teacher uses the appropriate module with the entire class.

Because Gardner left instruction to the teachers using his theory, teachers must select the most appropriate strategies. Once again, Marzano and Pickering's (2001) research on classroom strategies that work best comes to the multiple-intelligences-oriented teacher's aid. In project-directed work, the strategies of hypothesizing and summarizing come into play along with question asking and cooperative learning. These strategies lend themselves to lesson plans that differentiate learning in a project-based format that accomplishes individuation.

Sample Differentiated Multiple Intelligences Projects

In the following sample lesson plan, note how teachers selected strong instructional strategies such as hypothesis formation, cooperative learning, question asking, and summarizing so that they could individuate learning. Note also that individuated learning is distinct from individualized learning. Teachers in this lesson start with a common goal for the project before they use a variety of grouping tactics. Only at the end of the lesson, when it is time for each student to draw conclusions and make a personal learning statement, does any solo or individual work occur. Even there, the emphasis is placed on the students using their own internal decision power to maintain the locus of control.

MIDDLE GRADES LESSON

INTEGRATED MATHEMATICS/
LANGUAGE ARTS

Publishing a Classroom Newspaper

Standard
How to apply mathematical problem solving to establish a budget

Focus Intelligence
Verbal/Linguistic

Supporting Intelligences
Mathematical/Logical, Interpersonal, Visual/Spatial

Mediation Emphasis
Individuation

CHECKING PRIOR KNOWLEDGE

1. Students are arranged into groups of three to five students. Each student will have a specific job on the team matched to his or her abilities and interests. For this prior knowledge check, the group will select a recorder.

2. On newsprint, each recorder will write out (a) what the group members know/recall about newspapers, (b) what the group members hypothesize about the challenge of newspaper production, and (c) questions to ask.

3. After the know-hypothesize-question time is done, sample responses to each review item. Put the answers on the blackboard in three columns (K-H-Q).

4. Add items that are left out by asking questions that challenge. Conclude by asking each student to select three to five questions that are of most interest to him or her.

5. Let the class know that they are beginning a multiple-month project to produce two editions of a class newspaper as a vehicle for improving their ability to summarize information.

STRUCTURING THE TASK

1. Use the groups to start research about the targeted audience for the paper (parents, students, other grades, community) and how other newspapers work with their own audiences. Each group will develop a survey tool based on the 5W matrix (who, what, when, where, why). (Model its use before making this assignment.)

Person	1	2	3	4	5
Who					
What					
When					
Where					
Why					
Summary Statement					

2. Assign each group to a department. Group members will select an official recorder, a materials manager, a department manager, and staff roles. For the department, the group will select which of the following questions to answer:
   a. What is the paper's content going to be?
   b. What will the cost be?
   c. How will they market and sell the paper?
   d. Who will gather the news?
   e. What budget will they need?
   f. Who will have what responsibilities?
   g. What procedures will they follow in their jobs?

3. The executive management team will consist of the department heads. They will establish the overall budget first. Each department will determine its budget to show (a) all projected expenses, (b) anticipated income with sources, and (c) gross profit after taxes (5%–12%).

4. Identify parent or community volunteers to serve as resources (accounting, marketing, etc.).

5. The best source of revenue will be ads. Involve all groups in the selling of ads. They will turn revenues to the business team with the collected funds. The business team may use a spreadsheet or database to keep the records, invoices, and so on.

6. Journalists from the teams will write articles for the paper's first edition. The paper can include articles on class or student activities, current events, cartoons, sports news, community interviews, and surveys and editorials on hot topics.

7. The departmental teams will edit their own articles as well as have proofreading help from other groups. After all articles and ads are finished, the design team will assemble the paper.

8. After distribution, the department teams will review budgets and calculate profit and loss. If a profit is generated, the teams can budget for a celebration.

LOOKING BACK AND REFLECTING

Conduct a five-minute reflection by asking each student to write down responses to his or her original questions about producing a newspaper. Make random pairs in the class. Members of each pair will alternate for one minute, each sharing one "I learned." After both have shared, each will select a new "I learned" and share it with the same partner for 30 seconds. After a third 15-second alternate sharing, each will summarize what was learned in a wraparound. When this round-robin is done, ask each student to use the 5W model to write a summary of the "I learned" statements.

BRIDGING FORWARD

Before the second edition, make a summary on the blackboard or posted on newsprint of the following:

a. What I did well in publishing this edition

b. What I want to do better in the next edition

c. Help I need for doing my job better

Assessing Student Performance

To what degree can each student

1. Identify the purpose for publishing a newspaper?

2. Understand how to budget for a profit?

3. Write a newspaper story using the 5W's?

4. Sell and design ad copy?

5. Collaborate with a team?

6. Assess his or her job performance?

Not Yet	**OK**	**Strong**	**Super**

Materials

Sample newspapers for all students, budget outline sheets or computer software, graphic materials, or computer software.

Variation

Set up any business that interests the students and has local resources: the bank, drugstore, variety store, book publishing house, and so on. Differentiate subteams by the jobs required.

Enriching Secondary Content in a Multiple Intelligences Framework

In secondary classrooms that are content dominated, another useful application of Gardner's theory is found in lessons that allow for the development of many intelligences without detracting from the core content. Indeed, the different intelligences enrich the unit or lesson and extend the possibilities for the mediation of individuation. In the advanced American history lesson below, note how the different intelligences are integrated as the means (a) for developing a deep understanding of each decade, (b) for mediating individuation, and (c) for promoting transference.

SECONDARY LESSON

It's Your Decade

Standard
To apply research skills in a historic context

Focus Intelligence
Verbal/Linguistic

Supporting Intelligences
Mathematical/Logical, Visual/Spatial, Intrapersonal

Mediation Emphasis
Individuation

CHECKING PRIOR KNOWLEDGE

Select a decade that you will use to model the process for identifying its *distinguishing* (define this word for students) characteristics. Divide the class into groups of three. Review roles and responsibilities of each group member (recorder, materials manager, leader). Assign each group one point of focus from this list: cultural, economic, artistic, military, political. Each group will use the dictionary to identify the meaning(s) of the assigned word, make a symbol for the word, and sketch pictures that represent the word. Regroup students into groups of five, one person having each word to teach to the others. After each word is shared with symbols, pictures, and explanations, the sharer will check for understanding among all group members.

STRUCTURING THE TASK

1. Reassemble the original trios. Each group will select a combination of homework, reading, lecturette, video, and/or group tasks to gather information about the decade. Each group will study the chapter with a focus on its assigned word (e.g., *economic).* The members will gather as much information on the assigned word for this decade as they can find. Once they have reviewed the information, they will create an advertisement that sells the specific benefits of that focus word in this decade. Each individual in a group will select the means of gathering information that best fits his or her abilities.

2. Each group will do a poster presentation with its advertisement. After all presentations are completed, put an attribute web on the board with five rays. Mediate an all-class discussion, the purpose of which is to select the five characteristics of this decade that most make it unique:
    a. What are the characteristics you want to nominate? Any others?
    b. Explain why your choice should stay in the selected five. What other reasons?

3. After all are given, clarified, and explained, use a five-to-fist vote. Each student has one 5-point, one 4-point, one 3-point, one 2-point, and one 1-point vote. Five is the vote for the most important characteristics. Every person will vote on each item on the list. Have two students count and one student record each tally. Place and number the top five on the web.

LOOKING BACK AND REFLECTING

1. Give a quiz with one or two important facts related to each of the subtopics.

2. Ask each student to summarize in a journal entry what was learned about his or her group's subtopic and why this subtopic was important for the decade.

3. Invite each student to select a means of communicating the learning according to his or her favored intelligence(s).

BRIDGING FORWARD

Invite students to review the steps for selecting the characteristics of a decade. Reflect on what learning skills and strategies they each learned and write a summary statement about "How I learn best."

Ask individuals to discuss how they might benefit from using these skills and strategies in the study of future decades. Facilitate individual action plans.

Variations

1. Provide original requirement materials such as literature, music, essays, and other artifacts from a decade.

2. Add final products such as video, drama, or poem that capture the key characteristics of a decade.

3. Have each group select a single decade to study.

Individuating Assessment

In addition to lessons and projects that promote individuation through multiple intelligences theory, the teacher can mediate any given lesson by selecting end products that individuate the assessment of student learning:

1. A final exam that asks questions that require hypothesizing, comparing, and summarizing (verbal/linguistic) in a research project

2. A concept map of the project's key ideas (visual/spatial)

3. Sample mathematical problems requiring solution that test problem-solving abilities (mathematical/logical)

4. Self-assessment that demonstrates the ability to perform a learned task according to a set of criteria (intrapersonal)

5. A written essay on the content of the project (verbal/linguistic)

Individualizing Individuation

Finally, individuation comes down to the questions that a mediator poses to an individual student. Through this questioning process, the mediator can mediate individuation by connecting the student's dominant way of knowing to the student's personal understanding of the topic. In this way, the teacher helps students develop their best ways to think and to act and says to the student, "You're in control of your thinking. Having studied this topic, now tell us what *you* think."

- "If you were to express this idea in a short story, what would be the conflict?" (verbal/linguistic)
- "If you were to express this idea as a symbol, what would it look like?" (visual/spatial)
- "Explain this idea as a math formula." (mathematical/logical)
- "Where would I find examples of this concept in the natural world?" (naturalist)
- "How might a musician express that?" (musical/rhythmic)
- "How does this idea affect your life?" (intrapersonal)
- "How could this idea help us get along better?" (interpersonal)
- "Show me how to express the idea through mime." (bodily/kinesthetic)

KEY POINTS TO REMEMBER

- Gardner established guidelines for assessing the quality application of his theory. Like the Social Security number, every individual is unique; everybody does not have to do the same thing, nor do they need the same thing.
- Differentiation of instruction is the key to mediation of individuation; the process is as important as the finished product.
- The mediation of individuation empowers students to establish an internal locus of control, make their own decisions, and think before acting.
- Did your parent ever tell you something similar to, "So if your friend jumped off a bridge, would you jump too?" That is an example of a parent's attempt at mediation of individuation.
- Mediation of individuation requires balance while allowing children to be their own persons, working on controlling their own behavior (internal locus of control) and respecting children's right to privacy.
- Students with the desire to have the teacher's undivided attention would benefit from mediation of individuation. Utilize the eight guidelines to help students become self-directed learners through the use of the multiple intelligences.
- Allow students to select which intelligence they will use while completing interdisciplinary units that revolve around themes and concepts. This allows for differentiating instruction.

SAMPLE LESSONS

Individuation comes down to students' having the chance to frame their own destiny. Teachers can mediate this process by helping students establish an internal locus of control. This locus helps students build their sense of ownership and responsibility for decisions made. The lessons below model ways that teachers can integrate the mediation of individuation into rich interdisciplinary learning projects that align with the standards.

ELEMENTARY PROJECT LESSON

Safe in the Neighborhood

Standard
Practicing behaviors for safety

Focus Intelligence
Verbal/Linguistic, Interpersonal

Supporting Intelligences
Intrapersonal, Visual/Spatial

Mediation Emphasis
Individuation

CHECKING PRIOR KNOWLEDGE

Gather the children in a circle around you. Use a large sheet of butcher paper on an easel to record their ideas. Ask them, "What are your favorite places in our neighborhood?" Start by printing yours on the paper. Give every child a chance to pick a different example.

STRUCTURING THE TASK

1. Sketch the major intersecting streets in the community that are around the school. Sketch an outline of the school and label it. Ask the children to select other sites around the school and label them on your map.

2. Ask the students to tell you what they have learned about the dangers in the neighborhood and staying safe in the neighborhood. Use a T-chart on the easel headed Dangers and Staying Safe. After the chart is done, go back and ask why it is important they keep themselves safe.

LOOKING BACK AND REFLECTING

Ask each child to share one thing he or she is going to do today to stay safe in the neighborhood.

BRIDGING FORWARD

Give all the children a set of crayons and paper. Invite them to draw a picture of how to stay safe.

Assessing Student Performance

Collect the drawings and hang them on the bulletin board with each child's name.

Variations

1. Take the children for a walk in the neighborhood to see the places they have named. Invite a community service officer to come along and talk to the children about staying safe.

2. Invite the children to make their own sketches of the neighborhood.

MIDDLE GRADES PROJECT LESSON

My Heritage

Standard
Compare and contrast different attributes of ethnic groups

Focus Intelligence
Verbal/Linguistic, Interpersonal

Supporting Intelligences
Intrapersonal, Visual/Spatial

Mediation Emphasis
Individuation

CHECKING PRIOR KNOWLEDGE

1. Match the students into pairs. Explain the word *heritage*. Ask the pairs to identify heritage in their families and what signs there are in their homes that represented this heritage.

2. Ask for volunteers to share their responses.

STRUCTURING THE TASK

1. Gather a collection of books about the various ethnic and racial groups in your class. Provide fiction and nonfiction. Encourage all students to select a book that deals with their heritage.

2. Provide all students with a copy of this reporting form. As they read, they can fill in the information for the first question.

Name _____   Book Title _____

Author _____   Heritage _____

1. What does this book tell you about your heritage? (List ideas as you read.)
2. What surprised you about your heritage?
3. What are the most important things that you learned about your heritage?
4. Why are they important to you?

LOOKING BACK AND REFLECTING

Match the students into groups of three. In each group, students share via a round-robin what was most important and why. After three rounds of sharing, the groups will compare responses and pick those that were most alike. When all are ready, each group will share one point that all its members hold in common.

BRIDGING FORWARD

1. Ask each student to write a letter to a parent or significant adult. In that letter, students should summarize what they have learned about their heritage and tell how they will benefit from this knowledge.

2. Ask students to make a visual representation of what they learned about their heritage. Post these for all to see.

Assessing Student Performance

Give an essay examination with requests such as

1. Tell the most important things you learned about your heritage.

2. Imagine that you are giving a speech to your classmates. What would you tell them is most important about your heritage?

3. Prepare a three-minute speech on your heritage for presentation to the class. Provide a rubric to guide the speech.

Variations

1. Invite a series of community leaders to speak about their heritage. Ask students to identify what is the same and what is different from their own heritages.

2. Visit a series of ethnic museums on field trips. Give students a Venn diagram to illustrate similarities and differences with their own heritage.

SECONDARY PROJECT LESSON

My American Heritage: A Cultural Investigation

Standard
Compare and contrast attributes

Focus Intelligence
Interpersonal

Supporting Intelligences
Intrapersonal, Visual/Spatial

Mediation Emphasis
Individuation

CHECKING PRIOR KNOWLEDGE

1. Ask students to identify their family's cultural heritage. As much as possible, assemble them in groups of three from different cultural heritages.

2. Ask each student in a group to identify what he or she thinks are the unique attributes of his or her cultural heritage. When this chart is done, the members can look to identify which characteristics or attributes are similar and which are different. Post these for all to see.

   Our Heritage

   A. _____ B. _____ C. _____

STRUCTURING THE TASK

1. Assign all students to research books, articles, movies, and so on that tell how their ancestors contributed to forming and influencing the American heritage. Show students how to make note cards with the source and author identified and a short summary of the ideas gathered. Differentiate by difficulty and number of materials.

2. Establish a timeline for completion of this task.

3. Provide each group with butcher paper, markers and crayons, magazines, and glue. Invite them to create a collage or sketch that shows the contributions made to the American heritage. Each group must then be prepared to explain what it has included and why. When giving the whys, the group will make reference to its research.

LOOKING BACK AND REFLECTING

1. After the presentations, ask each group to review its work with this rubric. (It helps to provide the rubric at the start of the project.)

   a. To what degree did you (Score: 1 low–5 high)
      • Include your research in your collage or sketch? _____
      • Show similarities and differences? _____
      • Explain your reasons? _____
      • Communicate contributions to the American heritage? _____

- Work together? _____
- Make your contributions to the group? _____

BRIDGING FORWARD

1. Ask all students to prepare an essay telling how they could show pride in their dual heritage.

2. Ask students to make a visual representation of how their family heritage fits within the American heritage.

Assessing Student Performance

1. Give an essay exam with a question asking students to identify those elements of their family heritage that contributed most to the American heritage.

2. Invite students to write an autobiography that highlights their dual heritages.

Variations

1. To gather research, ask students to construct an interview questionnaire for their parents or others in their community. The questionnaire should seek information on how the adults that the students know think about their cultural heritage and the American heritage.

2. Have the class select a school wall and create a wall mural (with permission) showing the results of their study of cultural and American heritage.

10

Goal Planning

Indecision is like the stepchild: if he doesn't wash his hands, he is called dirty; if he does, he is wasting water.

—Madagascan proverb

In a high-tech society where instant gratification is the norm, many young people do not stop to think of planning their time, developing goals, or looking to the future. From TV they learn that it is easier to grab the moment or to steal what they like, rip off a professional sports jacket or a high-priced pair of shoes, drive by homes and shoot gang rivals or innocent children, paint empty walls with graffiti signatures and gang signs, snort cocaine or smoke marijuana, or hang out at the mall or on the corner. Impulsive behavior is more fun.

THE MEDIATION OF GOAL PLANNING

When students live in an instant-gratification culture, especially when they are bombarded with images of wealth that they lack, the mediation of goal planning becomes a critical tool for countering impulsive behavior. Mediation of goal planning occurs when the teacher guides and directs the student through the processes involved in setting and planning strategies and in achieving short- and long-term goals. The mediator increases the effectiveness of the process by making it explicit so that students can take responsibility for charting their own accomplishments in achieving the goals.

As with other interactions that promote behavior control and reduce impulsive actions, the most effective goal planning occurs when it is connected to academic achievement. For students alienated from academics, though, the mediator may still use goal planning successfully to delay gratification and to control impulsive behavior. (In this regard, the mediation of goal planning is connected to the mediation of competence, regulation of behavior, individuation, challenge, and self-change.) The mediator will understand that the greater the impulsivity of a student or class, the greater the need to mediate goal planning.

FOUR ASPECTS OF GOAL SETTING

In mediating goal planning, it is helpful for the mediator to start with an explicit introduction of the process, with material the students are familiar with, or with non-serious material that does not distract the students from the goal-setting process. To introduce the process, the teacher can prepare a bulletin board or handout that details the three criteria for goal setting as they are embodied in a four-aspect plan for carrying out the process:

1. Set a target that is realistic and appropriate and discuss how it meets the ABC criteria:

   A = Achievable. Do the students see the goal as possible to reach, given their talents and limits?

   B = Believable. Have the students seen a similar goal accomplished by someone like themselves?

   C = Conceivable. Can students understand what it will take to achieve the goal?

2. Develop a step-by-step action plan to achieve the goal.

3. Evaluate the process used.

4. Finally, evaluate the result and make needed adjustments.

Using an academic lesson that the students have already mastered, mediators will illustrate how to use the four aspects of goal setting. First, on the board they will write and label the goal. For instance, if the students have learned how to balance an algebraic equation, mediators will designate that as the goal and then label the goal statement. This is Aspect 1. Next, they will list on the board the procedures or steps for balancing an equation and label these as Aspect 2, the "step-by-step action plan." Third, they will work a sample problem and point out how they are performing each step as they do it and label it Aspect 3. Finally, they will check to see if the solution is correct and label this as Aspect 4. When the modeling is complete, mediators will check for the students' understanding of the goal-setting process before applying the same procedure to new content.

From this point forward, each time teachers introduce new material, they will start with a review of the four aspects by asking students to explain each aspect and give examples from their experience. During the lesson, the mediator will ask different students to label and explain the goal-setting aspects as they occur (here is a good opportunity to use the Teacher Expectation Student Achievement, TESA, skills). At the end of the lesson or unit, mediators can use a variety of assessment strategies that engage the students in evaluating their content mastery and their use of the goal-setting process.

THE RUBRIC FOR GOAL PLANNING: STANDARDS AND CRITERIA

As teachers set goals for activities, lessons, or units with the class, they can reinforce the goal-setting behavior by sharing with the students the rubric by which the teachers will assess the students' work. The rubric outlines the standards and criteria that will enable the students and the teacher to assess the quality of their work. When coupled with curriculum content, framed either by applications of Gardner's multiple intelligences theory or by transfer-of-thinking strategies learned from Feuerstein's Instrumental Enrichment, the rubric creates a road map for students and teacher alike. Instead of allowing students to sit passively in the classroom without holding the teacher accountable or the student responsible, the rubric announces early on the performance expectations for everyone and reinforces the goal-planning process.

First, the mediator selects a standard and discusses it with the students. The mediator points out that this is not a lesson in which the class will simply cover certain material, as, for instance, "Today we will read Chapter 13, 'The Age of Discovery'" or "Today we will discuss Chapter 5, 'Understanding Fractions'" or "This week we're going to read and discuss *Hamlet*." Instead, the mediator will discuss with the class what abilities or understandings they will develop during this unit of study. For instance, if the content standard states that, as a result of activities in the unit, all students will develop the abilities to perform scientific inquiry, the mediator will explain and give an example of scientific inquiry. Second, the mediator will list what the students will learn and then review the criteria for the levels of performance the mediator will expect. For instance, the unit in scientific inquiry will show each student how to plan and conduct a simple investigation, use simple equipment to gather data, use the data to construct an explanation, and communicate the results.

The finished rubric, posted in the classroom, will look like this:

RUBRIC

Standard

You will show me that you can *perform* a scientific inquiry.

Content

You will learn how to do the following:

1. plan and complete a project that shows how energy flows;

2. use water beakers and other tools to gather data on your project;

3. explain with a labeled drawing the data you accumulated; and

4. make a presentation to the class about what you discovered.

Rubric (continued)

Performance Criteria

You and I will decide on the pluses and minuses of four products: your plan, your use of the tools, your drawing, and your presentation. We will use the scales shown below. After you mark each one, think about what data you have to back up your assessment.

To what degree:

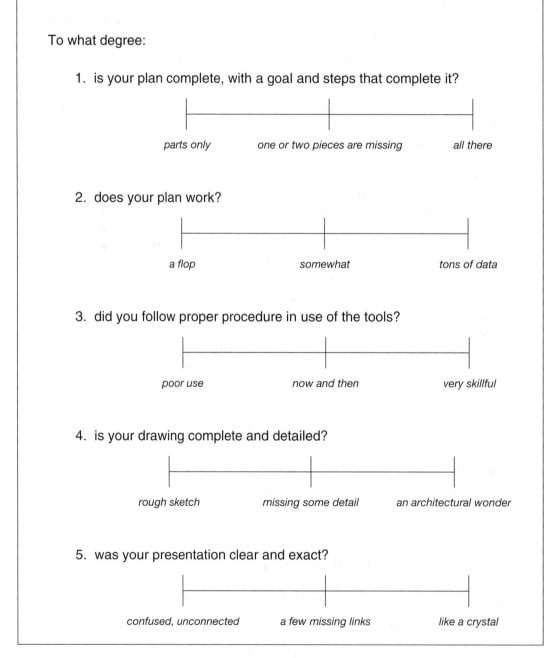

1. is your plan complete, with a goal and steps that complete it?

   parts only   *one or two pieces are missing*   *all there*

2. does your plan work?

   a flop   *somewhat*   *tons of data*

3. did you follow proper procedure in use of the tools?

   poor use   *now and then*   *very skillful*

4. is your drawing complete and detailed?

   rough sketch   *missing some detail*   *an architectural wonder*

5. was your presentation clear and exact?

   confused, unconnected   *a few missing links*   *like a crystal*

After mediators have reviewed the posted rubric, they have the option of providing samples of student work from previous years to illustrate the levels of performance. Finally, before they start the unit itself, they will convene a goal-setting session. A simple form for inclusion in students' portfolios, to use as a journal entry or to turn in for review by the teacher, will suffice.

Goal Setting

Name_____

Class_____   Date_____

Unit Title: Energy

My goals:

    1.

    2.

    3.

    4.

How I will achieve these goals:

    1.

    2.

    3.

    4.

Although it might benefit students for the teacher to mediate goal setting before every single lesson, it is most likely that time will not permit such coverage without a major abandonment of content in the curriculum. However, when starting new units of study, there is good evidence to support the use of time in introducing the goal-setting process at a unit's start and to revisit it through mediation as students work through and complete the project.

In the course of the project, the mediator may use such goal-planning interventions as

- "Let's review the process."
- "How does this step fit with your goal?"
- "What progress are you making toward the goal?"
- "Are there any steps you need to change?"
- "Are you running into any obstacles you didn't anticipate?"
- "Let's review our progress and redefine our aims."

REFLECTIVE GOAL-SETTING STRATEGIES

At the end of the project, the mediator can ask the students to assess the process used, the final products, and what content the students learned. This works best when the students take time to think or write in their journals before talking the project over. Here are some reflective strategies:

The 3-2-1 Goal-Planning Review

Direct students to form pairs. Each pair will have three minutes to review the goal-setting process as it was used in the unit just completed. Next, give the pairs two minutes to discuss what they learned from the experience about planning. Finally, each pair will develop in one minute a key question to ask the class about the completed goal planning. Write three to five questions on the board and spend three minutes sharing answers for each.

Five-Minute Think-Pair-Share

Give all students two minutes to think about and write down five things they learned about the goal-planning process in this unit. Next, pair the students and have each pair share their respective lists (allow one minute each). Partners should not repeat ideas heard from their partners. Continue the alternate talk for another 30 seconds each. Do a third alternate talk with no repeats for 15 seconds each. (Adapt this strategy to products or to content.)

Goal-Processing Wraparound

Give the students 30 to 60 seconds to think about and complete one of these stems:

"About goal planning I learned . . ."

"In this lesson, I improved my goal planning by . . ."

"In this lesson, the aspect of goal planning that I performed best was . . ."

Goal-Planning PMI

Present all students with a plus-minus-interesting questions (PMI) chart. Ask them to note what the pluses were about their goal planning in this unit. Repeat the notations for the minuses (Column 2) and interesting questions (Column 3).

P	
M	
I	

Three Questions for Reflection

Ask each student to think about or write about in a journal the goal planning used in this unit:

1. What was important about the goal planning you just completed?

2. How can you apply goal planning to other school tasks?

3. What steps will you take to use goal planning with another school task?

KEY POINTS TO REMEMBER

- The four main aspects of goal setting are to set a realistic target, develop a step-by-step action plan, evaluate the process, and evaluate the result; goals should be measurable, attainable, and in writing.
- Rubrics establish the standards and criteria prior to student work and shared with the students.
- The ABC criteria: goals have to be achievable, believable, and conceivable.

ELEMENTARY LESSON

Goal Setting Activity—Score

Standard
Develop strategies for decision making

Focus Intelligence
Bodily/Kinesthetic

Supporting Intelligence
Verbal/Linguistic

Mediation Emphasis
Goal Planning

CHECKING PRIOR KNOWLEDGE

Young students see many games on TV—basketball, soccer, football. They know that the object of most games is to score high. *Baskets, goals,* and *touchdowns* are common terms to them. Ask the class to brainstorm all the sports in which scoring points is important. List the sport and the way a player scores points (e.g., touchdown).

STRUCTURING THE TASK

1. Explain the connection between a goal in a game (e.g., touchdown, basket) and a goal in life (something we want).

2. Place a wastebasket on a chair. On the floor in front of the basket, mark thee lines (each two feet in length) that are at least three feet apart. Give each line a point value: one point for the line closest to the basket, two points for the middle line, and three points for the line most distant from the wastebasket.

3. Divide the class into four teams. Each team will have three minutes to get the highest score it can. All members must have a chance to shoot from one of the numbered lines.

4. Give each team three minutes to agree on a strategy. Points are scored by a "basket" times the line total (so, one shot scored from line 3 = 3 points, five shots from 3 = 15). Have a box of crumpled 8½" × 11" paper ready for each round.

5. Total the points on the board after each round for each team. Highest total wins.

LOOKING BACK AND REFLECTING

Ask each team to explain and judge its strategy in relation to its goal. Discuss what they would do differently the next time.

BRIDGING FORWARD

Each team will discuss and share this idea: "Scoring points in this game is like goal setting in life because _____ ."

Assessing Student Performance

Use a rubric to check students' knowledge and skill with goal setting.

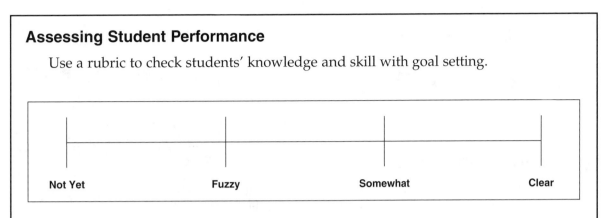

To what degree can the student

1. Explain the term *goal?*
2. Explain why goal setting is important (in general)?
3. Explain why goal setting is important in learning to read or do math?
4. Pick a strategy and explain its advantages and disadvantages?
5. Demonstrate the strategy in reading or math?

Materials

Wastebasket, crumpled paper, chalk

Variation

Each day for the next two weeks, allow the same teams to improve on their previous day's performance. Give three minutes to plan strategy beforehand and three minutes to evaluate after. At the end of the week, ask teams to explain in their own words the difference between a "strategy" and a "goal."

MIDDLE GRADES LESSON

Mapping a Plan

Standard
How to make a plan

Focus Intelligence
Visual/Spatial

Supporting Intelligences
Interpersonal, Intrapersonal,
Verbal/Linguistic

Mediation Emphasis
Goal Planning

CHECKING PRIOR KNOWLEDGE

Divide the class into pairs. Give each pair a large sheet of paper and a marker. On the board or overhead, list these situations:

1. Reaching the moon

2. Finding the Wizard of Oz

3. Discovering Atlantis

4. Traveling to the Antarctic

5. Visiting Grandmother's house

Ask students to identify the common elements in each (someone taking a trip, going someplace, having a goal based on a story, etc.). After you have discussed the items, tell each pair to select one as a basis for a planning task they will complete together.

STRUCTURING THE TASK

1. Identify and define each of the following words:

    Goal: a desired state or place

    Pitfall: a trap

    Barrier: a block or obstacle

2. On the paper, each pair will sketch its starting point and its goal. (Model on the overhead or board.)

    * The Goal

    * The Start

3. They will sketch at least three alternate paths from the start to the goal. Each path will have at least three different pitfalls or barriers. They should sketch these in place. No words are to be used.

4. They will sketch in a picture of the means by which they propose to avoid the pitfalls and bypass the barriers.

LOOKING BACK AND REFLECTING

After you have joined pairs into fours, instruct the pairs to use the ABC interview sheet (see sample lesson, The ABCs of Scoring Goals, below). Each pair will be in the focus for eight minutes to describe its chart and the thinking used to make decisions and to respond to the ABC interview.

BRIDGING FORWARD

Introduce these two stems:

About goal planning—

1. An idea I can use in other classes . . .

2. I wonder what will happen when . . .

Use an all-class wraparound to hear the responses.

Assessing Student Performance

Assign students to write an essay about the process of goal setting. They must use personal examples to illustrate. Provide a rubric for evaluating the essays.

Variations

1. Assign students to mixed ability groups of three. Give each group a target to find on a map of the school. Provide a goal that they must reach and select the class period when all groups will take their maps to find the target.

2. Invite students to interview a friend, family member, and so forth on the topic of professional or personal goals. How did the goal setting help or hinder the individual from achieving his or her goals? What advice would they share to help the interviewer meet his or her goals? Students can use this information while protecting confidentiality to discuss the goal-setting process.

SECONDARY LESSON

The ABCs of Scoring Goals

Standard
How to evaluate goals

Focus Intelligence
Visual/Spatial

Supporting Intelligences
Verbal/Linguistic, Interpersonal, Intrapersonal

Mediation Emphasis
Goal Planning

CHECKING PRIOR KNOWLEDGE

Ask students to define the word *goal* as they know it and list synonyms (*desires, wishes, wants,* etc.) and types of goals (career, educational, personal, etc.) that they have. Then have them fill in a copy of this chart in their logs:

Goals		
Meaning	**Synonyms**	**Types**

STRUCTURING THE TASK

1. Share this information with a jigsaw: realistic problem solving begins with the ABCs of goal setting: A = achievable, B = believable, and C = conceivable. These three criteria can help students measure the quality of their goals. Consider each of these criteria.

   First, *achievable:* an achievable goal is one that individuals can trace, step by step, from their current place to the actual attainment. This means that the goal is clear and explicit. On the long climb to the goal, individuals know each step in sequence, which steps are critical, and which steps may need some adjusting. For instance, Sue, an outstanding 15-year-old tennis player, wants to reach her goal of playing professional tennis. She has thought carefully about what she must do. She knows, for instance, that she might practice a minimum of four hours per day, continue her weight program, control her diet as prescribed by a nutritionist, strengthen her serve, and so on. By breaking her long-term goal into manageable sequenced steps, she makes her goal more achievable.

   Second, *believable:* a believable goal is one that is built on a careful assessment of what is within one's grasp. Each of us will refine our vision of what is possible to us by our experience. Direct experience can be the best teacher; indirect experience also helps. For instance, Sue's mother may not find her goal of a career in professional tennis to be very believable because the mother has neither known of nor heard about an "ordinary" young woman becoming a pro tennis player; the dream is virtually unbelievable. Sue and her mother both need concrete models. For Sue's mother, there are none. Sue, however, has read about women pros in *Sports Illustrated*, has seen women's tennis at Wimbledon, has watched Serena and Venus Williams on television, has attended a local tournament, has a Steffi Graf autograph, and has interviewed her next-door neighbor, a pro women's coach, for the high school magazine. Sue's firsthand contact with women pros makes her goal believable.

Third, *conceivable:* a conceivable goal is one built on solid assessment of one's strengths and weaknesses. The assessment is solid to the degree that one has good evidence from reliable sources of what one can and cannot do. Sue's coach is a reliable source. Weekly she reviews a videotape of Sue's practice. Together they keep a tally of how well Sue does with each different type of shot. They measure strength, accuracy, and attention. They can compare Sue's skills to others' in her ability class, as well as to women pros, to evaluate her capability.

The ABCs of goal setting will help students clarify their goals and make them more realistic. When taken together, the ABCs help the students form a more realistic picture of what is desired and the best means to that goal. By learning to use the ABC approach, the students give themselves a tool that will set a very positive and clarifying framework for substantive problem solving.

2. Divide the students into groups of three. Assign numbers 1, 2, and 3 to the students in each group.

3. Introduce the words *clarify, extend, focus,* and *support* by writing them on the board or overhead. Solicit several explanations and examples of each word. Instruct students to add the words to their vocabulary lists in the notes.

4. The person assigned the number 1 is the focus person. The other two in the group will focus their complete attention on the focus person for six minutes. After the focus person has had no more than three minutes to describe his or her goal with no interruptions from the others, they will ask goal-clarifying questions and extending questions to draw out the focus person. In no way will they argue with the focus person. They will use good eye contact, positive body language, and give nonverbal support to that person's responses. They will alternate questions for the final three minutes.

5. The focus person may select one of the following areas to share with his or her group:

   a. A career goal
   b. A skill goal
   c. An academic goal
   d. A product goal
   e. A task goal
   f. A personal relationship goal
   g. A personal improvement goal
   h. A family goal
   i. A spiritual goal
   j. A physical goal
   k. A financial goal

The focus person will describe the goal as specifically as possible in the three minutes. One member will keep time. The focus person may wish to describe the reasons for the goal, the advantages, how it was selected, what benefits it might bring, the hardships that it presents, and so on.

6. After listening for three minutes maximum, the others in the group will alternate with questions using the ABC approach. All questions must come from this area unless it is necessary for the listeners to ask a clarifying question such as "Can you be more specific?" or "Can you give us an example?" ("Why?" and "Do you think . . .?" questions are out of bounds.)

7. Conduct a model interview. Select a goal from your life and share it with the class. Have a timekeeper stop you after three minutes. Invite students to select questions from the list for you to answer. Do not forget the pass rule. In fact, this is a good chance to model that it is okay to say "I pass." After three or four questions, check for understanding by asking for thumbs up, and so on. On the instructions for the focus interview, clarify as needed and put the groups to work for the first round.

8. At the end of the time, instruct the focus person to give a specific "I appreciate . . ." to each partner for the assistance provided and to write into his or her log the original goal statement or any change made because of the clarification and support.

9. While the first focus person is completing a log entry, the others may prepare their goal statements. When you signal, the next person in the group will become the focus person. Complete this round as the first. When the second log entry is done, the third person will move to the focus and complete the round.

LOOKING BACK AND REFLECTING

Using a classroom wraparound, ask students in turn to respond to your processing lead-in: "From this goal-clarifying activity, I learned . . ." Encourage all to listen carefully to the ideas. Ask volunteers to identify the similarities between the ideas heard. Have a student list these on paper or the blackboard. When several are listed, seek multiple responses to the following questions: "What conclusions can you draw from this list of similarities? Why? What general statements can you make about the worth or value of asking goal-clarifying questions? What might be some appropriate times or situations for you to ask yourself goal-clarifying questions?"

BRIDGING FORWARD

Instruct students to use their logs. They might pick a different goal from the one first discussed in their groups. In their logs, have them write down one appropriate question they might ask themselves in each of the three ABC areas for that goal.

Assessing Student Performance

1. Assign students to plan a personal academic goal for the remainder of the year. Use the ABC model to structure the task. Require a weekly journal entry to monitor progress.

2. Assign students to write an essay or to create a collage that illustrates how they incorporate goal setting into their own lives. Provide an assessment rubric.

Variation

Hold an outdoor event with the wellness teacher. Have each student select three physical challenges. (e.g., sit-ups, a distance run). The students may work in pairs to chart their ABC goals and plans for the next two weeks. At appropriate times, they can record progress to their goals.

11

Challenge

When someone is taught the joy of learning, it becomes a lifelong process that never stops, a process that creates a logical individual. That is the challenge and joy of teaching.

—Marva Collins (Riley, 1993)

Researchers who try to understand what makes an effective teacher seldom seem to follow Marva Collins's advice about the joy of learning. Instead, they seem devoted to the behaviorist model and hold instead that the effective teacher has a pocketful of motivational tricks and techniques, the effectiveness of which can be easily measured. According to author Alfie Kohn (1993), these techniques fall into two categories: rewards and punishments. Rewards are good grades, gold stars, praise, and warm fuzzies; punishments are low grades, criticism, time-out or detention, and the forbidding "call home."

Kohn, Feuerstein, and others build on the tradition that prefers intrinsic motivation. In the mediation of challenge, the next criterion of mediating interactions, the mediator creates conditions and opportunities for students to achieve. These opportunities allow for the development of intrinsic motivation for completion of tasks that evoke feelings of interest, excitement, and determination, even though tasks may appear difficult. With support, encouragement, and mediation for challenge, students discover potentials previously unknown.

THE MEDIATION OF CHALLENGE

Consider students in two different elementary mathematics classrooms. In one, the teacher hands out a worksheet with 54 number problems. She tells the students what to do and then sits down at her desk. If a student has a question, he lines up to the right of the teacher's desk and waits his turn. In the other classroom, the teacher sits her students in groups of three. She gives each group a cup of dry corn and a cup of marbles. She asks each group to take out three pieces of corn and four marbles from the cups. The group has to agree quickly on the number of "pieces" they have. She repeats the process several times. Each time, the problem becomes more difficult. The children become more excited with each new chal-

> In the mediation of challenge, the mediator creates conditions and opportunities for students to achieve.

lenge. When all the corn and marbles are on the tables, she asks them to explain what they learned about adding the pieces. After their talk, she gives them the first numbers to add. Once again, as they succeed, she ups the ante with a more difficult problem.

When a teacher or parent mediates challenge, as in the second example, the students experience in their academics what novice skiers experience on the mountainside. First, there is the tension of the bunny hill. After the instructor coaches the skiers down the hill without a fall or picks up and restarts those who do fall, the novices return to the course on their own. As their confidence grows, the skiers tire: gone is the novelty of the initial challenge. Now they are sure and ready for the green runs. Once these are mastered, the skiers are ready for the tougher blue runs and, ultimately, for the double black diamond run. Do these students receive stickers and stars for each new triumph? No—their reward is the internal excitement and pleasure that comes with conquering fears, taking risks, and pushing their limits.

CREATING CHALLENGES

What do mediators do to create the challenges? First, they model an open and excited attitude about taking on the tougher word problem. As the student's body language and oral expression say, "Oh, my goodness, I'll never do that," the mediator encourages, "I know this is tough, but I also know what you can do. Together we can do this."

Second, mediators prepare a sequence of increasingly challenging and complex tasks. They chart the way for the students and show them how they will conquer the bunny hill to get ready for the tougher runs. And mediators give them a novel perspective: instead of the boring, repetitive worksheets that get "done" and filed, the mediator provides hands-on, activity-based situations that grow in difficulty, which the students see they will be able to conquer one at a time while their confidence grows.

Third, mediators encourage creativity, curiosity, and originality in performing the tasks. As students master the basic steps, mediators provide more difficult tasks and challenge the students to figure new ways to solve the problem: "Tell me another idea you have." "What's a different way?" The students try out their methods in search of the best approach.

Fourth, mediators encourage appropriate risk taking. They push the students to use new approaches in the strategies they want to try. "Will this stretch you? Will this take you out of your comfort zone?"

Fifth, mediators help students reflect on the reasons for their successes, identify their best work strategies, and build patterns of thinking into their methods.

Mediators communicate their observations of the students' work with enthusiasm and excitement about their satisfaction with their progress. They place special emphasis on what the students have chosen to do and what they have accomplished: "You picked this strategy; you made it work."

THREE THINGS NOT TO DO

What a parent or teacher does not do may be as important as what he or she does do to mediate challenge. First, the mediator does not rescue students by interfering with or performing the task or answering the question. A mediator who steps in too soon without good wait time and takes over the task is denying students the necessary practice and the opportunity to correct mistakes.

> What a parent or teacher does not do may be as important as what he or she does do to mediate challenge.

Second, the mediator *avoids* using extrinsic behavior modification, especially with conditional promises of rewards: "If you do this, then I'll give you . . ." Conditional rewards build a student's dependency on the reward. As the student is satisfied with a small reward, the expectation of a bigger reward soon follows: first, the new pair of shoes; next, an expensive dress—how long before the car keys? Once caught in the extrinsic reward trap, students lose focus on the fact that they had positive feelings about overcoming an obstacle that they had approached with uncertainty.

Third, the mediator *avoids* making the task seem insurmountable. Using the ski analogy, the mediator doesn't take the novice to the tip of the black diamond slope and say, "Ski down, I know you can do it." Risk that appears overwhelming is only discouraging.

INTEGRATING THINKING ACROSS THE CURRICULUM

In the mediated classroom, a skillful teacher may initiate the mediation of challenge by asking increasingly difficult questions. The three-story intellect model provides one approach.

At first glance, this model appears to be a mere simplification of Bloom's taxonomy. However, unlike Bloom's monumental list, which so many teachers, ironically enough, were asked to memorize, the three-story model is a useful tool for providing teachers with a challenging framework for increasing the challenge level of their mediational questions. All of the thinking skills detailed at each story were selected because of their regular and implicit use in the standard curriculum. For instance, it is a rare fourth-grade reading curriculum that does not ask students to begin making inferences, a "second-story" skill that is essential for reading comprehension. In algebra, introduced to most students in the ninth grade, students are called upon to learn about logic. In quality high school composition programs, it is a regular practice to expect students to write essays that compare and contrast characters, genres, and thematic treatments and to forecast story endings.

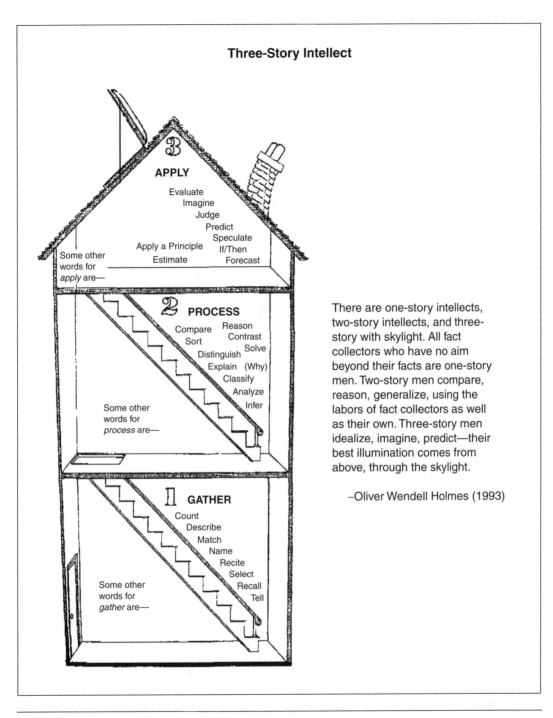

Three-Story Intellect

③ APPLY

Evaluate
Imagine
Judge
Predict
Speculate
Apply a Principle   If/Then
Estimate   Forecast

Some other words for *apply* are—

② PROCESS

Compare   Reason
Sort   Contrast
Distinguish   Solve
Explain (Why)
Classify
Analyze
Infer

Some other words for *process* are—

① GATHER

Count
Describe
Match
Name
Recite
Select
Recall
Tell

Some other words for *gather* are—

There are one-story intellects, two-story intellects, and three-story with skylight. All fact collectors who have no aim beyond their facts are one-story men. Two-story men compare, reason, generalize, using the labors of fact collectors as well as their own. Three-story men idealize, imagine, predict—their best illumination comes from above, through the skylight.

–Oliver Wendell Holmes (1993)

SOURCE: Bellanca and Fogarty (2003)

USING THE THREE-STORY INTELLECT MODEL

In the challenge classroom, the teacher can use the three-story intellect model to stretch how students interact with the content in three ways. First, the model can be used to ask increasingly difficult questions in a discussion of the content. The teacher can check for understanding of the material by asking first-story questions, followed by second- and third-story questions:

1. Name the country with the largest land area in _____.

2. Compare the exports of that country to the exports of _____.

3. Predict the impact on world trade if this country's exports were closed to U.S. buyers.

Second, a teacher can mediate challenge by using the three-story model to restructure his or her curriculum. There are two elements used for restructuring a curriculum: content and process. For each of these, the restructuring starts with the realignment of goals ("goal planning"). In current practice, much of what happens in many classrooms is coverage of the textbook and completion of workbooks. In the question-centered classroom, the center of attention is given to deepening the student's understanding of the key concepts in a course.

> In the question-centered classroom, the center of attention is the student's understanding of key concepts in a course.

To bring concepts into focus, the teacher who wants to mediate challenge will begin with the question, "When students finish this course, what will they know and be able to do?" After the teacher has answered this question, he or she will ask, "What resources do I have that will help students accomplish the key concepts and skills?" From the text and other materials, the teacher will select the supporting resources.

In a challenge classroom, the text provides the students with a major resource, not chapters to cover. The teachers will select the chapters and pages that will most help with answering their questions. For the material they select from the text, they will ask, "How will this material help the students achieve the objectives?" By implication, their choices will retain the most important information and throw out the unrelated or extraneous material.

This selection process, called selective abandonment, is one that most teacher candidates cover in their undergraduate preparation; unfortunately, they receive little practice in the art of selective abandonment. When they take their first jobs, the system gives little or no support to concept-based instruction. Immediately, the text-books and workbooks become the unselective guides that the novice must learn to cover chapter by chapter in 36 weeks. Indeed, the definition of *cover* as "to conceal" becomes a reality!

Take for instance a first-year teacher in a ninth-grade English class. On the first day of inservice in her career, she listens to a motivational speaker, attends a departmental meeting where she is handed her temporary list of students, the texts she will use, and her classroom number. The text looks familiar—it's the same one she used as a high school student. That night, she goes home and opens her lesson plan book next to the text. In the plan book, she jots down what she will do the first week: "Monday: take roll and hand out texts; review classroom rules. Tuesday: read about the Anglo-Saxon period; *Beowulf*. Wednesday: Anglo-Saxon slide show. Thursday: *Beowulf*. Friday: *Beowulf* test." To prepare for the class lectures, she pulls out the notes from her college survey course, English Literature 101.

M	T	W	Th	F
Roll Texts Rules	Read Anglo-Saxon History	Read *Beowulf*	Slides and *Beowulf* discussion	Test

How different it would be if she took the knowledge that she gained about literature and asked herself the question, "At the end of this course, what will the students know and be able to do?" Part of her answer might look like this: "My students will understand how great literature can inform our lives and help us make more thoughtful decisions in challenging situations" or "My students will be able to write a coherent three-paragraph essay explaining how the literature they read informed their lives." With these answers in mind, how much easier and productive it would be to restructure the first and subsequent weeks:

"Monday: take roll and ask students how literature may have informed their lives; give an example and use TESA [Teacher Expectation Student Achievement] behaviors to engage all; state expectations for course related to this discussion. Tuesday: introduce any writing expectations in a daily journal entry—each will react to literature read before we hold a classroom discussion. Tie their reflections to how literature informs our lives. Read and discuss Dr. King's *Letter From the Birmingham Jail* as it relates to their past knowledge and experience. Journal entry—'What meaning does this letter have for us?' Wednesday: discuss journal entry and provide a summary of *Beowulf*; discuss the story and its connection to the King letter. Journal entry—'How does *Beowulf* inform our lives?' Thursday: rewrite journal entries. Friday: introduce writing process. Do Venn diagram of two authors—informing our lives; review entries and discuss connection between the King letter and *Beowulf*."

M	Roll and Expectations Ask: How does literature inform our lives?
T	Journals: Reflections on literature
W	King's letter: How does it inform our lives?
Th	Compare *Beowulf* and King's letter New journal reflections
F	Writing lesson: Use Venn diagram to compare the two works with our lives.

Obviously, the second plan leaves out much that is offered in the textbook. The second plan, however, is more directly connected with the two objectives selected as a focus for the course. As the semester moves on, the teacher will ignore a lot of the literature and historic exposition in the 723-page text. As she proceeds through the course, she will select that literature that best helps the students relate literature to life as they develop their basic expository writing skills. By the end of the course, it is highly likely that these students will have a greater appreciation for, a greater understanding of, and a greater knowledge base about the required literature than they would have had if the teacher had stayed with the coverage method. In addition, by using the second core objective as a tool for communicating about the first, she will have students better able to produce a meaningful essay than if she had used the typical "fill-in-the-time" format with unconnected writing tasks.

In addition to restructuring curriculum so that less is truly more, teachers can take advantage of the three-story model to increase the challenge level of their tasks. For instance, in the ninth-grade example, teachers might spend the first quarter of the year structuring writing assignments that require students to improve the quality of their information gathering (first story). As they read the literature and background material, teachers can focus their attention on the story line, facts about the characters, and settings and historical background. Practice essays will ask the students to give details and describe with facts. As the students become more precise in these tasks, teachers can move the written assignments to the second story by asking them to use the gathered information to compare and contrast and to explain why. In the second half of the year, the students are ready to go to the third story and respond to essay tasks that require evaluation, prediction, and synthesis.

A third use of the three-story intellect occurs when teacher-mediators use the model to teach students how to inquire. After posting the three-story model, they can demonstrate to the class the techniques they are using to ask questions in the discussions and in structuring their writing assignments. To make use of what the students have learned about asking questions, the teachers can use think-pair-share groups, which begin with the students developing their own questions about the material they are studying. This can be as simple as allowing time at the end of each unit for pairs to structure questions about the material studied and posing them to the class.

OTHER QUESTION-ASKING STRATEGIES

Question-asking strategies that challenge students can take other forms too.

Question Web

At the end of the lesson, pair students. Each pair is to review the lesson material and form a question (what? why? when? where? or how?) about some part they don't understand or a part that is important to highlight. After all pairs have come up with a question (allow five minutes), call on students at random to provide questions. On the board or overhead, use a web to write the questions. After you have all the questions (don't duplicate any), guide a discussion to answer each one. Use your own extending questions so that students have the first chance to answer.

Three-to-One Technique

Ask questions that allow at least three possible answers. In trios, each student will give one possible answer for the recorder to write. Ask a follow-up question that challenges students to agree on the one best answer from the trio's list. They can rank or combine ideas. The checker checks to see if (a) all members agree (members signal thumbs up), (b) each member can explain the selected answer, and (c) each member can tell why that answer was selected. Members should rehearse (b) and (c) before signing the group's worksheet to indicate "I agree," "I can explain," and "I can tell why we decided on this."

Newspaper Graphic

Give each pair of students a copy of the following graphic with instructions to use the completed material as the source for the format.

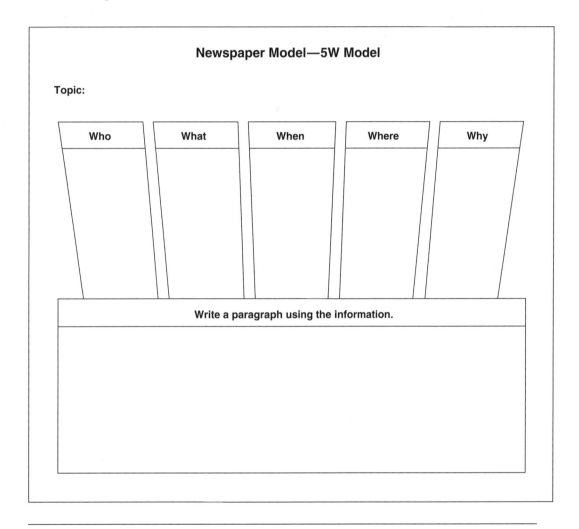

SOURCE: Bellanca and Fogarty (2003)

Beyond strategies that mediate challenge, the mediating teacher can build lessons that challenge students to rely on their own observations, thinking patterns, and ability to generalize in order to construct meaning and deepen understanding. Note in the following lessons how teacher-mediators have structured lessons that teach key curricular concepts (e.g., circumference, community) by starting with concrete experiences and ending with generalizations that challenge.

KEY POINTS TO REMEMBER

- In the mediation of challenge, the mediator creates conditions and opportunities for students to achieve at increasingly more difficult levels.
- The do's and don'ts of mediating challenge are identified: modeling excitement and enthusiasm, preparing a sequence of increasingly challenging and complex tasks, encouraging appropriate risk taking and originality in performing the tasks.
- Reflection after question asking are the keys for improvement through challenge.
- The three-story intellect model, similar in nature to Bloom's taxonomy, is a visual to assist teachers in developing questions, tasks, and tests that require students to think in response to more challenging questions from Levels 2 and 3 and not simply to regurgitate information (Level 1 questions).

ELEMENTARY LESSON

Problem-Solving Stories

Standard
Problem Solving

Focus Intelligence
Verbal/Linguistic

Supporting Intelligences
Interpersonal, Visual/Spatial

Mediation Emphasis
Challenge

CHECKING PRIOR KNOWLEDGE

Post a problem-solving observation study sheet for the students to use. Select a strong reader to read each behavior and lead the class in a choral reading review. Indicate that you will use the chart again as you observe them practicing the behaviors during the group work for this lesson.

Problem-Solving Worksheet

1. Name the problem.

2. Name solutions to the problem.

3. Check which are the best solutions.

4. Tell how the best solutions were made.

STRUCTURING THE TASK

1. Select a story on video. (You may use this same lesson outline for several problem-solving practice lessons.) Following is a selection of story videos. Be sure to pre-view each one to determine the spots in the story where you want to stop to have the students discuss the questions. (You may wish to substitute a story that you read to the class. Use the same questions at the appropriate spot in each story. If you have sufficient readers, before the video or in place of the video, have a reader in each group read the story and stop at the places you indicate so that the groups can discuss the questions.)

Stories Available on Video

How the Elephant Got His Trunk	*The Staunch Tin Soldier*	*Hansel and Gretel*
The Tinder Box	*Little Tom Thumb*	*Rumpelstiltskin*
The Emperor's New Clothes	*The Frog Prince*	*The Boy Who Cried Wolf*
Sleeping Beauty	*Tale of the Ugly Duckling*	*The Ears of King Midas*

2. Before you start the video, divide the class into trios. Use cards with colored dots to determine the jobs in each group. The reader will read the questions and the story, if you elect that approach; the recorder will write the answers; the checker will make sure that all members agree with each answer.

3. Give a copy of the problem-solving worksheet to each recorder.

4. Tell students that you will stop the video as soon as the problem or challenge is identified. Review the questions on the problem-solving observation chart that the group will use at this spot. After you have shown the video or told the story, allow five minutes for each group to fill in the first block on their problem-solving worksheet, The Problem.

5. Repeat the procedure for each of the remaining two blocks. Tell where you will stop, review the appropriate problem-solving behaviors, and allow five minutes after the video.

LOOKING BACK AND REFLECTING

Ask for sample responses to each of the blocks. Write the samples on the board and discuss the variations. Encourage the class to agree on a single response. Do not suggest or give an answer. Summarize what each group reports, and ask for agreements. Finalize the agreement for each block on the chart before you proceed to the next one. When you are gathering the data from the groups, avoid going back to the same groups.

BRIDGING FORWARD

1. Invite the groups to write the following on the back of the problem-solving worksheet: (a) a lesson they learned from how the character(s) in this story solved the problem and (b) what problem-solving behaviors from the chart they used well. Sample the responses to each question. After the groups have shared their answers to the second question, use the chart to give your feedback on the problem-solving behaviors you observed. Post it for the class to see.

2. Chart the students' uses of the problem-solving behaviors so they can see their own progress. You may wish to add an incentive for the class to reach certain milestones. Use of the chart will benefit the students most if you use this same lesson outline with a sequence of stories and mediate for challenge as each story becomes more difficult.

Materials

Problem-solving observation charts, selected video, TV, video player, index cards, colored dots, problem-solving worksheet, masking tape

Variations

1. If video equipment is not available, select a story to read to the class.

2. For Looking Back and Reviewing, mediate challenge by asking students to discuss (a) the challenges faced by the story characters, (b) how each dealt with the challenge, and (c) what students could learn from the characters about challenges.

MIDDLE GRADES LESSON

Heritage Heroes

Standard
Identify sources of information, including traits, behaviors, characteristics

Focus Intelligence
Visual/Spatial

Supporting Intelligences
Interpersonal, Verbal/Linguistic

Mediation Emphasis
Challenge

CHECKING PRIOR KNOWLEDGE

1. Create one or more webs on a bulletin board labeled Heritage Heroes. (Make one web for each culture represented in the class.)

2. Invite students to make a name card for each famous person they can identify by name. Place it on the appropriate web. Invite students to tell what they know about the nominees.

STRUCTURING THE TASK

To the webs already started, add names that were not nominated.

1. Invite each student to select one name from the web. Allow one week for each student to research the person. Have the student get the following information:
   a. Who is this person? (important dates and facts)
   b. What contributions did he or she make?
   c. What challenges did he or she overcome?
   d. What lessons can we learn from his or her life?

   Show students how to use index cards to record answers and identify the source of information.

2. Instruct each student to write a five-paragraph essay (one beginning, three middle, one end) that answers the questions. Discuss the indicators of success you will use. Discuss with each student the first draft and correct grammar, spelling, structure, and so on.

3. Collect, review, and post the final drafts.

4. Randomly assign three students to a group. The group will identify how the different heroes are alike and different in their thinking, beliefs, and attitudes.

5. Give each group time to plan and produce a five-minute meeting of the heroes on a TV interview show. The heroes will discuss a current event. Afterward, the group members will each explain why their characters argued for a certain point. (To allow time for this pageant, play only two or three presentations per day.)

LOOKING BACK AND REFLECTING

Ask the students to discuss what lessons they learned about facing challenges from the heroes. How might they apply the same resources in facing their everyday lives?

BRIDGING FORWARD

Invite all students to write a letter to their character. The letter will explain what lessons the students learned and how the students will apply that lesson to their own life. Be sure to review the indicators of success before they write.

Assessing Student Performance

1. To what degree does the five-paragraph essay respond to the four questions in a clear and concise manner?

2. To what degree does the group presentation capture the beliefs and ideas of the characters?

3. To what degree does the letter make a significant application of the character's best qualities?

Materials

Bulletin board, tacks or tape, multicolored paper, markers or crayons, index cards

Variations

1. Allow groups of three to do the research on a character.

2. Make a complete pageant with authentic costumes for each character.

3. In place of the essay, assign students to make a collage for each character.

4. In place of the current events discussion, give each group a current social problem to solve from the perspective of the heroes. Let them enact the solution in a miniplay.

HERITAGE HEROES

African Americans

Muhammad Ali
Marian Anderson
Maya Angelou
Louis Armstrong
Arthur Ashe
James Baldwin
Mary McLeod Bethune
Gwendolyn Brooks
Ronald Brown
Ray Charles
Dr. William "Bill" and Camille Cosby
Ossie Davis and Ruby Dee
W. E. B. DuBois
Paul Lawrence Dunbar
Medgar Evers
Min. Louis Farrakhan
Marcus Garvey
Nikki Giovanni
Berry Gordy
Dick Gregory
Alex Haley
Fannie Lou Hamer
Asa Hilliard
Zora Neale Hurston
John H. Johnson
Langston Hughes
Ron Karenga
Rev. Dr. Martin Luther Jr. and Coretta Scott King
Betty and Malcolm X (El Hajj Malik-Al-Shabazz)
Thurgood Marshall
Jesse Owens
Rosa Parks
Alvin Francis Poussaint
Colin L. Powell
Leontyne Price
A. Phillip Randolph
Lou Rawls
Jackie Robinson
Sojourner Truth
Harriet Tubman
Madame C. J. Walker
Ida B. Wells
Oprah Winfrey
Stevie Wonder
Andrew Young

Other World Figures of African Descent

Aesop
Sonni Ali
Richmond Barthé
Ludwig van Beethoven
Robert Browning
Paul Belloni Du Chaillu
Cleopatra
Samuel Taylor Coleridge
Samuel Crowler
Cheikh Anta Diop
Alfred Dobbs
Alexandre Dumas
Hannibal
H. H. Harrison
Queen Hatshepsut
Richard Hill
Imhotep
Makeda, Queen of Sheba
Nelson Mandela
Allesandro de' Medici
Joachim Murat
Queen Nzingha
Touissant L'Overture
Aleksander Pushkin
Haile Selassie
Charles Spaulding
Mary Church Terrell
Thutmose III
William Trotten
Desmond Tutu
Isaac Wallace-Johnson
Zenobia

Hispanic Americans

Lope de Aguirre
Pedro Antonio de Alarcón
Isaac Albéniz
Pedro de Alvarado
Everett Alvarez
Jorge Carrera Andrade
Pío Baroja
Garcia Calderon
Richard E. Cavazos
César Chávez
Roberto Clemente
Fernando De Rojas
Roberto Durán
Carlos Finlay
Fernanco García
Carlos Gomes
Cecilia Gonzalez
Jose Maria de Heredia
Julio Iglesias
Juan Ramón Jiménez
Agustín Lara
Diego Maradona
Ricardo Montalbán
Rita Moreno
Juan Ortega
Manuel Piar
Horacio Rivero
Chi Chi Rodriguez
Francisco de Zorrilla Rojas
César Romero
Arantxa Sanchez-Vicario
George Santayana
Lee Treviño
Fernando Valenzuela
Joseph White

Other World Figures of Hispanic Descent

Vasco Núñez de Balboa
Simón Bolívar
Jorge Luis Borges
Pablo Casals
Salvador Dalí
Plácido Domingo
Benito Juárez
Federico García Lorca
Pablo Neruda
Pelé
Pablo Picasso
Diego Rivera
Andrés Segovia
Fray Junípero Serra
Diego Velázquez
Emiliano Zapata

Native Americans

Dr. Charles Alexander
Bigfoot
Abel Bosum
Joseph Brant
Chief Cochise
Crazy Horse/Ta-sunko-witko
Dan George
Geronimo
Chief Joseph
Chief Naiche
Quanna Parker
Gregory Perillo
Chief Pontiac
Chief Red Cloud
John Ross
Santana
Sequoya
Chief Sitting Bull
Tecumseh

SECONDARY LESSON

Around and Around

Standard
How to use mathematical formulas to sharpen estimates of circular figures

Focus Intelligence
Bodily/Kinesthetic

Supporting Intelligences
Interpersonal, Verbal/Linguistic

Mediation Emphasis
Challenge

CHECKING PRIOR KNOWLEDGE

Invite one student from the class to determine which is greater, the circumference of a glass or its height. Give the student a sample drinking glass. After the student's "guess," ask the class to agree or disagree. Most will guess wrong and say "height." After several examples, they will begin to "estimate" with facts rather than "guesses." Solicit reasons for each different response. Repeat the procedure with two or three different glasses. List the methods for determining the correct answer. If no one contributes the terms *radius*, *circumference*, or *diameter*, add them to the list and provide their definitions. Conclude by presenting the word estimate. Ask for definitions, examples, and how knowing circumference and radius helped sharpen estimates of the glasses. Celebrate competence and prepare the students for transfer.

STRUCTURING THE TASKS

On the board make a map to show the connection of the key terms. Share the purpose of the lesson: "to learn how to use mathematical formulas to sharpen estimates of circular figures." Put students into trios. Assign the roles of calculator, checker, and encourager. Give each group a plastic bag containing (a) a calculator, (b) a tape measure, (c) three paper plates of different sizes, and (d) the worksheet. Groups will measure the radius of each plate and use the formula to calculate circumference. (Allow 15 minutes.)

LOOKING BACK AND REFLECTING

Allow each group to discuss these questions before you sample the total class:

1. What are your answers? How close were your estimates? What helped improve your estimates?

2. What did members of your group contribute to your teamwork?

BRIDGING FORWARD

For student journal entries, select one or more tasks from Item 1 below:

1. Solve these word problems:
   a. What will be the circumference of wheels having the following radii: 17", 36", 7", or 129"?

b. If you have a truck with 39" (diameter) wheels, how many times will the wheels turn in a three-mile trip? (There are ____ inches in a mile.)
c. Read the problem and give instructions for its solution. Mary's bicycle wheels have a 39" diameter. Mary rides her bike to school each day, taking the same 4.5-mile route each way. How many times will her front wheel turn in a round trip to and from school? Instructions must include (i) multiplying the mileage by 2 for the round trip, (ii) converting miles to inches, (iii) dividing 19.5" into mileage, and (iv) calculating circumference.
d. Invent your own circumference word problem and give instructions for its completion.
e. Explain the terms *circumference, diameter,* and/or *radius* and tell why each is important to know.
f. Make a list of objects in this room or your home on which you could use your math knowledge to estimate circumference. Pick one and show off your know-how.

2. After students have worked the problems, sample their work in a discussion.

Assessing Student Performance

How well can the student

1. Explain the mathematical vocabulary and give examples from daily life of how the concepts are connected?

2. Measure circular figures for radius and use the correct mathematical formula to calculate for circumference?

3. Explain why knowledge of the formula is important in daily life?

Materials

Several glasses with different heights and circumferences, overhead projector and transparencies, one calculator, tape measure, plates in three different sizes, worksheet in plastic bag, and student journals

Variations

1. Substitute triangles, squares, or any other geometric figure. Provide models in various sizes of the figure linked to the measurement formula for hands-on work.

2. Provide home-life follow-up measurement (e.g., for circumference: dishes, storage containers, garbage cans).

12

Self-Change

If you wait for tomorrow, tomorrow comes. If you don't wait for tomorrow, tomorrow comes.

—Sierra Leonian proverb

This tenth criterion for mediation, self-change, is like the final rush of energy and effort at the end of a marathon. All the other mediations are built on the assumption that the mediator's essential responsibility is to mediate and increase students' desires to change and to change how they learn throughout life. Students' recognition, acceptance, valuing, and monitoring of change within themselves, however, is what leads them to the finish line of independent and autonomous learning.

Feuerstein argues that the ability to change is the most stable characteristic of human beings. Whether a person wants to acknowledge that change is occurring all around and within, change is always present and ongoing. Many people resist this—it is often easier to stay in a comfort zone than to ease on down the road to self-change.

MEDIATING SELF-CHANGE

Mediators cannot force students to change. They can help students become aware of the dynamic potential for change. They can mediate the pluses and minuses of the change. From this awareness will come the self-control in learning that is the core of Feuerstein's work. This self-control involves the recognition that change comes from within, an expectation for growth in competence, self-monitoring for personal change, and an increased openness to helping oneself change and move through the comfort zones.

QUICK-START TACTICS

Some of the most beneficial classroom tactics in mediating self-change are the easiest to implement:

- Elimination of labels and categories that tell students they cannot change
- Increased respect for individual talents, and discouragement of comparisons among students
- Elimination of put-downs, slurs, and personal attacks
- Promotion of student self-evaluation and reflection
- Reduction of self-defeating behavior and language
- Development of an understanding of change within each student
- Use of personal standards and goals to help students guide their changes
- Increased monitoring of self through progress charts and portfolios
- Provision of helpful feedback
- Development of self-reporting parent conferences

Of these 10, the first 4 require special notice for use in the urban school.

Elimination of Labels and Categories

American educators are the first in the world with labels and categories. Their students, like animals in a zoo, are tested, prodded, grouped, and labeled. Meant to individualize education in a diagnostic-treatment mode, the labels create low expectations, isolation, and peer umbrage rather than raise performance or achievement levels. Students, long categorized and provided with "dumbed-down" curricula, cocoon themselves with excuses and rationalizations for doing less in learning quality and quantity. Classrooms without useless labels and categories, and schools without tracks and ability groups, free students from some of the sources of low expectations.

Respect for Individual Talent and Discouragement of Comparisons

Although much lip service is paid to individualized instruction, labeled students adapt readily to the low expectations held for them. Students with behavior disorders learn how to live up to that label by acting out; students with learning disabilities use "I don't have to do that because . . ." strategies with their teachers and parents; students at risk of failure assume a passive role with their academic work. There is little mystery about what is happening: these students are finding quick cover. Even though they may possess talents other than those used to make academic classifications, they know that their musical, visual, or interpersonal intelligences are not too highly esteemed. For survival among their peers, they often find it more expedient to adopt their label and perform according to their expected designation. However, when teachers fight the systematic negation of multiple talents and multiple intelligences, they create a

> When a teacher establishes a classroom climate that celebrates individual differences, student behavior moves to a higher plane.

classroom in which all students are respected for their individual talents. Even more, teachers create a new set of expectations that challenge students to use their talents to achieve higher academic and life goals.

Elimination of Put-Downs

> I have forgiven myself; I'll make a change. Once that forgiveness has taken place you can console yourself with the knowledge that a diamond is the result of extreme pressure. Less pressure is crystal, less than that is coal, less than that is fossilized leaves or plain dirt. Pressure can change you into something quite precious, quite wonderful, quite beautiful.
>
> —Maya Angelou (Riley, 1993)

Whenever a teacher establishes a classroom climate that celebrates individual differences, student behavior moves to a higher plane. Instead of accepting put-downs, slurs, and personal attacks that alienate students from each other, the mediating teacher is proactive in demanding verbal respect for all. This may require explicit social skill lessons, development of teamwork skills, celebrations of individual accomplishments, and public recognition of those who make extra effort to treat all peers with respect. Physical safety and security are the first right of every student in the classroom; emotional safety and security are the second. Without these foundation pieces, self-change will not begin.

Promotion of Reflection and Self-Assessment

When students are raised in an environment that promotes impulsive reactions and incidental experience, young students fail to form the habits of mind that lead to high achievement. Recent brain research accentuates the value of guiding students to learn how to plan what they will do, how to monitor their own progress, and how to make judgments on the quality of their work. When these three elements apply to their thinking processes and they begin to "think about their thinking," gains on achievement are remarkable (Bellanca & Fogarty, 2003, pp. 191–192). However, students need the time and the guidance of a teacher-mediator to develop these reflective habits.

> Students raised in an environment that promotes impulsive reactions fail to form the habits of mind that lead to high achievement.

There are a variety of strategies that provide simple yet powerful facilitation of student reflection and self-assessment. In the BUILD model of cooperative learning (Bellanca & Fogarty, 2003), these strategies are described as the tools that motivate students to "look back and reflect." These look-backs include a review of (a) what students learned in terms of facts, concepts, or insights in the curriculum and in terms of how to work successfully in a team and how to solve problems, (b) how students learned the content and used their team-building and thinking skills, and (c) how they might improve their learning, cooperating, and thinking dispositions. Introduced and modeled through direct instruction techniques, these strategies provide an opportunity for the mediator to extend student reflection from simple, short responses into elaborate self-assessments that encourage each student to monitor his or her own cognitive and affective growth.

Reflective journals are an excellent medium for continuous self-assessment. Laminated feedback cards promote select dialogue between mediator and student (see samples below). Index cards are easy to collect and review.

```
┌─────────────────────────────────────────────────────────────────────┐
│                           Feedback Card                               │
│   ┌───────────────────────────┐     ┌───────────────────────────┐    │
│   │         (Side 1)          │     │         (Side 2)          │    │
│   │                           │     │                           │    │
│   │  Topic_____    │     │  Mediator Reflects Here:  │    │
│   │  Name_____    │     │                           │    │
│   │                           │     │                           │    │
│   │  Student Reflects Here:   │     │                           │    │
│   │                           │     │                           │    │
│   └───────────────────────────┘     └───────────────────────────┘    │
│                                                                       │
└─────────────────────────────────────────────────────────────────────┘
```

When mediators provide the framework for student responses, they make it easier for students to avoid writer's block and to provide increasingly more elaborate responses. There are three especially easy-to-use tactics that provide helpful self-assessment frameworks for content, cooperation, or cognition: the stem, Mrs. Potter's Questions, and plus-minus-interesting questions (PMI).

In a conventional classroom inculcated with behaviorist practices, there is no time for student self-assessment. The teacher dispenses, judges, rewards (with stars, stickers, and high grades), and punishes (with time-outs, red ink, and low grades). In the mediated classroom, the teacher establishes performance criteria and indicators of success before key lessons. As students work, they take time to check progress against the criteria, listening to the teacher's corrective feedback on how well their work in progress matches the criteria.

> Patient redirection by the mediator will encourage both reflective thought and honest sharing behaviors.

Time for learning how to use reflective strategies and to build a disposition for self-assessment is a long-term task. It can begin in the primary grades in small increments with simple "I learned" stems in a wraparound. At the end of a lesson, the teacher says, "I would like each of you to take a turn saying one thing you learned in this _____ lesson. Do not repeat or copy someone else's words. Use your own idea. Listen to each other."

```
┌─────────────────────────────────────────────────────────────────────┐
│                          "I Learned" Stems                            │
│                                                                       │
│   Today, I learned that …                                             │
│   I discovered …                                                      │
│   I understand why …                                                  │
│                                                                       │
└─────────────────────────────────────────────────────────────────────┘
```

Scheduling reflective time each day will add to the benefit derived from the mediation of self-control and the mediation of sharing. Egocentric children will interrupt each other, jump out of turn, and forget about listening to others. Patient redirection by the mediator will encourage both reflective thought and honest sharing behaviors. As the students become comfortable with reflection, setting learning goals, and assessing their own progress, the process of individuation approaches its zenith.

In the middle grades, regular use of de Bono's (1985) PMI or Bellanca and Fogarty's (2003) Mrs. Potter's Questions (p. 205) provides the opportunity to develop deep reflection. Whether tying these strategies to the completion of an essay in language arts, a science experiment, a fine arts project, or a wellness challenge, the mediator structures the development of students' disposition to learn.

Mrs. Potter's Questions

What was I expected to do?	What might I change in the future?
What did I do well?	What help do I need?

PMI

P Pluses	**M** Minuses	**I** Interesting Questions

KEY POINTS TO REMEMBER

- Use reflective journals to promote reflection and self-assessment; without reflection, the saying "If you keep doing the same stuff, you'll keep getting the same stuff" comes into play.
- Respect individual talent and discourage comparisons and put-downs; no more "Hellllllllllllllo, earth to learner" and "Are you in there?"

ELEMENTARY LESSON

Famous People Who Have Changed Our Lives

Standard
Using the writing process to understand the contributions that people of color have made to the history of the United States

Focus Intelligence
Verbal/Linguistic, Visual/Spatial

Support Intelligences
Interpersonal, Intrapersonal

Mediation Emphasis
Self-Change

CHECKING PRIOR KNOWLEDGE

Ask the class to help you complete a K-W-L chart (know, want to know, and learned) about famous African Americans. (If the class has students of color or ethnicity other than African American, adjust the list you provide.) After the first two columns are complete, let the class know the problem they will solve in this lesson. For the person you choose, select a specific challenge this person faced that blocked his or her equitable access to his or her full constitutional rights. What was the problem it caused?

STRUCTURING THE TASK

1. Divide the class into groups of three. Each group will select one name from the K list and three questions from the W list.

2. Provide age-appropriate print and/or video materials about each selected person. The group will use the materials (a) to find a picture of the person, (b) to answer the questions about the person, and (c) to pick out ways that person changed his or her own life and the lives of others by solving the problem or challenge identified.

3. Using poster board and markers or crayons, the group is to depict the change experienced by this person or left as a heritage for other African Americans (or appropriate group).

4. Display the completed pictures.

LOOKING BACK AND REFLECTING

Make an all-class list of the various ways the featured persons made changes in their own lives. Discuss the importance of taking charge and changing your own life.

BRIDGING FORWARD

Invite all children to write a short essay telling how what they learned from the featured persons could help them complete the essay. Use the PMI chart as a self-assessment tool. Collect the essays and charts.

Assessing Student Performance

Students will identify people of color who changed their lives. Each student will

1. Identify and tell one important way to change for the good.

2. Write a short essay to discuss an idea learned about self-change.

Materials

Newsprint and markers (for KWL charts); books, articles, and videotapes about people of color; poster board and markers for groups; masking tape or tacks; essay paper and pencils

Variations

1. Select a short biography about one famous person of color. Read the story to the class.

2. Direct each student to interview a person of color he or she admires. Questions should include, "Who or what are you? What do you do? How have you changed your life for the better?" Use the data to make posters.

3. Adapt the KWL chart so it represents the cultural background of the students. If the class is predominantly Hispanic, focus the K-W-L on famous Hispanic Americans. If there is a mixture of student cultures in the class, be sure that the K-W-L groups reflect the mix.

4. To use the K-W-L with the World Wide Web, add a D column (for Data) before the L column. "What data words will help us answer the W questions?"

5. For bridging forward, have each child make a personal improvement goal.

6. Have each student select a person of importance, a hero or heroine, who made significant self-change. After research, students will select ways to show how the person's willingness to change carries an important message for everyone.

MIDDLE GRADES LESSON

Valuing Respect

Standard
How to eliminate put-downs, slurs, and disrespect in the classroom and other environments

Focus Intelligence
Interpersonal

Support Intelligences
Interpersonal, Visual/Spatial

Mediation Emphasis
Self-Change

CHECKING PRIOR KNOWLEDGE

1. Divide the class into groups of three. Assign a recorder for each group. The recorder will copy your whiteboard double T-chart.

Looks Like	Sounds Like	Feels Like

2. With all members contributing, each group will list three or more ideas in each column based on their experience with disrespect in the school. Give specific examples for each column (Looks Like—obscene gesture; Sounds Like—"nerd"; Feels Like—anger). Allow five minutes for this listing before you ask the reporters to help you construct a list on the board or newsprint with no items duplicated. After the list is composed, show two signs and ask which they believe ought to mark this list in the classroom. Encourage random volunteers (refer to the Teacher Expectation Student Achievement, TESA, strategies) to explain why. After hearing students' responses, give your reasons for "thumbs down" to disrespect.

Thumbs Up	Thumbs Down

STRUCTURING THE TASK

1. Keep the same groups. Instruct each group to construct a double T-chart for "respect in the classroom." (Provide a 24" × 36" piece of newsprint or poster board per group.)

2. After the groups have finished the T-charts, invite them to make a magazine ad for R-E-S-P-E-C-T with ideas taken from the chart. Show sample ads that have simple, clear, and strong messages.

Looks Like	Sounds Like	Feels Like

3. Post the ads around the classroom. Select two or three ads per day for the class to brainstorm what they like about the ads. They may use only respectful responses as generated on their T-charts.

LOOKING BACK AND REFLECTING

After reviewing all the ads, use the double T-charts to make a class list of the 10 most important respectful behaviors for this classroom. Vote by giving each student a red dot (five points), a blue dot (three points), and a yellow dot (one point). After the master list is made, each student has three votes. Tally the score for the top 10. Post the final list.

BRIDGING FORWARD

Ask each student to write a reflective essay. In the essay, the student will discuss (a) "what I have learned" about giving respect to my classmates and (b) "how I can change" to show more respect.

Assessing Student Performance

To what degree can the student

1. Identify three to five respectful behaviors?

2. Explain why respect is important?

3. Demonstrate improvements in respect within the classroom?

Materials

Newsprint or poster board, markers or crayons

Variations

1. Replace the group-made ads with other media (such as essays, videos, Web home page design, games, collages, rap songs).

2. Allow each group to select its product.

3. Make the products a home assignment.

4. Hold an exhibition of the products for parents and/or other classes.

5. Using Aretha Franklin's "R-E-S-P-E-C-T" or Janet Jackson's "Control" songs, change the words to apply to the information generated on the double T-charts, and then perform the song.

SECONDARY LESSON

Reflective Journals

Standard
How to introduce students to reflective thinking as a process to manage self-change

Focus Intelligence
Intrapersonal

Support Intelligence
Verbal/Linguistic

Mediation Emphasis
Self-Change

CHECKING PRIOR KNOWLEDGE

1. On the overhead or with a handout, show Nikki Giovanni's (poet and children's book author) poem "The Funeral of Martin Luther King, Jr."

2. Using TESA strategies (see Chapter 2) that encourage all to participate, ask this sequence of questions (ask one student to list the responses on the board):
   - In your own words, what does this poem say?
   - In what ways does this poem connect you to what you already know about Dr. King?
   - What new or different ideas and feelings does the poem stir?

STRUCTURING THE TASK

1. Provide each student with a journal. (This can be 20–30 stapled blank pages, a purchased notebook, or loose-leaf pages at the back of a class notes binder. It is a book that you want students to bring daily or to keep in the classroom.)

2. Explain the purpose of the journal—to enable them (a) to think deeply about the material/content they are learning in this class (yes, a math journal, science journal, art journal, as well as English journal), (b) to think how they might apply what they are learning, (c) to understand how the course content ties together, and (d) to see how they are making continuous improvement.

3. Provide the standard and criteria that you will use in reviewing the journal. You will have to decide what criteria you want for quantity (daily entry?), quality of thoughtfulness, completeness of responses, spelling and grammar requirements, and so on. Provide a rubric or scale if you intend to grade the journal.

4. Explain "confidentiality." At times you will read private entries; at other times, you will call on volunteers to share their ideas with the class. Ask that the volunteers share their entries with you before they share them with the class.

5. Let students know that you will provide a structure for each entry. If they elect to make additional entries, allow them an open structure.

6. Start with the three-question structure used for the poem above. If you teach in the arts or English, entries will best be made before class discussion.

   a. In your own words, what does this _____ say?

   b. In what ways does it connect you to what you already know about _____?

   c. What new or different ideas or feelings does the _____ stir?

If you teach math, science, social studies, or other courses, follow the same sequence after students have viewed or read introductory material.

    a. In your own words, what does this information say?

    b. What do you already know about this topic?

    c. What do you predict you might be learning new or different?

7. After time is given for entries, you may wish to ask several volunteers to share responses to each question (this is a good time to practice appropriate mediation skills!).

8. A second time to use the reflective journal is at the end of a lesson or unit. Again provide stems to prompt the students' reflections. Be sure to remind students that you prefer thoughtful responses over the quick answers that they might think you want to hear. Here is a basic three-cue sequence:
   - I learned [today, in this lesson, in this unit] . . .
   - This information is important because . . .
   - To use this information [skill], I intend . . .

LOOKING BACK AND REFLECTING

After students have made several entries in their journals, ask them to review what they have written and share entries:

- In my entries, I am pleased that I . . .
- In my entries, I think I can improve by . . .
- In future entries, I intend to . . .

BRIDGING FORWARD

At the back of the journal, invite students to construct a course concept map. As the course progresses, have students reflect on the connections between the course topics, subtopics, and facts and create the map. Show them an example while reminding them that each map will be unique.

Assessing Student Performance

To what degree does the student

- Use multiple sentence responses to each cue?
- Individuate his or her responses?
- Communicate an understanding of the material?
- Show continuous improvement in mastery of the course content?
- Edit his or her verbal responses?

Materials

A journal and pencils or pens for each student

Variations

1. Depending upon the interaction(s) you want most to mediate, review the chapter and design appropriate entries. For instance, if you want to stress meaning, you can have students use appropriate graphic organizers with your course content. If sharing behavior is important for a class, focus your reflection on cues on the group process and social skills.

2. Encourage students to use a variety of media that fit individuated intelligences, especially as unique entries. Poems, songs, sketches, and so on are welcome!

3. Teach Mrs. Potter's Questions and end each week with a journal entry that assesses one area of the students' class lives: content, cooperation, cognition.

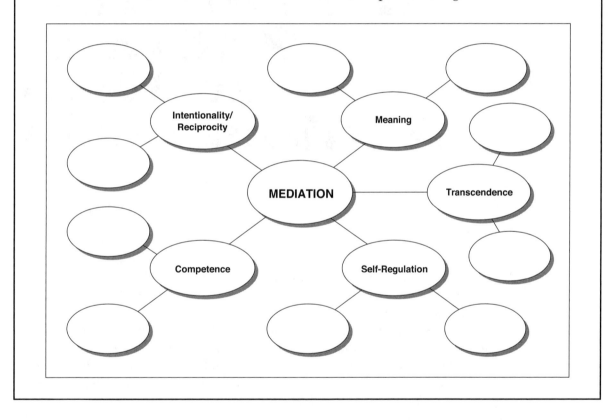

13

The No-Frills Pathway to High Achievement

Karen looked at the path leading to the school's front door. The cement was cracked and the grass on either side was uncut and littered with empty plastic water bottles, gum wrappers, and a soda can. Ahead, the faded gray metal door, edged with rust, blocked her way into the school.

Today was Karen's first day at Juarez School as a teacher. She had spent the summer after her graduation planning for this day. Her bag, loaded with books, her new laptop, and her letter to the principal, hung heavily from her shoulder. "What a day this was going to be!" A day she had dreamed about in every college class. She was going to teach. She was going to make a difference, a huge difference in her students' lives, and it was all starting today.

MAINTAINING THE DREAM

How many young teachers approach their first day of teaching with energy, enthusiasm, and an unbounded desire to make a difference in their students' lives? They can do anything. They can teach any child under any circumstance. There is nothing and no one that they can't teach.

For too many, that dream, as playwright Lorraine Hansberry (1989) wrote, "dries up like a raisin in the sun." It becomes a "dream deferred." More than one third leave the profession before they receive tenure, burned out and disillusioned. For many, the image of the shiny, well-kept, and bright school building gives way to falling plaster, litter, and unvarnished doors. For others, the mind-picture of neatly arranged computer banks, glossy new textbooks for every student, and packed classroom libraries that they recall from their halcyon days in their well-funded sub-urban enclaves is replaced with 10-year-old texts to be shared, a closet of unboxed six-year-old computers, and a note telling them that the classroom supplies for the year haven't yet arrived. And then there are the students. Instead of 20, there are 35. Instead of reading at grade level, most are years behind. These are definitely not the students discussed in Education 101.

There are no easy answers that ensure that all teachers in urban schools keep their dreams alive, especially when the schools' budgets trickle funds for new books, technology, and professional development. In spite of these obstacles, however, there is much that school leaders and the teachers themselves can do, especially in preparing to meet the learning challenges unique to these children.

Politicians love to talk about high expectations for all children. Teachers live with the reality of acting on those expectations. From the first day new teachers walk up the pathway to a school's front entrance, they are embarking on a journey of great challenge and great opportunity. Given budgetary constraints and other obstacles, these novices must accept that they may have to leave some of their dreams behind and accept the tough realities that come with the territory. However, they never have to abandon the dream that they can make a significant difference in their students' lives.

Walking the Pathway

The first task of new teachers is to get a strong grip on the hands of their new students and resolve never to let go as together they walk along the pathway of learning. Although this pathway may not look and feel like the sunny, flower-carpeted pathway they experienced in their college days, it is the pathway they are walking. On this pathway, some children may stumble; others will cower in fear at the monsters that hide in the bushes; and still others will collapse, exhausted. But with a firm grip, young teachers will look to their side and see the many students who walk with them, the students they pick up and nudge along, and the students they carry piggy-back along the rough road to success for all.

Finding Help and Support

A second task for new teachers is to seek out sensible, practical, and cost-effective ways to expand their professional know-how to meet their new challenges. For this, it is helpful, although not always possible, to find at least one other colleague, preferably a seasoned veteran in the same building, who has retained the spark of the dream that he or she is going to impact all of the children he or she teaches. The second choice is another novice teacher who shares the same dream.

The third task calls for these colleagues to start walking their own learning pathway, the pathway of professional development. Meeting once a week, these teachers will begin a conversation about their goals for the children they teach and what it is they can learn together to be most successful in this task and to make certain that no students will ask, "What is it about me you can't teach?"

MAKING SIMPLE CHANGES . . . SIMPLY

In the second chapter of this book, the importance of "high expectations" not only stated in words but put into daily practice was highlighted. The literature has shown for many decades how high expectations practices, garnered from the TESA (Teacher Expectation Student Achievement) research, are fundamental tools for effective teachers' tool kits. Over the last several decades, many other studies have added to this list. Most recently, meta-analyses have provided the information that indicates to teachers which of these very simple and easy to use tools work best to increase student achievement in various subject areas.

At the same time, as educational researchers have helped teachers see what instructional strategies will most help them in their quest to teach every child well, other improvements have provided valuable information about children's learning, especially the learning of children of poverty. Foremost among these has been the work of Reuven Feuerstein's studies of these children's learning deficiencies and the means to eliminate the deficiencies and transform these students into able learners.

More Knowledge Than Ever

The result of these studies is that today's teachers, both the novice and the seasoned veteran, have new knowledge about what it takes to best help urban students succeed with the expanding challenges of learning they face. Teachers no longer have to rely on pet theories of educational professors who may have not ever visited an urban classroom or who think it is more valuable to survey the sociological characteristics of urban children. Nor do they have to stick to worksheets and workbooks from educational publishers in order to keep their students busy. In fact, all teachers, especially those who have the desire to keep their first-day-of-school dreams alive, have more than enough tools available to ensure that every student they teach becomes an excellent learner.

No Excuses

In a closer to ideal world, such as in those school districts that have a wealth of funds to provide for professional development, teachers do not have to rely on their own means to deepen their own learning. However, shortage of school funds doesn't mean that individual teachers or cadres of teachers cannot put together their own no-frills professional development.

NO-FRILLS PROFESSIONAL DEVELOPMENT FOR ALL

No-frills professional development begins with one or two teachers reading and discussing the concept of high expectations summarized in the second chapter of this book. Following their initial discussion, these teachers each can make a simple plan to assess which of the TESA behaviors they do well and which they need to add to their instructional repertoire. They will keep a weekly log, shared with their colleague, on the impact they observe as they practice and perfect the selected strategies. In the log, stories of what went well, what do they want to improve, and questions for discussion become the fodder for a weekly support meeting. If the teachers can resolve the logistic issue of class coverage, the colleagues should visit each other's classrooms to observe and take notes on students' reactions to the teaching behaviors. At the end of a unit, the teachers can also look for indicators of improved student performance.

GETTING STARTED

1. Review TESA. Assess pluses and minuses for self.

2. Maintain log of impact.

3. Share with colleague.

4. Visit each other's classrooms and give feedback.

5. Make adjustments.

6. Continue to improve selected TESA behaviors.

The High-Effects Strategies

Going beyond the teaching *behaviors* that impact achievement, teacher teams can identify which of the high-effect teaching strategies—cooperative learning, graphic organizers, homework, and so on—they can add to their instructional repertoires (see Chapters 3 ff). Following the "less is more" approach, the teachers each should select one strategy per nine weeks to introduce or improve in their classrooms. As with the "asking questions" strategy found in the TESA model, it is more helpful if the teachers work together in weekly peer support teams to plan how to integrate these strategies into daily lessons and to assess the impact on student learning.

Time to Include Content

In the middle and secondary grades, teachers of similar content can band together into peer support groups of two or three. In addition to working with selected instructional strategies, these groups can focus on content. Content inquiries can include such questions as "What are the most important concepts in this unit that align with the standards?" and "Which instructional strategies from the high-effects group will most help the students learn these concepts?" Although many of the responses may be hypothetical, the teachers can "test" their hypotheses, observe the results, and refine their instruction.

Focus on Learning

In the first year, the peer support teams meeting weekly may focus on instructional strategies and content. At least by the second year, they should begin switching the emphasis from "teaching" to "learning." For this, they can return to Chapters 3–12 and review Feuerstein's criteria of mediated learning. After making a priority ranking of which criteria most match their students' needs, they can begin a review. In this review, the groups can ask three basic questions: What are the criteria? Why are they important? What means do we have for mediating this criteria?

Individuals may start classroom work as mediators by integrating questions that focus student attention on the selected criteria. "How much better do you think you are in solving this type of problem?" (competence). "What do you think is the meaning of this paragraph?" (meaning). Others may want to start with strategies that mediate a specific criterion such as cooperative learning for developing "sharing behavior." Still others may feel the need to embed either mediating questions or strategies into whole lessons (see sample lessons at the end of each chapter).

Whichever starting point team members select, it is important that they keep the focus on student learning by asking, "How will these questions improve the way students make sense (meaning) of the lesson?" "What changes do we see in student learning about this material as a result of this mediation?" and "What are the problems students are experiencing?

Eliminating Learning Deficiencies

In the time spent focusing on learning in their peer support meetings, teachers should make sure that the dominant amount is spent on analyzing the learning deficiencies that block individual achievement. Because there is not a specific test, the eyes and ears of the teachers make the best tools for this task. In the rubric below, the first column notes the most common deficiencies. In the second column there is space to write the indicators of the deficiency that they see and hear from students. In the remaining columns are the point ratings (low to high). Teachers can complete this chart with two targets in mind: individual students and a classroom. The high scores will tell them which deficiency needs the most mediation. By referring back to Chapters 2–11, they can identify the tools and strategies that will most help students eliminate the deficiencies.

Eliminating Learning Deficiencies						
Deficiency	Indicators	1	2	3	4	5
1. Blurred and sweeping perception						
2. Unplanned, impulsive responses						
3. Impaired label making						
4. Impaired time concept						
5. Impaired spatial orientation						
6. Imprecise data gathering						
7. Inaccurate observations						
8. Piecemeal data gathering						
9. Lack of inferential thinking						
10. Weak problem-solving orientation						
11. Episodic viewpoint						
12. Lack of comparative behavior						

SOURCE: Adapted from Feuerstein, 1980.

Teachers must take care with the word *deficiency*. Unlike the behaviorist's pessimistic orientation, which assumes that internal and cognitive changes are not possible and that intelligence and learning capability are "fixed," Feuerstein holds the opposite point of view. He notes that a deficiency is an undeveloped propensity that proper mediation will strengthen. He also notes that with proper intervention in the form of a mediated learning experience, any student can become a more efficient thinker and learner. Indeed, the research literature is full of evidence that supports his optimistic theory for a wide range of young and adult learners.

A Question of Will

When novice teachers take it upon themselves to do no-frills professional development, they are "giving to get." What they give up is one period per week of individual lesson planning time in order to take time to work with a colleague. Rather than go through the motions of outlining a sequence of activities prescribed by someone else's script, they begin their walk on the self-directed professional development pathway. This requires only an act of will. In return, what these teachers get from their own sharing behavior is a feeling of professional collegiality, increased motivation and competence in ensuring that they can teach every child, and pride in making sure that their own dreams are fulfilled. On the toughest of days, when neither teaching nor learning seems to go well, this is the wellspring that sustains them. Such sustenance goes a long way in helping to overcome any temporary disappointments.

No Frills and the Seasoned Veteran

No-frills professional development need not be limited to novice teachers. Seasoned veterans who desire to keep their dreams alive can benefit as well. Self-directed investigations, mutual encouragement, and collegial problem solving are far more effective in renewing tired spirits than top-down mandates or endless sit-and-get workshops on topics unrelated to student needs.

CRITICAL ELEMENTS IN THE NO-FRILLS MODEL

Not too long ago, the predominant professional development tool was the opening day of school inservice. Time for a speech from the principal, a motivational pitch from an edutaining consultant, and an afternoon to fix up the bulletin board and unpack. "Go and do. Have a great year."

Today, there are many models for professional development and a growing recognition that teachers, like doctors, dentists, and other professionals, must continue their education if they are to keep up. For many, this means an advanced degree. For others, it means piling up course credits to get step-and-scale raises. Although there is nothing inherently wrong with these approaches, what they fail to do is focus teachers on the needed collaborative effort to bring the changes in instruction, curriculum, and assessment that will ensure that all children are taught with the highest expectations.

Among all the different models that exist, including study teams, action research, learning communities, and so forth, there are a few key ingredients that are always in the recipe for success. These include peer support teams, the principal's leadership, and district coordination.

The Principal Is the Instructional Leader

Critical to professional development targeting changes that will impact all students is the principal. Much has been written about the principal as instructional leader. Many principals do this well, others delegate it away, while some ignore it and others take a laissez-faire stance. If the principal chooses to spend more time supervising the lunch hall, blowing the time whistle between classes, counting books, and so forth, that is fine. But principals who do so to the detriment of overseeing the instructional improvement process will never see improvement in teacher performance and in student performance.

More than 50 years ago, Madeline Hunter made it a point in her many talks to teachers and administrators that the standard for time spent in leading instruction in a building was 50 percent. Today, some principals do more, and some do less. Those who do more, it is safe to say, usually see the results in what teachers do in the classroom that matches the research on effective teaching and what students do in the way of increased learning.

A self-directed teacher or an inquiry team may have the chance of involving additional leaders, especially the principal, in a variety of ways. Most important, these teachers can involve department chairpersons, grade-level leaders, and site administrators, especially the principal. To do this, the teachers can create a portfolio. In the portfolio, they will include samples of their observations, samples of student artifacts showing changes in performance, and test scores showing the results from their work. They can invite the principal to observe student learning in their classrooms and to a follow-up conference to discover the benefits to the school (and the principal) of raised achievement scores in other classrooms with minimum budget impact.

What do these instructional leaders do in the no-frills approach? First, they budget sufficient funds for their professional development plan. Second, they see that professional development schedules are made for the year. The schedules will include sufficient time for the planned activities. Third, they form a team of teacher leaders or department chairs to give input, guide the plan, and overcome the bureaucratic obstacles. Fourth, they communicate to the central office on the progress of the plan, problems that arise, and successes to celebrate. Fifth, they mediate each teacher's progress, guided by the criteria for a mediated learning experience. As mediators, they take time to assess how well each teacher is implementing the targeted instructional improvement plan and what help mediators can provide.

A Schoolwide Plan

What teachers can use as no-frills professional development, principals can formalize for schoolwide achievement gains. The following guidelines will help principals facilitate a schoolwide approach for instructional improvement.

1. Principals best serve the teachers and students as instructional leaders who guide collegial decision making with an insistence that whatever the school community does, it does to increase achievement for all students. For these principals, high achievement for all must be a nonnegotiable effort by all.

2. Principals expect and support all staff members to actively participate in the improvement effort. They hold teachers individually accountable for the effort to improve learning. They hold the school team accountable for the results. To help all teachers succeed, principals schedule time for peer team and grade-level meetings that focus on the improvement goal. They also allow time for teachers to visit each others' classrooms.

3. In addition to the district's standardized evaluation, these principals assess how teachers are applying research-based best practices and programs to the issue of student achievement.

4. Principals encourage teachers to work together for the school's achievement goal. They celebrate accomplishments and communicate to parents, the community, and the district the good work of the schoolwide team.

5. Principals model strong mediation with the faculty. This begins with the mediation of intentionality (school vision and mission) and reciprocity (engaging all staff). It includes goal planning, sharing behavior, and self-change as priority interactions.

As formalized: schoolwide professional development, no-frills activities do not require a large budget. New information is gathered from selected how-to books (no external consultants). Teachers meet during planning periods in the school day (no stipends or substitute teachers). Teachers reflect on the information they gather, make their plans, use the plans in the classroom, and look to the standardized test results. In this model, everyone is in the same boat; the principal facilitates the oar strokes and the faculty team pulls together.

Keeping It Simple With Peer Support Teams

Peer support teams have a simple task: learn together. It is important that they keep the process simple as they dialogue with each other to make sure that no child ever asks, "What is it about me you can't teach?" The following guidelines will help teams keep it simple.

1. Meet for one period at a time. Start and finish on time. Start with one planning period a week.

2. At each meeting, agree on roles: Who will record? Who will summarize? Who will keep us on task?

3. Operate by a premade agenda with a goal.
   a. Week 1: review research on_____.
   b. Week 2: make implementation plans for using_____.
   c. Weeks 3–4: gather data on implementation and discuss problems.
   d. Week 5: assess impact on learning.
   e. Week 6: identify most struggling learners and make remediation, intervention, and prevention plans.

4. Respect each other's ideas. No moaning or griping.

5. Use interpersonal skills to facilitate positive communication.

6. Think outside the box.

7. Assess your progress: What have we learned? How are we benefiting? How are our students benefiting? How can we do better?

Using External Consultants

Although the no-frills model places emphasis on a faculty's self-directed change effort, there are times when it is appropriate to call on the expertise of the external consultant. What are these times?

1. To kick off the improvement effort with a person whose credibility lends motivation to the effort

2. To provide special expertise in resolving difficult implementation issues

3. To provide guidance for the principal in the institutionalizing of a program selected by the faculty

4. To demonstrate more difficult methods

5. To deepen teachers' understanding of content, learning challenges, or special methods relative to a particular subject

6. To develop deeper understanding of curriculum content

7. To maintain enthusiasm and interest in the implementation

In addition to these, a school may have to use a consultant who is certified to prepare teachers in the use of a method or program. For instance, when a school elects to implement Instrumental Enrichment, Feuerstein insists that they do so only with a trainer certified after three years' training and classroom use. In this way, he feels comfortable that novice users will adhere to the integrity of the program, which can be difficult to use without proper training and coaching.

When using an external consultant to provide information, principals should insist that teachers use the material presented, at least in a "try out" mode. This is accomplished best with a schedule of peer support meetings, as described above, and a method of assessment. If the consultant is helping the teachers use a new program or new content, the principal should schedule the consultant for follow-up demonstrations, classroom visits, and teacher conferences. In the school improvement field, information is necessary but insufficient to instigate change. As Joyce and Showers (1983) pointed out in their groundbreaking research more than two decades ago, structured follow-up is essential to change. Without coaching and support over time, workshop information dies on the vine, with less than 10 percent finding its way to the classroom. With appropriate follow-up, including regular consultant visits, 90 percent of workshop information results in instructional changes.

A District Connection

Although self-directed learning will help individual teachers and their students, it is not the be-all and end-all of professional development. The most important professional development makes sure that all students in a school and in a district are benefiting from better ways of learning.

If it is important to a school's achievement effort that teachers not be left on their own to implement the best that research is telling them in how to improve learning, it is likewise important that the district assure every parent, no matter where he or she lives in the district, that all children will have an equal chance to learn more, better, and faster. All will have an equal chance at the resources, and no school will fall through the cracks.

At the first level, district leaders help the process of improvement in a school by supporting and applauding the effort. Support and applause, however, mean little if the district fails to (a) budget sufficient funds for the no-frills effort and (b) ensure that any contract allows sufficient time for teachers to meet and make instructional decisions and that a key central office administrator is available to meet at least four times a year to review the project's progress and solve bureaucratic problems.

At the second level, a district can adopt the no-frills approach for all schools. The no-frills principle works as well in a district as it does in a small school. It is a matter of planning and leadership. First, the district needs only to set up the no-frills model in each building. Within a day, all principals can learn how to structure a school's no-frills model. Several half-day visits to a site by a consultant with other district leaders can provide the support and encouragement for getting the program started. After that, no more than one district person will be needed to monitor and facilitate each school's programs. To implement the study of content in the curriculum or a significant program such as Feuerstein's Instrumental Enrichment, the district can plan on a training of trainers model that places a program facilitator in each building to coach and coordinate the follow-up.

Bottom Up, Top Down

In the no-frills approach, professional development is neither top down nor bottom up. It is both. At the district level, high expectations for every school to attain high achievement are presented without apology as nonnegotiable. The district then provides the resources, especially the allotment of time, for teachers to assemble in each school and focus on a long-term process that they carefully plan and control.

What are the conditions that are needed to make this dual approach succeed? First, there must be mutual trust and respect. If the district or school leaders cannot trust the teachers to self-direct their learning within the framework of the district's aim to raise achievement for all students, or if they don't respect the teachers' ability to reach all children, no frills will fail. In a like manner, if teachers, or their representatives, cannot trust administrators to provide the leadership, then no frills will fail.

Facilitating the No-Frills Process

To make this process work in a school, it is the district's responsibility to supply teachers with the standardized achievement data, usually collected in March, before the end of the school year. Admittedly, many test data reports are not designed to inform the teachers. Much data goes to the state office of education so it can determine how badly or well a school is doing. It may not be in a form that helps teachers understand how individual students are progressing or how the school is doing to improve achievement. Likewise, many schools receive their data reports in mid-summer, or worse, in mid-autumn. Neither situation has to be. Neither helps data-based decisions about individual students.

There is another danger with a no-frills approach. Using a no-frills approach does allow a district to avoid budgeting for professional development. Budgets reveal values. If a district wants to say "no dollars" for professional development, it speaks its values. Without professional development, it is highly likely that there will be no improvement in scores. For student improvement, especially in the very difficult area of achievement, teachers and administrators must learn to use new and better ways to improve their knowledge of content and the skill to upgrade student learning.

One way for a district to target sufficient dollars to the achievement goal is to make a strong plan that focuses all professional development on the goal of increased test results. A district can review what it already spends on all the different activities that fall under the label "professional development," eliminate those that show weak results, and consolidate all activity to focus on improving student achievement. In this context, administrators should deny all requests for money to attend conferences and workshops, subsidized course work, and one-day "sit-and-get" workshops outside the goal of improving achievement.

Last, the school or district can adopt a common form to guide the peer support meetings that are the heart of the no-frills approach. These forms will help the district put the emphasis on staff development where it belongs: at the implementation stage. Rather than focus on "seat time" and the acquisition of information, a strong peer support program will enable the district to communicate that the hallmark of quality in professional development is in successful implementation of research-strong programs and strategies targeting achievement.

BUILDING A HISTORY OF IMPROVEMENT: A YEARBOOK OF PROGRESS

With all the emphasis on standardized test results, other snapshots of change can be forgotten. In a no-frills school, the faculty and parents want to see how well the students are learning. Yes, the report card gives a snapshot. Yes, the standardized test gives another snapshot. Although both are necessary, neither gives the whole picture. Thus in the no-frills school, the faculty maintains an annual portfolio: its yearbook of progress on its instructional improvement plan.

This yearbook contains multiple snapshots, including standardized test scores, grade-level statistics in reading and math, photographs of important events, and a collection of forms and artifacts that document student progress, peer team successes, and the like.

IDENTIFYING STUDENT LEARNING NEEDS

Team Name ———————————— Grade ————————————

School ———————————— Date————————————

Member Names ——————————————————————————

Priority Needs:

Identification Method Used:

Comment:

PLANNING INTERVENTIONS FOR ACHIEVEMENT

Team Name _____ Grade _____

School _____ Date _____

Member Names _____

Goal:

Objectives:

Learning Needs to Target:

Strategies to Use:

Timeline:

Responsibilities:

Assessment:

LESSON DESIGN

Team Name _____ Grade _____

School _____ Date _____

Member Names _____

Learning Need:

Goal:

Mediation Focus:

Materials:

Timeline:

(Lesson Design, Continued)

Action Steps:

Checking Prior Knowledge:

Structuring the Task:

Looking Back and Reflecting:

Bridging Forward:

Assessing Student Performance:

ASSESSING STUDENT LEARNING

Team Name ———————————— Grade ————————————————

School ———————————————— Date————————————————

Member Names —————————————————————————

Rubric:

Artifacts Collected:

Comments:

TEAM ASSESSMENT

Team Name _____ Grade _____

School _____ Date _____

Member Names _____

In this lesson, what we did well:

What we should do differently in the next lesson:

What help do we need? What questions do we have?

KEY POINTS TO REMEMBER

- Professional development should focus on student achievement, regardless of whether it is developed at the individual, team, school, or district levels.
- School budgets reveal school district values. To see how much your school or district values professional development for achievement, review how much money is allocated to such professional development.
- A no-frills professional development includes low- to no-cost activities, including developing support and inquiry teams, writing in journals and logs, using graphic organizers for reflection and self-directed investigations, having book clubs and weekly meetings with job-alike grade levels and periodic across grade-level or content areas with collegial problem solving as the goal; quite simply, learning together.
- Effective and efficient professional development will be the cause of improved scores and the elimination of the achievement gap.
- Teacher burnout suggests that, at one point, teachers were well-lit. Take advantage of the professional development made available or create your own to continue to serve a viable role in educating all children.
- Focus discussions on
  1. What you want students to know.
  2. How you know they have learned it.
  3. Your plan if they did not learn it.

IN CONCLUSION

There is no real conclusion to this book. Every teacher who is searching for the best ways to help all children succeed marches on a non-ending timeline of lifelong learning. Every child is eminently teachable. All should hear that there is nothing that any teacher can't teach them. Some students come to the teachers with greater challenges. These serve only as the impetus to acquire more knowledge, deeper understanding, and more refined skills for the lifelong search to ensure every child the fullest development of the right to learn.

Bibliography

Alleyne-Johnson, J. (1995). Life after death: Critical pedagogy in an urban classroom. *Harvard Educational Review, 65*(2), 213–230.

Anderson, K. (1989). Urban coalition encourages minority youth to "say yes" to math and science. *Black Issues in Higher Education, 5*(21), 6–8.

Angelou, M. (1985, March 5). *USA Today*.

Anyon, J. (1995). Race, social class, and educational reform in an inner-city school. *Teachers College Record, 97*(1), 69–94.

Apple, M. W. (1991). The politics of curriculum and teaching. *NASSP Bulletin, 75*(532), 39–50.

Aronson, E. (1978). *The jigsaw classroom*. Beverly Hills, CA: Sage.

Ascher, C. (1993, February). Changing schools for urban students: The school development program, accelerated schools, and success for all. *Trends and Issues No. 18*. New York: ERIC Clearinghouse on Urban Education.

Atwater, M. M., Wiggans, J., & Gardner, C. M. (1995). A study of urban middle school students with high and low attitudes toward science. *Journal of Research in Science Teaching, 32*(6), 665–677.

Ausubel, D. (1978). *Educational psychology: A cognitive view* (2nd ed.). New York: Holt, Rinehart & Winston.

Ball, A. F. (1995). Text design patterns in the writing of urban African American students: Teaching to the cultural strengths of students in multicultural settings. *Urban Education, 30*(3), 253–289.

Banathy, B. (1991). *Systems design of education: A journey to create the future*. Englewood Cliffs, NJ: Educational Technology.

Beckum, L. C., Zimny, A., & Fox, A. E. (1989). The urban landscape: Education for the twenty-first century. *Journal of Negro Education, 58*(3), 430–441.

Bellanca, J. (1992). *The cooperative think tank: Graphic organizers to teach thinking in the cooperative classroom*. Arlington Heights, IL: SkyLight.

Bellanca, J., & Fogarty, R. (2003). *Blueprints for thinking in the cooperative classroom* (3rd ed.). Arlington Heights, IL: Pearson/SkyLight.

Ben-Hur, M. (Ed.). (1994). *On Feuerstein's instrumental enrichment: A collection*. Palatine, IL: IRI/SkyLight.

Binet, A. (1886). *Psychology of reasoning*. Paris: Thoemes Continuum.

Bloom, B. (Ed.). (1956). *Taxonomy of educational objectives: The classification of educational goals, by a committee of college and university examiners*. New York: Longmans, Green.

Brookover, W., et al. (1982). *Creating effective schools: An inservice program for enhancing school learning climate and achievement.* Holmes Beach, FL: Learning Publications.

Brophy, J. (1986). Research linking teacher behavior to student achievement: Potential implications for instruction of Chapter 1 students. In B. Williams, P. Richmond, & B. Mason (Eds.), *Designs for compensatory education: Conference proceedings and papers.* Washington, DC: Research and Evaluation Associates.

Carter, R. L. (1995). The unending struggle for equal educational opportunity. *Teachers College Record, 96*(4), 619–626.

Chapman, C. (1993). *If the shoe fits . . . : How to develop multiple intelligences in the classroom.* Palatine, IL: IRI/SkyLight.

Cohen, E. (1986). *Designing groupwork: Strategies for the heterogeneous classroom.* New York: Teachers College Press.

Cohen, M. (1993, April). *Patterns of school change.* Paper presented at the Annual Meeting of the American Educational Research Association, Atlanta, GA.

Cooper, E. J., & Sherk, J. (1989). Addressing urban school reform: Issues and alliances. *Journal of Negro Education, 58*(3), 315–331.

Costa, A. L., & Garmston, R. (1985, March). *The art of cognitive coaching: Supervision for intelligence teaching.* Paper presented at the Annual Conference of the Association for Supervision and Curriculum Development, Chicago.

Cziko, C. (1995). Dialogue journals: Passing notes the academic way. *The Quarterly, 17*(4), 1–5, 11.

Dahl, K. L. (1995). Challenges in understanding the learner's perspective. *Theory Into Practice, 34*(2), 124–130.

Dahl, K. L., & Freppon, P. A. (1995). A comparison of inner-city children's interpretations of reading and writing instruction in the early grades in skills-based and whole language classrooms. *Reading Research Quarterly, 30*(1), 50–74.

Darling-Hammond, L. (1996). *What matters most: Teaching for America's future.* New York: National Commission on Teaching for America's Future.

Davis, B. (1995). *How to involve parents in a multicultural school.* Alexandria, VA: Association for Supervision and Curriculum Development.

de Bono, E. (1985). *Six thinking hats.* Boston: Little, Brown.

Deutsch, M. (1949). An experimental study of the effects of cooperation and competition upon group processes. *Human Relations, 2,* 199–232.

Dewey, J. (1933). *How we think.* Boston: D. C. Heath.

Eisner, E. W. (1983). The kind of schools we need. *Educational Leadership, 41*(2), 48–55.

Feuerstein, R. (1980). *Instrumental enrichment.* Baltimore: University Park.

Feuerstein, R. (1996). *Instrumental enrichment.* Jerusalem: International Center for the Enhancement of Learning Potential.

Flanders, N. (1964). Interaction models of critical teaching behaviors. In F. R. Cyphert & E. Spraights (Eds.), *An analysis and projection of research in teacher education* (pp. 197–218). Columbus: Ohio State University Research Foundation.

Fogarty, R. (1989). *From training to transfer: The role of creativity in the adult learner.* Doctoral dissertation, Loyola University of Chicago.

Fogarty, R., Perkins, D., & Barell, J. (1992). *How to teach for transfer.* Palatine, IL: SkyLight.

Frymier, J., et al. (1992). *Phi Delta Kappa study of students at risk: Final report* (Vol. 1). Bloomington, IN: Phi Delta Kappa.

Fullan, M., & Stigelbauer, S. (1991). *The new meaning of educational change.* New York: Teachers College Press.

Gardner, H. (1983). *Frames of mind: The theory of multiple intelligences.* New York: Basic Books.

Glasser, W. (1986). *Control theory in the classroom.* New York: Harper & Row.

Gonzales, M. R. (1995, April). *Multicultural education in practice: Teacher's social constructions and classroom enactments.* Paper presented at the Annual Meeting of the American Educational Research Association, San Francisco.

Good, T. (1970). Which pupils do teachers call on? *Elementary School Journal, 70,* 190–198.

Good, T. (1987). Two decades of research on teacher expectations: Findings and future directions. *Journal of Teacher Education, 36,* 32–47.

Goodlad, J. I. (1984). *A place called school: Prospect for the future.* New York: McGraw-Hill.

Gottlieb, J., Alter, M., Gottlieb, B. W., & Wishner, J. (1994). Special education in urban America: It's not justifiable for many. *Journal of Special Education, 27*(4), 453–465.

Grubb, W. N. (1995). Reconstructing urban schools with work-centered education. *Education and Urban Society, 27*(3), 244–259.

Hansberry, L. (1989). *A raisin in the sun.* New York: Vintage.

Harris, H. W., Blue, H. C., & Griffith, E. E. H. (Eds.). (1995). *Racial and ethnic identity: Psychological development and creative expression.* New York: Routledge.

Harris, J. J., III, & Ford, D. Y. (1991). Identifying and nurturing the promise of gifted black American children. *Journal of Negro Education, 60*(1), 3–18.

Hendricks-Lee, M. S., et al. (1995). Sustaining reform through teaching learning. *Language Arts, 72*(4), 288–292.

Holmes, O. W., Jr. (1993). *The poet at the breakfast table.* Boston: Houghton Mifflin.

Hunter, C. (1991). On the case in Resurrection City. In C. Carlson, D. Garrow, G. Gill, V. Harding, & D. Hine (Eds.), *The eyes on the prize civil rights reader* (pp. 426–438). New York: Penguin.

Hunter, M. (1971). *Teach for transfer.* El Segundo, CA: Tip.

Ishikawa, K. (1985). *What is Total Quality Control?* Englewood Cliffs, NJ: Prentice Hall.

Iwaszkiewicz, S. M. (1995). Gunfire in the night. *English Journal, 84*(7), 82–83.

Jackson, M., et. al. (1991). Class, caste and the classroom: Effective public policy vs. effective public education. *Western Journal of Black Studies, 15*(4), 242–247.

Jenlink, P. M. (Ed.). (1995). *Systemic change: Touchstones for the future school.* Palatine, IL: IRI/SkyLight.

Johnson, D. W., et al. (1984). *Circles of learning: Cooperating in the classroom.* Alexandria, VA: Association for Supervision and Curriculum Development.

Johnson, D. W., & Johnson, R. T. (1999). *Learning together and alone: Cooperative, competitive, and individualistic learning* (5th ed.). Boston: Allyn & Bacon.

Johnson, V. R. (1990). Schools reaching out: Changing the message to "good news." *Equity and Choice, 6*(3), 20–24.

Joyce, B. R., & Showers, B. (1983). *Power in staff development through research and training.* Alexandria, VA: Association for Supervision and Curriculum Development.

Kagan, S. (1977). Social motives and behaviors of Mexican American and Anglo American children. In J. L. Martinez (Ed.), *Chicano psychology.* New York: Academic Press.

Kagan, S. (1992). *Cooperative learning.* San Juan Capistrano, CA: Resources for Teachers.

Kermin, S. (1972). *Teacher expectations and student achievement.* Los Angeles: Los Angeles County Office of Education.

King, S. H., & Bey, T. M. (1995). The need for urban teacher mentors: Conceptions and realities. *Education and Urban Society, 28*(1), 3–10.

Kohn, A. (1993). *Punished by rewards.* New York: Houghton Mifflin.

Kozol, J. (1991). *Savage inequalities.* New York: Crown.

Kozol, J. (1992). Inequality and the will to change. *Equity and Choice, 8*(3), 45–47.

Lee, C. D. (1995). A culturally based cognitive apprenticeship: Teaching African American high school students skills in literary interpretation. *Reading Research Quarterly, 30*(4), 608–630.

Lundquist, S. (1995). The urban partnership program: A new model for strengthening communities through educational change. *Community College Journal, 65*(7), 28–32.

Luria, A. R. (1976). *Cognitive development: Its cultural and social foundations.* Cambridge, MA: Harvard University Press.

Lyman, F., & McTighe, J. (1988). Cueing thinking in the classroom: The promise of theory-embedded tools. *Educational Leadership, 45*(7), 18–24.

Marcus, S. A., & McDonald, P. (1990). *Tools for the cooperative classroom.* Palatine, IL: IRI/SkyLight.

Marzano, R. J., Pickering, D., & Pollack, J. E. (2001). *Classroom strategies that work: Research-based strategies for increasing student achievement.* Alexandria, VA: Association for Supervision and Curriculum Development.

Musial, D. (2002). [Cleveland report]. Unpublished study.

National Center for Effective Schools. (1993). *Multiple intelligences theory in action: Research and the classroom.* Madison: University of Wisconsin.

Noddings, N. (1993). For all its children. *Educational Theory, 43*(1), 15–22.

Ogle, D. (1986). K-W-L: A teaching model that develops active reading of expository text. *Reading Teacher, 39*(6), 564–570.

Parchen, E., Peacock, M., & Neches, N. (Eds.). (1996). *Poetry in motion: 100 poems from subways and buses.* New York: W. W. Norton.

Raiser, L., & Hinson, S. (1995). Writing plays using creative problem-solving. *Teaching Exceptional Children, 27*(4), 59–64.

Resnick, L. B. (Ed.). (1976). Metacognitive aspects of problem solving. In *The nature of intelligence* (pp. 231–235). Hillsdale, NJ: Lawrence Erlbaum.

Riley, D. W. (Ed.). (1993). *My soul looks back, "Less I forget": A collection of quotations by people of color.* New York: HarperCollins.

Rosenshine, B. (1971). *Teaching behaviors and student achievement.* London: National Foundation for Educational Research in England and Wales.

Rowe, M. B. (1969). Science, silence and sanctions. *Science and Children, 6,* 11–13.

Rubovits, P., & Maehr, M. (1973). Pygmalion black and white. *Journal of Personality and Social Psychology, 25*(2), 210–218.

Sadker, D., & Sadker, M. (1985). Is the OK classroom OK? *Phi Delta Kappan, 66*, 358–361.

Sarason, S. B. (1990). *The predictable failure of educational reform: Can we change course before it's too late?* San Francisco: Jossey-Bass.

Schmuck, R., & Schmuck, P. (1988). *Group processes in the classroom.* Dubuque, IA: William C. Brown.

Senge, P. (1990). *The fifth discipline: The art and practice of the learning organization.* New York: Doubleday.

Sharan, S., & Sharan, Y. (1976). *Small-group teaching.* Englewood Cliffs, NJ: Educational Technology.

Sharan, S., & Sharan, Y. (1992). *Expanding cooperative learning through group investigation.* New York: Teachers College Press.

Sharron, H. (1987). *Changing children's minds: Feuerstein's revolution in the teaching of intelligences.* London: Souvenir.

Slavin, R. E. (1983). *Cooperative learning.* New York: Longman.

Sperling, M. (1995). Uncovering the role in writing and learning to write: One day in an inner-city classroom. *Written Communication, 12*(1), 93–133.

Tribus, M. (2004). *Improving the quality of teaching according to Deming and Feuerstein.* Jerusalem: International Center for the Enhancement of Learning Potential.

Vygotskii, L. S. (1962). *Thought and language.* Cambridge: Massachusetts Institute of Technology Press.

Walker, A. (1983). *In search of our mothers' gardens.* San Diego, CA: Harcourt Brace Jovanovich.

Index